Redcoats Against Napoleon

Redcoats Against Napoleon

The 30th Regiment During the Revolutionary and Napoleonic Wars

Carole Divall

with a Foreword by
Lieutenant Colonel John Downham

Pen & Sword
MILITARY

First published in Great Britain in 2009 by
Pen & Sword Military
an imprint of
Pen & Sword Books Ltd
47 Church Street
Barnsley
South Yorkshire
S70 2AS

ISBN 978-1-84415-851-5

A CIP catalogue record for this book is available from the British Library.

Typeset in 11/13 Ehrhardt by Concept, Huddersfield, West Yorkshire
Printed and bound in England by CPI UK

Pen & Sword Books Ltd incorporates the imprints of Pen & Sword Aviation, Pen & Sword Maritime, Pen & Sword Military, Wharncliffe Local History, Pen & Sword Select, Pen & Sword Military Classics and Leo Cooper, Remember When, Seaforth Publishing and Frontline Publishing.

For a complete list of Pen & Sword titles please contact
PEN & SWORD BOOKS LIMITED
47 Church Street, Barnsley, South Yorkshire, S70 2AS, England
E-mail: enquiries@pen-and-sword.co.uk
Website: www.pen-and-sword.co.uk

Contents

List of Maps

List of Illustrations

Preface

In the autumn of 1787 a 16-year-old ensign, Alexander Hamilton, joined the 30th Regiment of the Line (the Cambridgeshire). He retired forty years later as lieutenant colonel of the same regiment. In between lay one of the most cataclysmic periods of European history which embraced the French Revolution and the subsequent Revolutionary and Napoleonic Wars. Hamilton had been born into a Britain predominantly rural. Industrial processes were only just beginning to transform the structure of a largely agricultural economy. Britain was acquiring an empire and still held the most important of its colonies, the seaboard states of North America; but was intermittently at war with its traditional enemy, France. When he died in 1838 he left a world essentially global in which Britain was the principal player, a world where technology and ideology were undermining the certainties of life at a bewildering rate. The *ancients regimes* of the eighteenth century were no more. The proletariat was stirring; democracy was the new watchword; Europe and the world were set on irresistible change.

The young Hamilton was typical of his time and his class. He had actually been commissioned in 1784, aged 13, as an ensign in the 84th Foot, although it is unlikely that he ever served with this regiment. Indeed, his obituary makes no reference to this connection, although Hamilton himself mentioned it in his record of service. But it was normal practice in the eighteenth century for the sons of the gentry to receive commissions long before they were able to perform the duties of an officer. Hamilton was the grandson of a Scottish landowner, and the great-grandson of the second Marquis of Lothian. This gave him a social status he shared with many of the officers of the British army before war and expansion led to the admission of the sons of the rising middle classes.

His arrival in 1787 was not coincidental, since an order of that year ordered the augmentation of the 30th Foot, so that 'each of the eight companies . . . shall be forthwith augmented by adding One Sergeant One Drummer and Fourteen Private Men, as also that Two Companies each to consist of One Captain One Lieut. One Ensign Three Sergeants Three Corporals Two Drummers and Fifty-six Private Men, and also One other Company to consist of One Captain One Lieutenant One Ensign Eight Sergeants Eight Corporals Four Drummers and Thirty Private Men shall be added to Our said Regiment.' An expanding regiment was a good place for a young man to begin his military career, although it is unlikely that Hamilton realised at the time that forty years later he would still be serving with the same corps, having seen action in France, Iberia, two islands of the Mediterranean, Egypt and India, on land and at sea.

His experience was the experience of the regiment, and it is his and their story which will be narrated in this work. Theirs was a workaday existence. They were not one of the crack regiments like the Guards or those of the Light Division. They do not live on in a host of letters and journals. Yet their experiences through the turbulent twenty-six years which began with the storming of the Bastille and ended at Waterloo were shared by many of the regiments which made up the British army of that time. Nor were such regiments incapable of inspiring the devoted loyalty of those who served with them. Writing in 1817, at a point when the Napoleonic crisis was over and the army was being reduced by the disbanding of many second battalions, Lieutenant Edward Neville Macready maintained that the junior battalion of the 30th – 'This brave corps – . . . will be remembered as long as the names of Fuentes d'Onor, Badajoz, Salamanca, Muriel, Quatrebras and Waterloo are emblazoned on the pages of British achievement.'

What follows is the biography of one of Wellington's many unassuming but reliable regiments and the story of a talented officer who distinguished himself throughout his long career. An obituarist described him as a 'gallant and distinguished' officer and referred to his 'long and arduous' service. This narrative seeks to demonstrate how those epithets may equally well be applied to the regiment in which he served with such distinction.

Author's note:
Because of the inconsistency over time in the spelling of Spanish and Portuguese place names it has been decided to use the modern spellings at all times except in quotations.

For further information regarding the author, please go to <u>www.caroledivall.co.uk</u>

Acknowledgements

The men of the 30th Regiment live on in official records, in journals and newspaper reports, and in the comments and recollections of their contemporaries. Researching their story across such a wide range of primary sources would have been impossible without the help of the staff at the archives, museums and record offices which hold much of this material. Particular thanks are due to the archivists of the Queen's Lancashire Regiment, and to the staff of the National Archives and the National Army Museum, without whose assistance this book would not have been written. Similarly, the staff of the records offices in Dublin, Limerick and Mullingar (Westmeath) and of the National Library in Dublin provided me with a wealth of information about the time the regiment spent in Ireland, while at the Cornish Records Office the staff willingly trawled through local newspapers to find accounts of the wreck of the *Queen*. It is such material which, I hope, brings the story of the 30th to life.

On a more personal level I have to thank the many friends and acquaintances I have made during the past ten years. Enthusiasts all, they have been generous in their willingness to share their own knowledge so that I could develop mine. I have particularly valued the interest in all things Napoleonic of Mick Crumplin FRCS, and the help of Mike Robinson in putting together the story of Quatre Bras from the perspective of 'The Old Three Tens'. I also appreciate the generosity of John Macdonald in allowing me to reproduce the likeness of Thomas Walker Chambers, and of Colin Yorke in letting me share his detailed research into the life of his ancestor, John Yorke, who served with the 30th from 1803–1817.

It would have been impossible to contemplate a history of the regiment during the Revolutionary and Napoleonic Wars which went beyond the magisterial account of Neil Bannatyne without the enthusiastic support of Lieutenant Colonel John Downham of the Queen's Lancashire Regiment. The material he found for me in the early days of my research gave me the starting points I needed, and the interest he has shown ever since has encouraged me to continue. I am, therefore, doubly grateful, for all his help during the past ten years, and for his willingness to write a foreword for this present work.

Nor can I end these acknowledgements without expressing a similar debt of gratitude to my husband. Whether extracting information from the many sources we have consulted or driving through Spain and Portugal in the footsteps of the 30th, drawing maps or reproducing illustrations, he has been unfailing in his support. Indeed, he must have felt at times that there were several thousand intruders in our marriage, men in scarlet coats who have occupied so much of our life over the past decade.

This work is dedicated, therefore, to John Downham and John Divall, and to the memory of all the men, officers, NCOs and other ranks, who served with the 30th Regiment of the Line, redcoats against Napoleon.

Foreword
by Lieutenant Colonel John Downham

This is the story of how a second-line draft-finding battalion of an ordinary Infantry Regiment of the Line, little more than a holding and recruiting battalion of old soldiers past their prime and of immature youngsters, was transformed by its campaigns in the Peninsula and by careful nurturing to become one of the handful of veteran regiments on which Wellington's victory at Waterloo so largely depended.

The battalion sprang from proven stock, for it was raised in 1803 by a division of the old 30th Foot, a regiment with over a hundred years of achievement by land and sea behind it. It had been on active service overseas for most of the previous decade, most recently at the capture of Malta and the remarkable (and underestimated) Egyptian campaign of 1801 when it gained its Sphinx badge.

For the first six years of its short but glorious existence the 2nd Battalion fulfilled the primary role for which it was originally intended, raising and training recruits, who were periodically sent off in drafts to the 1st Battalion, and holding those soldiers whose age, state of health or limited terms of enlistment rendered them unfit for overseas service in the higher readiness 1st Battalion. Its secondary role at that time was to support the Civil Power in Ireland, and as such the battalion was often dispersed in detachments, a situation generally accepted as inimical to good discipline, administration, and in particular training, which was largely confined to annual camp at the Curragh or elsewhere.

Everything changed when the 2nd Battalion embarked to join Sir Arthur Wellesley's army in Portugal. On arrival at Lisbon in March 1809 the battalion was quite rightly judged to be unready for active service, with a large gap of experience and maturity between the old soldiers and the young lads, and it was accordingly sent to garrison Gibraltar. By September 1810, after a further period in the rather more operational garrison environment of Cadiz, the 30th were judged fit to join Wellington's field army in the Lines of Torres Vedras. There followed over two years of campaigning in Spain and Portugal, in the course of which the officers and men of the 30th had good reason to be proud of their parts in the bloody storming of Badajoz, the great victory of Salamanca and the successful delaying action at Villamuriel.

Unfortunately, the regimental manning structures were based on an assumption that the 1st Battalion, in the East Indies from 1806, would be fed by a home-based 2nd Battalion; the dispatch of the 2nd Battalion to an operational theatre made this impossible to sustain for long, and indeed after two campaigns in Spain the 2nd Battalion was sent home to recruit. Its extraordinarily rapid regeneration between September and December 1813, and consequent selection to join Sir Thomas Graham in Holland, are a testimony to the organisational skill and determination of the Commanding Officer, Lieutenant Colonel Alexander Hamilton.

Despite its chronic lack of experienced officers and a shortage of casualty replacements in the Peninsula, by the time of the Waterloo campaign the 2nd Battalion of the 30th was indeed a veteran unit by any standard, and should not be confused with those home-based second and third battalions, full of youngsters and recently volunteered militiamen, that were rushed over to the Low Countries in May 1815, causing Wellington to regret the absence of much of his 'Old Spanish Army'. An extreme example of this 'infamous army' was the 3rd Battalion of the 14th Foot, in which fourteen officers and some 300 men were under the age of twenty. In the 30th, by contrast, only six officers and rather fewer than one hundred soldiers were under twenty, all the latter having at least two years' service and 412 of them (over 82%) had more than five years' service (comparable to the 28th Foot, another acknowledged 'Old Spanish Army' battalion, who had 371 soldiers (71%) with more than 5 years). An average private soldier of the 30th at Waterloo was about 29 years old with over 6 years' regular service, mostly in the Peninsula and the Low Countries. He was also, incidentally, some 5 feet 7 inches tall (exactly the same as his regimental successors 150 years later) and was more likely to have been recruited in Ireland than in the Eastern Counties of England.

The 30th has been well served by its historians of the Napoleonic period. The first of these could be said to be Edward Macready, whose vivid journals of the last three years of the 2nd Battalion, including Waterloo, are extensively quoted in the current publication. Macready not only wrote his own detailed account very shortly after the events described, but subsequently, having taken it upon himself to correct some major errors relating to the 30th in the first edition of Siborne's great history of the Waterloo campaign, took great pains to check his impressions of the Waterloo campaign against the recollections of his surviving contemporaries. His letter to them seeking confirmation, or otherwise, of his enclosed view of events at Waterloo is a model of open-minded academic investigation:

> I will thank you to return the paper to me with your marginal comments on it stating with what you coincide, wherein you differ from me. What did you see? What you did not? Wherein you think I

am deceived? In short, anything that may assist me to come at the actual truth and to lay it before Captain Siborne.

Edward Macready's widow left his copious journals to the regiment, and by the 1880s they were being used within 1st Battalion The East Lancashire Regiment, successor to the 30th, as a basis for historical lectures to the regiment in India. This appears to have prompted several officers to begin further research, for in 1887 a regimental committee published *The Historical Records of the XXX Regiment*. This was no mere extraction from the *Regimental Digest of Services*, but bears the evidence of extensive and diligent enquiries in the Public Record Office and the Library of the Royal United Services Institute and, in the editor's words, 'it is as far as possible made up of the narratives of officers and others who actually served in the operations they describe'. In the years before the Great War, this material was amplified and worked up for publication, in 1923, as *The History of the XXX Regiment* by Lieutenant Colonel Neil Bannatyne, whose own service in 'The Old Three Tens', 1864–91, was close enough to the Napoleonic period for him to be able to tap into a living tradition. The result remains one of the more readable of the old regimental histories, invariably accurate as to fact and seldom less than persuasive in interpretation.

The present work builds on these sure foundations, but in the century or more since Bannatyne and his contemporaries carried out their researches our knowledge has been greatly enlarged by new material, such as the journal of Lieutenant and Adjutant William Stewart. In addition to making excellent use of such first-hand sources, Carole Divall (ably supported by her husband John) has further mined and analysed the rich resources of the Public Record Office to trace the evolution of the 2nd Battalion. Of particular interest to many military historians will be the author's use of court martial records, an under-exploited source of great value to anyone wishing to understand the inner workings and social mores of Wellington's army; the verbatim witness statements in this class of record give an authentic voice to soldiers of all ranks, recording strange stories and revealing much fascinating detail. Equally good use has been made of the biographical information to be found in such records as Officers' Half Pay and Soldiers' Pensions, which also offer many illuminating glimpses into their service. The result is a well-rounded portrait of one of Wellington's regiments and those who served in it.

It is a universal truth that the character and ethos of a military unit is to a remarkable extent shaped by that of its commander, and the 2nd Battalion of the 30th Regiment was always fortunate in its commanding officers, in particular Alexander Hamilton.

Hamilton was a seasoned soldier who had served under Abercromby, Moore, Nelson, Wellington and Graham, and had, like Napoleon, won early distinction at Toulon in 1793. He was an admirable example of that cadre of dedicated and professional regimental officers to whom the British Army, then as now, owes a very large part of its success. Personally modest, or perhaps too proud to lobby for honours and preferment, Hamilton took good care of his officers and men. He was a sound trainer who set great store on practice with ball ammunition and whose practical battlefield injunction to 'fire low boys – hit 'em in the legs and spoil their dancing' showed a good understanding of both the limitations of contemporary musketry and the sardonic humour of his soldiers. Although his men reckoned that 'nothing will hit him', he was in fact wounded three times, twice seriously. His coolness and resolution under fire is exemplified in an anecdote recorded by Bannatyne:

> Colonel Hamilton, like most old campaigners, chewed tobacco, and tradition says that in action it was his custom when he saw any sign of nervousness or impatience in the ranks to ask audibly if anyone had any tobacco. Half a dozen brass boxes were of course offered to the great man, who, with all eyes fixed on him, would select one and cutting a convenient quid, insert it in his cheek, nor until he had it comfortably under weigh would he deign to notice the enemy. He thought a thirty-yard range quite long enough.

It was a tribute to the exertions of Hamilton in particular, and his company officers, that in 1817 young Lieutenant Edward Macready could write the following disbandment obituary on his beloved 2nd Battalion:

> This brave Corps . . . was not more distinguished by its professional exertions than by the cordial and brotherly unanimity which pervaded its internal regulations. The men were devoted to their Colours and their officers; never, while the Regiment existed, had they been known to shrink from either. The officers, scrupulously attentive to their soldiers, entered with feeling into their wants and wishes, and received a pleasing return when circumstances threw the power of obliging into the hands of the private.

To which he added that

> it was not a brutal fierceness, but a truly noble feeling for the honor of their country and Corps, that excited their energies in the day of action.

Since those words were written the Infantry of the Line, backbone of every British military operation, has suffered many structural changes and, over the past sixty years, a succession of drastic reductions. Some of the organisational changes, in particular those of Cardwell and Haldane, were necessary and useful; others have been driven by the time-honoured prejudice of the British political classes against military expenditure and a complacent diversion of resources in favour of projects offering more immediate electoral gratification. Despite these vicissitudes, in the course of which the legacy of the 30th Regiment of Foot has been inherited in succession by The East Lancashire Regiment (1881–1958), The Lancashire Regiment (1958–1970), The Queen's Lancashire Regiment (1970–2006) and The Duke of Lancaster's Regiment, such is the potency of tradition that a seamless web of *esprit de corps* connects today's soldiers with those who fought at Waterloo.

In the mess of 1st Battalion The Duke of Lancaster's Regiment, young officers are surrounded by material reminders of 'The Old Three Tens', from battle paintings and medals on the walls to a fragment of the Regimental Colour and even a twig from the hedge near which the regiment stood on the field of Waterloo, while among the cherished trophies in Regimental Headquarters are the Eagle taken at Salamanca and a French drum captured at Waterloo. But such relics carry little meaning without the stories of human endeavour, fortitude and gallantry which lie behind them, and so those officers and soldiers who have the honour to be the lineal descendants of the 30th Foot, and all who support them, will be truly grateful to Carole Divall for this new, definitive history of the regiment at one of the most critical periods of its long history.

Spectamur Agendo

Chapter 1
The Thirtieth Regiment of the Line

When Ensign Hamilton joined the 30th Regiment, he became a member of a corps with a hundred years of history, going back to 1689 when Sir George Saunderson, baronet, of Saxby, Lincolnshire, who was also Viscount Castleton in the Irish peerage, received a commission from William III to raise a regiment of foot. Saunderson's estates were in Lincolnshire and Yorkshire, which became the source of the earliest recruits. This Lincolnshire connection was still flourishing a century later, and Hamilton began his military career recruiting there while the rest of the regiment was in the West Indies. In June 1689 the new regiment mustered at York, clothed and armed. What might the red-coated ensign have made of his forebears? Their grey coats, waistcoats and breeches, all with purple facings, and their broad-brimmed hats would have seemed curiously outlandish. He would not have envied the laced and plumed hats, the elaborate wigs, lace cravats, knots of ribbons on the shoulders of coats seamed with gold, the embroidered baldrics and silk sashes of his predecessors. Uniform, and war itself, had changed dramatically in the intervening years.

For the next hundred years the new regiment was intermittently on active service, in Europe and beyond. Particularly notable for its uncanny resemblance to the assault on Badajoz more than a century later was the attack on Namur in 1695. 'The grenadiers marched straight up to the palisades of the covered way and discharged their grenades over them. The 23rd and Saunderson's [that is, Castleton's regiment] were the next to come up, the enemy's fire from the covered way was terrific and while the batteries of the Allies galled the French in their works the French redoubts Epinoise and St Fiacre fired with fatal effect upon the English regiments as they marched up the glacis, but the assailants could not be driven back. Then the French sprang four fougasses on the glacis. The English fled backwards as the earth opened and belched forth its deadly load; no man knew whether his next step might place him again on the very nest of one of those fearful messengers of death, yet even this did not deter the British troops from again advancing.'[1] The attack was ultimately successful and Namur was carried, but it was a baptism of blood and fire for the young regiment.

Disbanded in 1698, the regiment was then reformed in 1702 to serve as marines. There were plenty of old faces, but they wore a new uniform, with yellow facings, earning themselves the nickname 'yellowbellies', a name still given to Lincolnshire people. Only later did the regiment acquire its more famous title, 'The Old Three Tens'. After eight years, however, and service across the globe from the West Indies to Spain, they were once more disbanded when the Peace of Utrecht brought the War of the Spanish Succession to an end; a disbandment which brought about the only mutiny in the regiment's history when the men found themselves seriously in arrears of pay.

The Jacobite resurgence of 1715 saw an urgent need for more troops and the regiment was re-founded for the second time, taking its position as the 30th in the line. As such it continued until 1881. Military memories are long and tenacious, however; even during the second Boer War a sergeant of the first battalion, the East Lancashire Regiment, into which the 30th had been transformed, wrote: 'We were soldiers, fit successors of the men who, in the Peninsula, at Waterloo, and in the Crimea, had helped to make, and uphold, the proud record of the old XXXth.'[2]

Once again there was active service, in the Mediterranean, in France, and eventually in the American colonies, but there were also extended periods in Ireland. The army was not popular among civilians unless it was fighting and winning victories abroad, when it was lauded from a distance and its commanders, like the Marquis of Granby or General Wolfe, became national heroes. At home it was regarded as licentious, unruly and expensive, and its numbers were quickly reduced, while as many regiments as that country could reasonably sustain were sent to Ireland where their presence supported the Protestant Ascendancy.

There were other activities which were typical of the period: serving for eight years in Gibraltar; recruiting, mainly in the Eastern Counties and Scotland; even some road-making in Scotland. In 1775, the composition of NCOs and other ranks was 266 English, ninety-eight Scottish, twelve Irish and two foreign. The influx of Irish Catholics had just started as the long-standing embargo on Irish recruits was lifted, but was yet to become a torrent. One other feature of the period was the acquisition of a light company. In 1772, when the regiment was reviewed at Ferrybridge, the light company skirmished in front of the other companies, a novel development of infantry drill.

The War of American Independence broke out in 1775, but the 30th were not involved until 1781. In September of that year they saw action at the battle of Entaw, which produced the heaviest casualties of the war. Both sides claimed victory, but the British held the field. The war against the colonists was stuttering into defeat, however, and in 1782 the regiment was sent first to the Leeward Islands, and then to Jamaica, which was under French attack. Finally, in 1784, it was posted to Dominica. It had also been designated the

Cambridgeshire Regiment in a move which gave all the regiments of the line county appellations, although the titles were rarely used outside official correspondence. Nevertheless, the Eastern Counties remained a prime source of recruits until well into the next century.

At this point an impression of the regiment can be gained from the jaundiced recollections of a private soldier, who identifies himself as James Aytoun. He joined the 30th in 1788, and served with them certainly until 1807, since there are references to India in his memoirs. In his opinion the regiment was commanded by officers who were unfit for the purpose. The adjutant was often the only officer present at exercise, while the captain of the light company, Satterthwaite, was a 'paper' officer whom Aytoun never saw. His recollections constitute a list of beatings and floggings, stories of officers indifferent to the welfare of their men, and examples of exploitation. It is no wonder, therefore, that he failed to understand the anti-slavery movement in Europe. 'The negroes have more liberty than the soldiers. The men, as often as may be convenient, trot six or seven miles to a plantation to see a favourite black wench or to dance ... A soldier is liable to be flogged if more than a mile from barracks, camp or quarters and if out of barracks after tattoo they are liable to be tried by a court martial and punished.'[3] Slaves were too valuable to be ill-treated: soldiers were dispensable. Nevertheless, even Aytoun conceded that matters improved after the outbreak of the French Revolution. New regulations of 1792 and 1797 meant that men were no longer beaten randomly with rattan canes. Instead, all soldiers had to be tried by a court martial, with sworn evidence both for and against. Furthermore, humane officers recognised that contented soldiers were more effective soldiers.

The regiment returned to Europe in 1791, arriving at Portsmouth in March to find Europe on a knife-edge. Things could never be the same after the storming of the Bastille in 1789, and two years later it was obvious that the increasingly extreme position adopted by the revolutionaries in France would prove a threat to all those states which hoped to preserve the status quo. With Europe poised for war, the British anticipated extensive naval activity. In 1793 the 30th was broken up and distributed by company through the fleet to serve yet again as marines. Two companies were on HMS *Swiftsure* and HMS *St Albans*, and a detachment was sent to HMS *Bellona*. All three ships, and others on which men of the 30th subsequently served, were part of the Channel fleet. A further four companies served with Hood's fleet in the Mediterranean where, according to Aytoun, they were 'joined by the Spanish fleet and I believe we were in all more than forty ships of the line, besides frigates, sloops and tenders. We cruised on the coasts of Genoa and France till August 28 and then stood in to a landing place a considerable distance from Toulon. We were on boats embarked on the *Robust* at the time commanded by Commodore Elfinstone [sic] and the *Robust* pushed into the shore as the pilot advised. We were landed in boats without interruption. We marched through vineyards and the grapes were ripe and French girls brought us, as we passed along, bunches of fine black grapes, which was new to British soldiers.'[4]

Aytoun was among the first British soldiers to be landed in the south of France, in a body of 1,500 marines and soldiers who had been acting as marines. Their purpose was to give support to the Royalists in Toulon who had risen against the revolutionary government in Paris and now depended upon British help to keep them safe from reprisals. The port, which was vital to the French Mediterranean fleet as a supply depot, had already been under Anglo-Spanish blockade before the rebellion broke out. On 27 August the British ships were invited into the harbour. After a day's hesitation, Admiral Lord Hood went one step further and landed the 1,500 marines, although he had no long-term strategy. Shortly afterwards the Spanish ships joined the British.

The Republican reaction was immediate; a force of 12,000 men under General Carteaux, later augmented by 5,000 men from Italy under General Lapoype, was sent to deal with the situation. Meanwhile, their opponents were also gaining in strength, eventually rising to 15,000 men. This all took time, however, and the first engagement, when a French force was defeated at Ollioules by an Anglo-Spanish detachment, involved only 500 invaders against about 750 Republicans. It was, perhaps, a lucky success; ill-disciplined troops caught in a narrow defile by experienced regulars.

Overall, the allied situation was not particularly secure. Their line of defence extended for eight miles around Toulon, describing a U-shape which had as its three crucial points Fort la Malgue, Mount Faron and Fort Malbousquet. From this defensive position, with resources thinly stretched, it was impossible to take offensive action against the gathering strength of the Republicans. Nevertheless, the Anglo-Spanish forces had guns and ammunition, and ships in support, so that the weakness of their situation was not immediately apparent.

After the fall of Marseilles, which had also risen against the Republicans, the defence of Toulon became increasingly perilous, particularly when a rising star of the French military, Captain Napoleon Bonaparte (still known as Napoleone Buonaparte), arrived on 16 September to take command of the artillery bombardment. At the same time, Hood depleted his forces by sending some of them to Corsica. Fortunately, Lord Mulgrave had reached Toulon on 6 September and under his command the expedition acquired greater military coherence, even though Mulgrave was primarily a politician. One significant step was the organisation of the British forces into two battalions, one of which was commanded by Captain Brereton of the 30th.

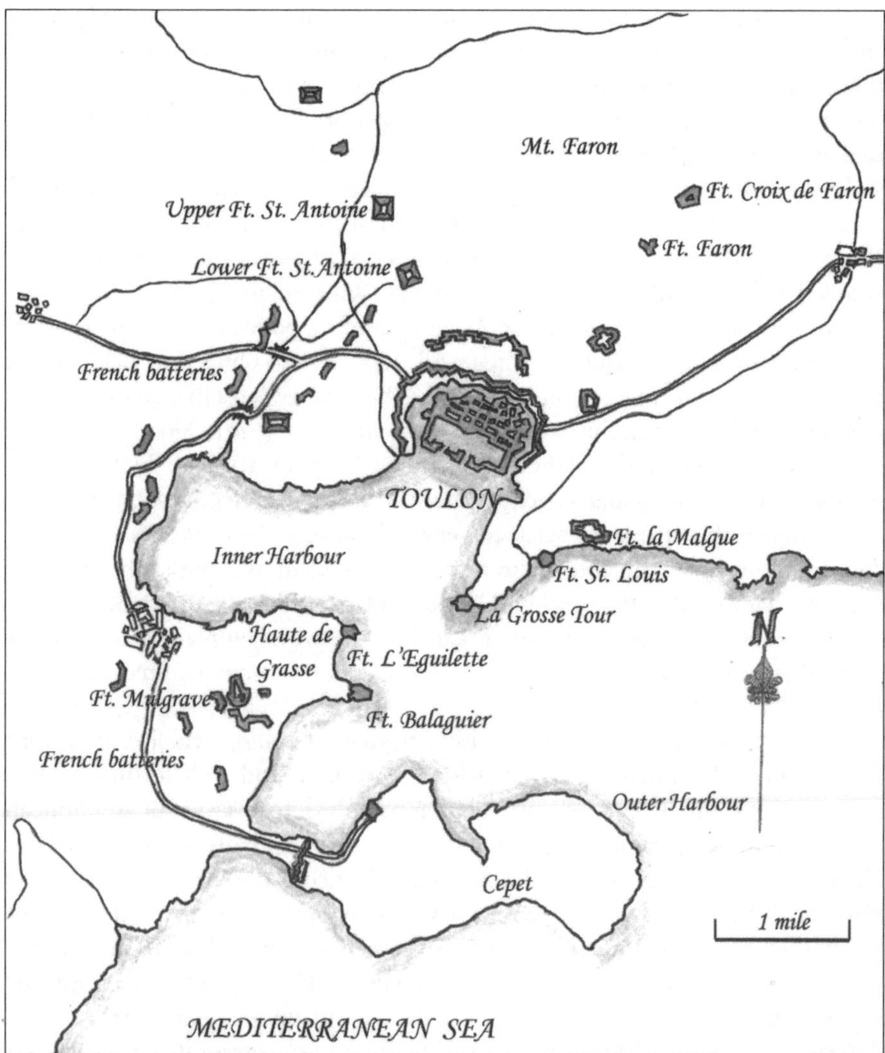

The Siege of Toulon, 1793

Initially, on the French side, there was a dispute about strategy. Napoleon wanted to focus on Pointe l'Eguilette, a position which would make the ships in the harbour vulnerable to French guns. General Carteaux, however, preferred a land blockade, hoping to pick off the earth forts which the allies had built and then attack the main, Vaubanesque defences of the town. As overall commander, his view prevailed, although Napoleon had the ear of the *representants du people*, Augustin Robespierre and Christophe Saliceti.

The initial French bombardment, across several days, concentrated on the ships in the inner harbour, inflicting damage and casualties. Lord Hood decided, therefore, to occupy the heights of Grasse, on the south side of the harbour. Sir Thomas Graham, serving as a volunteer and Lord Mulgrave's aide-de-camp, sent the following account of what happened on 21 September to his brother-in-law, Lord Cathcart: 'Both Admiral Gravina and Lord Mulgrave went, and I accompanied them; the detachment consisted of 150 British and 350 Spaniards. We embarked at midnight and landed near Fort Balaguay, and gained the wooded heights without seeing any enemy. The Spaniards were all against occupying the westernmost and most commanding point, as being too distant to receive any support from the ships, and Lord M. was obliged to yield, and to return to the easternmost point of the hill. The post was established there about daybreak, and we returned to breakfast on board the *Victory* [Hood's flagship].

'In the afternoon, they [the Anglo-Spanish] were attacked by 600 men, who got near them under cover of the wood, but were repulsed with some loss. Some of the Spaniards behaved very well, others ill – ours all well; we had an officer of the 25th and eight men wounded. In the night the Spanish Commandant wanted to abandon the post, but our officer (Captain Brereton of the 30th) refused to go, and sent to Lord Hood, who complained to Langara [second-in-command of the Spanish forces], and another commandant was immediately sent.'[5]

Crucial to both sides were the hills beyond Toulon, principally Mount Faron and Le Hauteur de Grace, which were high and well fortified. They were held by the defenders until September, despite a series of Republican attacks. On 30 September, however, the enemy set up batteries above Mount Faron. In response Lord Mulgrave tried to drive the French from their redoubt. The night was foggy, which undoubtedly helped the allies as they began their attack at 2.00 a.m. Graham, in another letter to his brother-in-law, provided a detailed account of what happened. Having reminded Cathcart of the difficulty of bringing forces up in column under heavy fire, he then described the action. 'The British and Piedmontese were quite mixed at this period, and the rear of the columns from the higher ground still kept on firing. During this check, the Neapolitan grenadiers advanced . . . and began to draw off the attention of the left of the enemy's line, to which the advance guard had fallen back. At the critical moment our people charged from behind the rocks, and ran on without firing. The enemy began to give way, and very soon took to their heels, and, being closely pursued, never attempted to rally; but as it was up hill and one continued bed of angular stones, it was impossible for any of our troops, faint with hunger, thirst, and fatigue, to get up close with them. The Neapolitan grenadiers and the head of our columns of British and

Piedmontese entered the redoubt at the same moment, where only three or four hundred men attempted to resist. The rest fled by the lunette towards La Vallette, or tried to hide themselves among the perpendicular rocks on the north side of the redoubt, from whence many of them fell or were tumbled down by the foreigners, especially the Spaniards, who had no notion of giving quarter, as their great object seemed to be to get possession of the spoils of the dead, for which every consideration of humanity was laid aside; the conduct of the British was strikingly different. From the redoubt, the lunette, and rocks near both, a heavy fire was kept up on the enemy, who could not get very fast away as the descent was so rapid, and a party from Fort Faron went much lower down the hill, and pursued them closely, till brought up by the fire of some guns they had on the side of Coudon. The success of this attack was no doubt much owing to Elphinstone's attack, originally intended as a diversion only; but when he heard the firing become general in all the points to his left, he left only 30 men in the fort, and went out with 460; of these the Spaniards and French hardly ever came into action, but about 160 of the 30th and 69th Regiments behaved with uncommon steadiness, climbing up the face of an excessive rugged and steep hill (exactly a cairn) without returning a shot till near the top, though exposed to the enemy's fire from the moment they left the fort, which is within musket-shot of the top of the hill.'[6]

Elphinstone, in his report to Lord Mulgrave, particularly noted that Captains Torriano of the 30th and Beresford of the 69th behaved with particular gallantry as they led their men up the mountainside under fire. It is interesting to compare this eulogy of Torriano with a view from the ranks. According to Aytoun, 'We had a company in Dominica that was called Captain Torriano's but I never saw him until we came to Liverpool. He was a remarkable proud man and very seldom was with the regiment . . . Major Campbell had a whim which the men called Transportation into Captain Torriano's Company. If a man was very ill-behaved he was transported into that company so that it was the sink of the regiment.'[7] Such is the significance of perspective when evaluating a man's character.

The Republicans had also placed a battery at Quatre Moulins, south of the village of La Seyne, and two batteries at La Hauteur de Reinier, but these were disabled on 8 October when Brereton successfully led 300 British troops, including 225 rank and file of the 30th, and various foreign detachments on a mission to spike the guns.

A week later the position on Cap le Brun, which had only been established the previous day and was weakly held by French Royalists, was attacked by Republican forces and taken after a fierce struggle. Lord Mulgrave, convinced that the Republicans had extended too far in advance of their lines, launched a counter-attack from his position at La Malgue. Elphinstone wrote to Lord Hood. 'On the 15th before day, the report of musquetry was heard, which increased with the light, and induced me to order 100 of the 30th Regiment, 100 Neapolitans, 50 Spaniards, and the remainder of the Royal Louis, to follow me there. By the time I got to the bottom of the hill, the fire was become very brisk, and I had some difficulty to get up by the road. The troops from La Malgue were nearly up, by a shorter road through vineyards. I detached Captain Torriano of the 30th to go round the left of the hill, and take the enemy on their right flank. This had the desired effect and they gave way. On the top of the hill I found the Royal Louis defending themselves gallantly, although hard pressed, but the outposts driven in, and the men in want of cartridges. I advanced with the fresh troops, and recovered our outposts, after an obstinate resistance, and placed Captain Tomlinson of the 30th in the advance, the Neapolitans in the centre, Captain Torriano on the left, with the Royal Louis and the Spanish troops on the right, and it was near an hour before the enemy retired.'[8]

Unfortunately, Elphinstone then himself retired to organise reinforcements. He returned to discover that the enemy had advanced in strength under cover of the woods. Supported by artillery, they attacked the post on all sides and successfully overwhelmed the defenders. Among those killed was Captain Torriano, whom Elphinstone described as one of the most respected officers in Europe. He also praised the 30th for their stout resistance. As well as the loss of Torriano, the regiment suffered Lieutenant Alexander Hamilton, wounded, and Lieutenant Shewbridge, temporarily posted missing. As a result, two sergeants brought the men safely off the field.[9] Eventually, Cap le Brun was saved for the Royalist cause not by the advance of the additional troops, whose movements lacked co-ordination, but because the Republicans recognised that they were cut off from their own lines. Common sense, therefore, recommended a speedy retreat.

Two successes should have given heart to the Royalist cause, but on the British side at least there was an awareness that co-operation with the Spanish was proving increasingly difficult. Furthermore, few British reinforcements could be expected; the 750 men who arrived from Gibraltar on 27 October made little difference. However, the end of the month also saw the arrival of 1,500 Neapolitans, although the replacement of Lord Mulgrave by General O'Hara, a man inclined to pessimism, was an unfortunate development.

Meanwhile, matters were improving for the Republicans. The Royalist stronghold of Lyons had fallen, releasing troops for the attack on Toulon, and on 7 November Carteaux had been relieved of his command, possibly at the prompting of Napoleon. His successor was General Doppet, but more significant was the arrival of Baron du Teil as artillery commander. He recognised Bonaparte's acumen and gave him virtually a free hand. The subsequent increase in skillfully placed batteries exposed the vulnerability of the principal allied forts, Mulgrave and Malbousquet.

On 26 October an order arrived directing the 30th to Gibraltar preparatory to their departure for the West Indies but the squadron which should have transported them to Gibraltar was delayed in Genoa. A posting to the West Indies was unlikely to have been popular; too few would have returned if it had actually happened. Nevertheless, remaining where they were must have caused some discontent since by this time rations consisted of rotten meat and bread full of maggots.

Events now swung in favour of the attackers under Doppet's more aggressive command. On 15 November, after some probing sorties, a committed attack was made on Fort Mulgrave; this was only beaten off by determined defensive action. The Republican failure, however, led to Doppet's replacement by the more competent General Dugommier. Further Republican reinforcements, bringing their strength to something like 35,000 men, tipped the balance even further. The defenders were outnumbered two to one and the fall of Toulon was inevitable.

With Bonaparte granted the freedom by Dugommier to direct the artillery bombardment as he chose, Fort Mulgrave remained the principal objective, although Fort Malbousquet was also a tempting target. On the night of 27 November the latter fort was bombarded by guns which had been brought forward and carefully concealed. The gunners in Fort Mulgrave and on Hood's ships launched a counter-bombardment, thus preserving the fort in allied hands for a while longer, but its weak position had been all too clearly demonstrated.

Meanwhile, allied forces were concealed in woods around La Grasse, the height on which Fort Mulgrave was situated, and at 4.00 a.m. on 29 November they advanced in three columns, the British, about a sixth of the total, on the left, against the Republican battery position at Poudrière, where among the guns was a long cannon which could fire into Toulon itself. This battery was successfully taken, as were two further batteries, although such a move was against the tactical intentions of the attack. Having advanced too far, the allies then found themselves under counter-attack from the rallied and reformed Republican forces and suffered heavy losses. The capture of General O'Hara may have been a mixed blessing, however, since his pessimism did not inspire the troops. The allies rallied on a Sardinian line which had stood its ground but retreat was the only option. A further stand was made at Fort Malbousquet but overall the action was a disaster.

For most of the 30th, their interest in the fate of Toulon ended at this point, 300 of them being detached to serve as marines. The lethal struggle continued a little longer, however.

Republican tactics now focused on pinning down the garrison of Fort Malbousquet, while attacking Fort Mulgrave. Feints against the former fort and the forces on Mount Faron, and a long-range bombardment of Cap le Brun would prevent the allies coming to the assistance of the beleaguered Fort Mulgrave. The bombardment started on 15 December, and the actual attack was launched two days later at one in the morning. Aytoun recalled that: 'we had constant skirmishes with the French and the most tremendous cannonading and bombarding that can be conceived. When I was in Fort Mulgrave we were both cannonaded and bombarded. The French threw four bomb shells and we returned the favor [sic] with three. So it often happened that those who were coming and those who were going were seen passing just over our camp at the same time and if the French artillery had been as good as they were willing, we should have suffered greatly but many of their shot and shells passed over us and fell half a mile beyond us.'[10]

According to the report of Lieutenant General Dundas, now in command, which was written on board the *Victory* on 21 December, 'Captain Connolly 18th Regiment abandoned the post entrusted to his care, at the moment he saw the British and Spanish picquets retire into the Fort [Mulgrave] and the command devolved upon Capt Vaumorel of the 30th Regt, but on the enemy entering on the Spanish side, the British quarter commanded by Capt Vaumorel of the 30th Regt could not be much longer maintained, notwithstanding several gallant efforts were made for that purpose. It was therefore at last carried, and the remains of the garrison of 700 men (Spaniards) retired towards the shore of Balaquier . . .' After the fort had been taken, Captain Vaumorel, Lieutenant Cuyler, five sergeants, three drummers and 140 rank and file and seamen attached to the 30th were posted missing. 'The fate on the above Officers and Men is not nor cannot be known, but, from all the intelligence that can be gained, it is to be apprehended that they fell before day-break, gallantly defending the post they were entrusted with, when abandoned by other troops.'[11]

This report relates to the events of 17 December, when Fort Mulgrave was finally lost. Further attacks gave the French command of Pointe l'Eguilette so that, just as Napoleon had always intended, the allied fleet was vulnerable to artillery fire. The Petite Rade had to be abandoned, and it was only a matter of time before the ships would have to depart. On land, Mount Faron had also been taken by the Republicans. Although the first attack was repulsed, the Republicans were able to establish themselves in the centre and on the western

end of the ridge, which obliged the garrison to surrender. At the same time, Fort Malbousquet was evacuated by the Spanish.

Departure was both inevitable and difficult to effect. The only position still held by the allies was Fort La Malgue. Being crucial to a successful embarkation, it was only abandoned at the last minute. The arsenal was destroyed, and the soldiers of all nations retreated to the ships, accompanied by as many of the local citizens as could make their escape. On 19 December the Tricolour flew over Toulon.

It was just another sorry chapter in the wretched sequence of expeditions which characterised British military involvement in the Revolutionary Wars, but for the 30th it was a first taste of fighting the enemy who would dominate their lives for the next twenty-two years, and also a first glimpse of the brilliance of a man they would not meet again until 1815.

What about the men who were posted missing at Fort Mulgrave? Vaumorel, adopting a third person voice, wrote the following account. 'Orders in writing had been received on the morning of the 16th by the officer commanding the fort to do his utmost in defending the same for the protection of that part of the fleet anchored in the inner harbour, and should the ammunition be expended to receive the enemy on the bayonet. Captain Vaumorel's predecessor, at variance with this order, abandoned the post during the first attack without being followed by a single British soldier, or even by his own servant, in consequence of which Captain Vaumorel decided to defend the place to the last extremity.

'After daylight on the 17th, the enemy made a third attack and succeeded in getting possession of a Spanish battery of five 24-pounder guns divided by an epaulement from the British side. After a feeble defence the Spaniards, 700 men under a lieut-colonel, gave way and retired to the shore at Balaguier; the enemy entered through the embrasures and the British were obliged to surrender half-an-hour after daybreak.'[12] The surviving defenders were made prisoners of war but were well treated by the Republicans during their period of captivity, which lasted twenty months.

Hamilton also referred to his experiences at Toulon in his statement of service of 1810. He cited a wound he had received at Mount Faron, and the more serious wound which incapacitated him at Cap le Brun and nearly cost him his leg. For both Hamilton and Vaumorel this was the beginning of a distinguished military career, although they would eventually serve the British cause in very different capacities.

Chapter 2

Battle Honours – 'Egypt'

The ignominious departure from Toulon marked for the 30th the end of their presence in mainland France for more than twenty years. Admiral Hood, however, now directed his attention to another area of potential French weakness, the island of Corsica. Vulnerable to naval attack, and with a disaffected population, it seemed a weak point in Republican defences and a useful base for the British Mediterranean fleet. There were only three French garrisons on the island, at Bastia, Calvi and the Bay of San Fiorenzo, so that it represented a tempting target for British occupation, despite the failure of an earlier attempt to blockade these strongholds.

In January 1794 Hood landed 3,000 soldiers and marines on the island, including men of the 30th, to challenge a French force of much the same strength. Their first objective was to seize the town and citadel of Mortello[13] on the western shore of San Fiorenzo Bay. Battered by four guns, Mortello surrendered on 10 February after an assault led by Lieutenant Hamilton. A

Admiral Hood's attack on Corsica, 1794

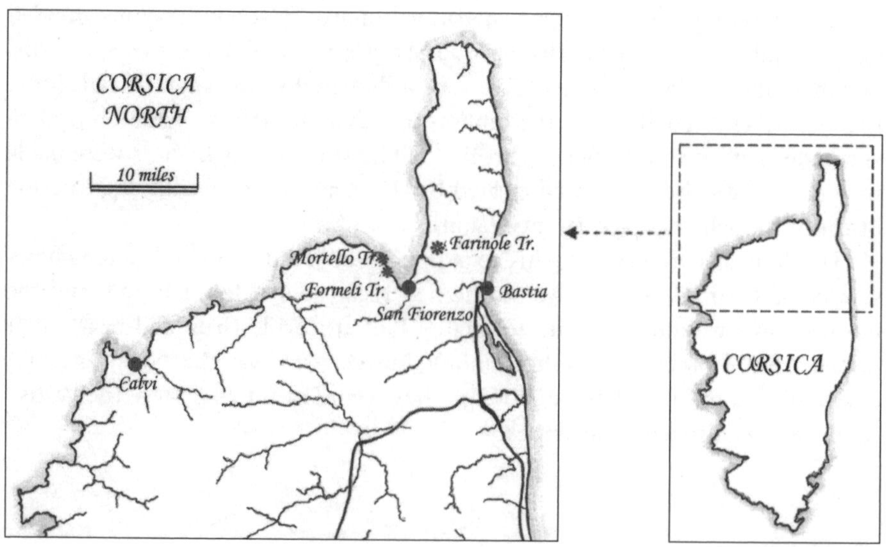

week later the Convention redoubt, higher up the bay, was carried with all its guns. As a result, the enemy abandoned Formeli, where they were manning two batteries, and retreated to Bastia, which was then besieged by the British. Attempts to take the three forts which guarded the town failed dismally, but the French garrison was eventually starved into submission and surrendered on 15 May. The 30th won praise from Lord Hood for their part in this short campaign: 'Major Brereton of the XXX Regiment and every officer and soldier ... are justly entitled to my warmest acknowledgements. Their persevering ardour and desire to distinguish themselves cannot be too highly spoken of, and which it will be my pride to remember to the latest period of my life.'[14] Of the 1,200 men who took Bastia, often regarded as a naval force, 1,000 were from regiments serving as marines, not least among them the Mediterranean detachment of the 30th. This action also brought the regiment into contact with one of the heroes of the age, Horatio Nelson, captain of the *Agamemnon*.

Having secured San Fiorenzo Bay and Bastia, Hood turned his attention to Calvi, although he himself departed at this point. He had heard that a French fleet was sailing from Toulon to relieve the garrison, and put to sea to prevent its arrival. Failing in this objective, he sailed on to Genoa, where he remained until the attack on Calvi was well under way. In his place, Captain Nelson was responsible for transferring the troops from Bastia to Calvi, landing them at Port Agro, two and a half miles south-west of Calvi on 19 June. Calvi itself was a formidable place, situated on a rocky peninsula and protected by two forts and several well-placed gun batteries. All these defences, however, could be attacked from higher ground, although only after roads had been built so that the guns could be dragged into position. By 4 June the first battery was in position, and opened fire on Fort Monteciesco. A further battery was positioned to attack Fort Mozzello, and both batteries maintained a fierce cannonade. In the counter-attack Nelson suffered the wound which cost him the sight of his right eye. By 18 June, however, the breach at Mozzello was deemed practicable, and the following day both Mozzello and the nearby Fountain Battery were carried with minimal loss. The town itself held fast, and further batteries were constructed to force its surrender. Finally, after some protracted negotiations, it was agreed that Calvi should capitulate on 10 August unless relieved from France. When no relieving force arrived, the surrender was completed, and Corsica passed into British hands for the next two years.

A year later Lieutenant Hamilton, on board HMS *Terrible*, took part in two naval actions, on 14 March and 2 July. In the former, fought off Genoa, there were also officers and men of the 30th aboard *Egmont* and *Princess Royal*, as well as women and children. As well as these actions, Hamilton also received the thanks of Captain George Campbell for putting down a mutiny on board

Terrible while at sea. Elsewhere in the Mediterranean, members of the regiment, acting as marines, were involved in the capture of the French ships, *Ça Ira* and *Censeur*, while others saw service in the West Indies.

Indeed, the regiment might well have thought themselves destined to act as the military arm of the navy, even though this had blessed them with successes which more than outweighed the disaster at Toulon. The staff and headquarters under the rapidly promoted Lieutenant Colonel Lockhart had joined the detachments in Corsica, but their return journey in 1795 proved more hazardous than their experiences on the island. Their convoy was attacked off Cape St Vincent, and they were taken as prisoners to Bordeaux. At the beginning of the following year, however, they were exchanged by cartel and Lockhart was able to resume his command, at Colchester and then at Bandon in Ireland, of a regiment still depleted by the absence of the marine detachments. Ireland was considered particularly vulnerable to French attack, as General Hoche's arrival in Bantry Bay in 1796 demonstrated. Although Hoche did not land, the French fleet being dispersed by storms, invasion was anticipated for the next two years and beyond. The convulsions of 1798, when the long-threatened Irish rebellion finally erupted, might have had even more serious consequences if the French had launched their attack a month earlier, when the rebellion was at its height. Also, if they had landed in a less isolated area than County Sligo, they might have influenced events even at that late stage.

The 30th remained detached from the violence of the uprising and its brutal consequences. Their posting at Bandon kept them well away from the epicentre of the disturbances, for what was probably another period of tedium, as they watched for a French fleet that never arrived.

The men of the Mediterranean detachment, meanwhile, were drafted into the ships of Jervis's fleet, later the victors at the battle of Cape St Vincent, reminding us that the government saw the war with revolutionary France as essentially naval. Toulon and the disastrous expedition to Flanders had demonstrated how little could be achieved on land, so that it was better to become paymaster of the armies of reactionary Europe, and focus British aggression on what could be achieved at sea.

In accordance with the government's strategy, the 30th left Ireland at the end of 1798, embarking at Cove (Cork) for Minorca, and then sailing on to Palermo, where Nelson needed reinforcements to hold Sicily. This proved another period of inaction but the promise of conflict came a year later when the 30th sailed under the command of Sir Thomas Graham to Malta, which was held by the French. Major Lockhart remained in Messina with a small detachment but on 6 December 1799 the rest of the regiment, about 400 men, under the command of Lieutenant Colonel Wilkinson, embarked along with the 89th on HMS *Culloden* and HMS *Northumberland*, arriving at St Paul's Bay three days later. Initially the 30th marched to Birchirkara, but were then transferred to Ta'Bulebel, on the outskirts of Zetjun, where they took up entrenched positions. As the campaign continued, the French were forced to withdraw into Valletta, where their hopes of reinforcements were frustrated by the intervention of the British navy. One ship carrying 1,700 troops was taken and three others were put to flight. Meanwhile, Graham raised a Maltese levy, the first companies being given temporary officers from the 30th and the 89th. Wilkinson was offered command of the whole levy but declined, perhaps out of loyalty to the 30th.

In June 1800 Graham was superseded at General Abercrombie's command by General Pigot, who brought 1,500 extra troops. Abercrombie himself arrived in July, and praised Graham's efforts. By early September the French, holed up in Valletta, were ready to surrender, and on 8 September they were taken off the island by British ships. Before he also left the island, Graham wrote of his gratitude to the regiments he had commanded, praising them for their perseverance and discipline. The 30th had enjoyed a moment of glory, when the two flank companies, along with those of the 89th, and part of the 25th, stormed Fort Riscali, a French outpost, just before the surrender of Valletta.

The fall of Malta made Abercrombie's force, which was about 15,000 strong and based at Gibraltar, available for further action in the Mediterranean. An obvious objective was Egypt. The French still held Alexandria and Cairo, despite the precipitous departure of Napoleon a year before to pursue his political ambitions. A long-standing French dream of using Egypt as a route to India had not been abandoned, but the stranded French army represented a tempting target. The plan was contemplated even before Malta had fallen, and took definite shape in early autumn. In October the 30th sailed to Gibraltar to join the main force and then returned to Malta in November as part of the expedition. Finally, in December, the British troops, now in two divisions, embarked yet again.

There was some slight readjustment to the structure of the regiment as they prepared to move into very different territory from anything they had previously experienced. Lieutenant Colonel Lockhart returned to take overall control and the recently promoted Captain Hamilton rejoined, having served as brigade major to Brigadier General John Moore while in Malta.

An interesting and contemporaneous source for the Egypt campaign was published in 1803 as a *Journal of the Late Campaign in Egypt* by Thomas Walsh, captain in the 93rd Foot, and aide-de-camp to Major General Sir Eyre Coote. His observations vividly supplement an account of the part played by the 30th in the expedition. In complete contrast to Walsh's perspective of events is the view from the ranks found in the diary of Daniel Nicol of the 92nd. Many of his perceptions and experiences must have been shared by the men of the 30th.

The 30th finally set sail from Malta on 20 December, after the winds had settled. Nine days later they reached Marmorice Bay with the rest of the fleet of 200 ships, thirty-eight of which were serving as transports. On the way they survived a violent storm off Rhodes. The arrival in the bay certainly impressed Walsh: 'The sight of so many vessels sailing between the two narrow ridges of elevated mountains, which formed the intricate entrance into this bay, joined by the dismal and lowering aspect of the atmosphere, rendered more awful by the long and repeated flashes of lightning, made the scene impressively grand and solemn.'[15] A vast expanse of calm water, surrounded by tree-clad hills and bare crags, with barren mountains rising behind, created an awe-inspiring scene.

The troops were landed and remained for eight weeks practising manoeuvres in a novel fashion. Brigades were landed from flat-bottomed boats and then, in response to signals from naval officers, kept in lines of advance and retreat. This was to instruct them how they were to move and conduct themselves when the real landings took place. Not everything was perfect, though. Bread, in particular, left much to be desired. 'Some vessels were dispatched to Macri Bay for bullocks and others to Smyrna and Aleppo for bread which was furnished us by the Turks, a kind of hard dried husk. We were glad to get this as we were then put on full rations and our biscuits were bad and full of worms.'[16]

On 6 February there was a storm of rare violence which inspired both Walsh and Nicol to awestruck wonder. Walsh wrote: 'This morning was unusually dark and gloomy, and thick clouds continued to gather over the adjoining mountains, the summits of which were soon entirely hidden from our view. About eleven a tremendous thunder storm came on, accompanied with as heavy hail as ever known. The stones were considerably larger than pigeons' eggs; and came down with such terrible force, as soon to level several of the tents; the rain fell in torrents; and the wind blew furiously from the south east ... The rain continued with unabated violence all day, and likewise during the night, which was the most blowing and tempestuous I ever passed on shore. The lightning was incessant, and, breaking through the extreme darkness, increased the horrors of the storm.'[17] Nicol's response was similar. He commented on the size of the hail, larger than anyone had ever seen. As a result, the tents looked as if they had been riddled with musket balls.

On 17 February General Abercrombie explained his plans to his general officers, and three days later everything was ready for re-embarkation, although the actual departure was delayed for another two days by contrary winds.

Bearing in mind the reputation of British soldiers at the time, it is interesting that not a single complaint about their behaviour was received from the local population. The expedition now sailed for Egypt, through increasing gales, which may explain why on 25 February, when the gales were at their height, the 30th took several casualties, Lieutenant James, Paymaster Sergeant Matthews, two sergeants, two corporals and eight privates all being returned as wounded. Finally, on 1 March, they anchored in Aboukir Bay, famous as the scene of Nelson's victory of the Nile. A landing was impossible. Furthermore, any ships which approached too near the shore were fired upon by enemy artillery, the whole shoreline being well-fortified. The troops, however, were in good spirits and eager to get into the boats, but high winds and a dangerous surf meant that plans for landing had to be delayed, to general disappointment.

On 7 March the weather eased, and the following day a landing was made, signalled by the firing of a rocket. The 30th, in the second wave of the assault, suffered no casualties, but the battalions of the reserve, which made the first landings, took heavy losses against determined French resistance. The flat-bottomed boats, each with fifty men and a complement of sailors to row them, waited for the order to push off. The soldiers sat with their muskets between their knees. A solemn silence was preserved as the boats moved towards the point of rendezvous, the only sound being the splash of oars in the water. It took over four hours to get all the boats into position, at which point Captain Cochrane of the navy gave the signal to advance. Immediately every boat was rowed vigorously towards the shore. Shells were thrown at the French positions, but there was no response from the invisible enemy until the British boats were within firing range, when a tremendous bombardment of artillery opened up. This changed from shot and shell to grape as the boats neared the shore, and heavy casualties were taken. Walsh himself witnessed a boat carrying some Coldstream Guards struck by a shell, so that all were either killed or drowned. The landing continued, however, despite the battering, and although the French advanced to meet the attack they were quickly repulsed.

The 30th formed part of the fourth brigade, along with the 2nd, 44th and 89th, under General Doyle, 'A true and hearty Irishman, and well fitted to have command of men. He had none of that pride and sullenness which too often attend those in authority. He was ever attentive to our wants and his affability and kindness can never be forgotten by any soldier in the brigade.'[18] The strength of the 30th was forty-one sergeants and 433 other ranks, with thirty officers, while the whole British force numbered 17,512. Fit for immediate action were 15,463 infantry, two regiments of cavalry (472), and 578 artillery manning forty guns.

The main objective of the expedition was Alexandria, which General Menou was holding with a force of 10,000 men (out of a total French force of 25,000 in Egypt). On 12 March the British advanced towards the city, and the next day an attack was made near Mandorah Tower. Doyle's brigade, including the 30th, was in the third line, to the left of the Guards, and only came into action when General Hutchinson, second-in-command to Abercrombie, was ordered to attack the French right. As the result of a turning movement, Doyle's brigade was brought into the front line, with the 30th at their head. They advanced across swampy ground towards a little green hill. Their light company, with the light company of the 44th, and supported by the rest of that regiment, charged and seized a canal bridge held by infantry and cavalry, with two guns in support. Although the details of the action are not clear, it would seem that the rest of the 30th supported the 44th. One ensign (Rogers) and two privates were killed, and Captain Douglas, a corporal and five privates were wounded. (Eighty years later a military working party dug up two skulls, and a breastplate of the 30th, in the style of the early nineteenth century.) As a result of this action, the French withdrew behind their defences in Alexandria. Since the enemy enjoyed superiority in artillery, Abercrombie contented himself with entrenching his forces and bringing up supplies. Taking Alexandria seemed a simple objective to the men in the ranks who, according to Nicol, expected to assault the city as soon as the siege guns and ammunition arrived. Their optimism was misplaced, however.

The castle of Aboukir fell on 20 March but at the same time warning was received of an imminent French attack. The battle of Alexandria was fought on the following day, when the French attempted to drive the British into Lake Maadie. It was also rumoured that an order subsequently found in the pocket of a dead French general stated that no quarter was to be given. The 30th, still part of Doyle's brigade, were in the second line behind the Guards, and, like the rest of the force, were under arms by three o'clock in the morning, this state of readiness having been imposed as a general order three days before in response to a French raid from Alexandria. The attack began half an hour later. The French planned to create a diversion on the left, before attacking the reserve and overwhelming the centre, thus driving the British force into Lake Maadie. The initial French attack was successfully beaten off. The Guards then received a determined assault which they held off with steady and equally determined musketry. At this point the 30th advanced in support, although the rest of the brigade played little part in the battle. Eventually, as every fresh French attack was beaten off with considerable loss, Menou had no choice but to withdraw. The British victory, however, was marred by the death of General Abercrombie. He had suffered both a contusion to the chest and a bullet to the

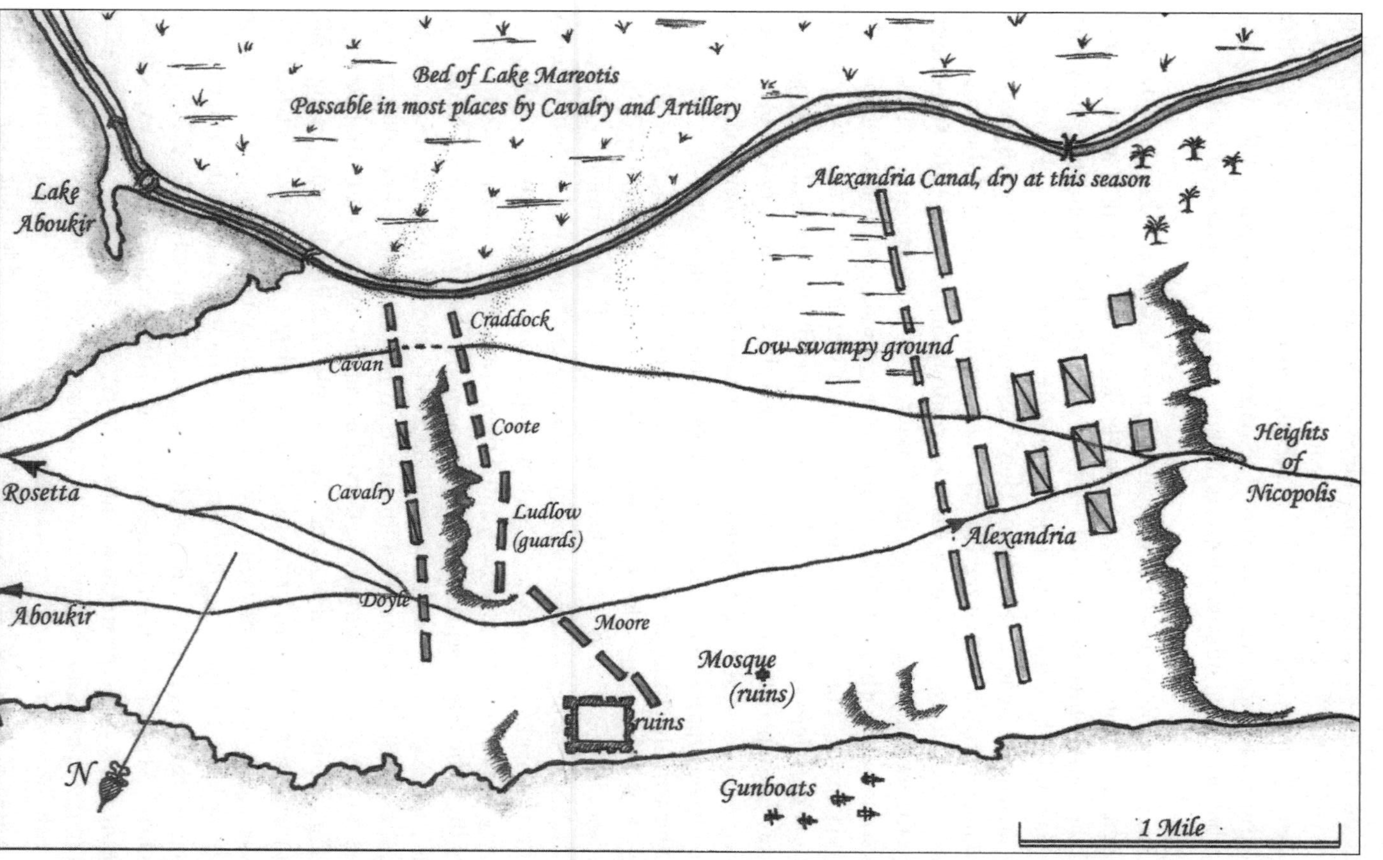

Initial troop dispositions at the Battle of Alexandria

thigh during the battle. Gangrene set in, and he died on 28 March, mourned by the whole army. As for the 30th, they lost three rank and file dead, while two officers, three NCOs and twenty-one rank and file were wounded, casualties which seem to have occurred while the regiment was supporting the Guards. As a bonus, all the officers involved in the actions so far received gold medals from Selim III.

Overall, by this stage of the campaign British losses were about 3,500 killed, missing and wounded. In addition to the losses in the action at Mandorah and the Battle of Alexandria, the 30th lost a man on 18 March, and another on 23 March, both returned as 'killed before Alexandria'.

Lieutenant General Sir John Hely-Hutchinson was now in command. Leaving 6,000 men to pen the French in Alexandria, he diverted the remainder of the British force to Cairo. It was not a comfortable advance. 'The succeeding days the weather was extremely unpleasant. The wind, being very high, blew the sand about with great violence into our faces and eyes, so as to incommode us very much. This was a circumstance, from which we had not yet suffered, though we afterwards experienced it too frequently, before we left Egypt: and to this cause perhaps may chiefly be ascribed the complaints of the eyes, with which so many men were afflicted, and by which many lost their sight, though some have happily recovered it since their return from Egypt.'[19]

The British advanced to Rosetta, which was taken on 14 April after the French abandoned it. The 30th arrived there with the 89th three days later, followed the next day by the 8th and the 79th. On 17 April nearby Fort Julien was taken, making it safe to continue the advance on Cairo in two columns along the banks of the Nile. There was an action at Rahmanieh on 9 May, during which the French concentrated their attack on a Turkish force that had recently joined up with the British. At one point the Turks were put to flight. The French pursued them, but were checked by the fire of the gunboats on the river. General Doyle put the 30th and 92nd into an oblique line and they too fired on the French who now retreated as rapidly as they had advanced.

The action at Rahmanieh, which Walsh called a skirmish, ended at nightfall, but the British did not enter the town because plague was endemic. Instead, the advance continued to Shibrighite, which was reached on 11 May. Here the men were ordered to abandon their knapsacks, which were then transported by water so that the pace of the march could be accelerated.

On 17 May a French column heading for Cairo after a foraging expedition, finding itself at the mercy of a Turkish force, surrendered to Doyle's brigade without a fight. Thus 600 men, with supplies and 550 camels, were lost to the French forces in Cairo. The advance on the city continued with yet more hard marching as they sank into the sand with every step, and lost one pace for every three advanced. Some days the sun beat down without a breath of wind to cool them; at other times the Kamsin, or sirocco, blew, nearly suffocating the men as they marched. By 16 June, however, they were almost within range of the enemy's guns, and two days later they sighted the Pyramids for the first time, an experience which raised their spirits.

The most serious problem at this point was sickness. Two officers of the 30th (Ensigns Barry and Arbouin, who had only reached Egypt on 25 March) and forty men were lost during a period of three months, which finally saw the French trapped in Cairo. On 21 June, Gizeh, opposite to Grand Cairo, was invested, and preparations were made for a general siege. The next day, the French offered to surrender, although only to British generals, and on 27 June, after terms had been agreed, General Belliard signed the capitulation. His dispirited troops evacuated Cairo on 7 July and were escorted back to Rosetta, from whence they embarked for France at the expense of the British Government. It took three weeks to complete the evacuation of the French, but on 28 July the last of Belliard's force finally left Egypt.

The British troops now enjoyed a brief respite from marching. They were reviewed by the Grand Vizier on 6 July, and three days later the 30th occupied the citadel of Cairo. Some of the regiment, like Nicol of the 92nd, may have visited the Pyramids. On 15 July, though, the British left Cairo, marching to Rahmanieh and then on to Rosetta, which they reached two weeks later. At this point they rejoined the main army, which had remained before Alexandria. A somewhat bizarre situation subsequently developed. Effectively blockaded, General Menou obstinately refused to communicate with the British by land, although he permitted communication by sea. He also flooded the canal in front of the town, a move the British countermanded by building a dam and creating a sizeable inundation.

Doyle's brigade finally took up a position before Alexandria on 8 August. Despite the easy victory at Cairo, it had been a gruelling experience for officers and men alike. The heat was so intense that the men had to stop every so often and wring the sweat out of their clothes. Furthermore, when Doyle was taken ill, command passed to Colonel Spencer, a poor substitute in Nicol's opinion. 'Our brigade was inspected by Lord Hutchinson who ordered us camels to carry our packs to Alexandria but Colonel Spencer said there was no need for it. This officer had had command of the brigade since General Doyle left and what different treatment we received, the one always looking out for the comfort of the soldiers, the other [Spencer] harassing us as far as he thought we would bear it.'[20] There was some reward, though, if only for the officers. On 19 July General Hutchinson sent a puncheon of Sicilian wine to the officers of each regiment after a particularly arduous march, with the compliment that he had never known such an abstemious and well-conducted army.

Doyle's brigade was reorganised, and was now made up of the 50th, 89th and 92nd, as well the 30th. Of these four regiments, the 30th was the weakest, with a strength of only 269, which demonstrates the cost of campaigning in such alien conditions.

With no risk of a counter-attack from Cairo, the British could now concentrate on the capture of Alexandria. A two-pronged assault was planned. While one division, under Sir Eyre Coote, sailed west from the city before making a landing, the main body of the army, including Doyle's brigade (once more under Doyle's command), prepared to advance on the city from the east. The attack was made on 17 August. Brigade orders, received the previous day, stated that the 30th would 'oblique to the right for the attack of the French redoubts in that direction . . . As the attack will be made before daylight, firing will only create delay and probably confusion. The redoubts must therefore be carried with the bayonet. The General knows too well the troops he has the honour to command to feel any anxiety on the score of their conduct before the enemy, but he must impress on them the necessity of the most perfect silence.'[21] The regiment was under the command of Lieutenant Colonel Lockhart, who proved himself more than capable of fulfilling these orders.

Walsh's account vividly describes the ensuing action. 'Sir John Hutchinson had ordered an attack to be made along the whole of the enemy's front to the eastward of the town. This movement took place about four in the morning, and it was intended not only to gain ground, but as a diversion in favour of Major-Gen. Coote.

'The attack of a green hill, a little advanced on the right of the enemy's position, was confided to Major-Gen. Cradock, and the Brigade, under the command of Gen. Doyle, was destined to carry it into execution. The thirtieth regiment was to march up to a small redoubt on the right, and the fiftieth to another on the left, the ninety-second remaining in central position in the rear, to support either, if necessary. The two battalions of the twentieth were also placed in such a manner as to be in readiness to move up to any point required.

'On the left of the enemy there was a small hill of sand, called by us the Sugarloaf Hill; of this Major-Gen. Moore took possession with very little resistance, and thence he was enabled to reconnoitre the enemy's works. This position, however, it was not possible to retain, as it lay completely exposed to the enemy's cross-fire, and from its size afforded little or no shelter.

'The green hill was ascended by Major-Gen. Cradock without the loss of a man, the French having fled on our first appearance. But, finding that we did not keep the ground which we had gained on our right, they made an attempt to drive us from the green hill.

'For this purpose, five hundred men of the seventy-fifth demibrigade, their Colours flying, drums beating, and confident of success, moved with two guns rapidly across the plain, toward the post which the thirtieth Regiment occupied. They advanced with their bayonets fixed, and without firing a shot, until they got very close to the thirtieth. The corps, though not more than two hundred men, did not wait their arrival, but ordered by Colonel Spencer and headed by Lieutenant-Colonel Lockhart, pushed forward in the most gallant and intrepid manner, to meet the enemy, who immediately gave way, and were driven back to their entrenchments in the greatest confusion. They had several killed and wounded in their retreat, and eight men were taken prisoners, being literally dragged out of the ranks by our victorious troops.'[22]

So effective was Lockhart's control of his men that he was able to check their enthusiasm and bring them back into order when French artillery opened fire to protect their own retreating infantry. The whole action had lasted only five minutes, but it cost the regiment twenty-nine casualties, three of them fatal. Nevertheless, its effect had been critically decisive, and the 30th returned to the cheers of the whole army, something remembered by John Colbourne, later Field Marshal Lord Seaton, many years later when he presented new colours to the regiment. He took particular pleasure in recounting the details to the then commanding officer, Lieutenant Colonel Mauleverer. Yet all Nicol observed was that 'The 30th Regiment advanced to check a party of the enemy advancing from the bridge to the hill when a smart firing commenced. General Doyle desired us to lay close to the ground until the order to rise, telling us in an Irish whisper to level low, for said he, one bullet in a Frenchman's shin bone this day is as good as two in the head some other time. The enemy drove in the 30th Regiment.'[23]

General Hutchinson, in his dispatch of the 5th September, made his own comments on the action: 'it afforded one more opportunity to display the promptness of British Officers, and the heroism of British soldiers. A part of Gen. Doyle's Brigade, the 30th Regiment (but under the immediate orders of Col. Spencer) had taken possession of a hill in front of the enemy's right. Gen. Menou, who was in person in that part of the French entrenched camp directly opposite to our post, ordered about 600 men to make a sortie to drive us from our position. The enemy advanced in columns, with fixed bayonets, and without firing a shot, till they had got very close to the 30th Regiment, to whom Col. Spencer gave an immediate order to charge, though they did not consist of more than 200 men; he was obeyed with a spirit and determination worthy of the highest panegyric. The enemy was driven back in confusion. They had many killed and wounded, and several taken prisoner.'[24]

A brigade order of 20 August made the following observation: 'Brigadier-General Doyle ... wishes to return his thanks to Lieutenant-Colonel Lockhart and the officers and men of the 30th Regiment for their gallant conduct in charging and putting to rout a superior force of the enemy and he has the pleasure to acquaint the Corps that their spirited behaviour has met the most marked approbation of His Excellency the Commander-in-Chief. It is difficult to particularize individuals where all deserve praise, but Captains Hamilton and Grey of the 30th Regiment from their particular situation had more the opportunity of distinguishing themselves and the Brigadier-General requests these gentlemen to accept his thanks for their energetic and efficient exertion.'[25]

Despite this success, Alexandria did not fall on 17 August, and for the next few days the British found themselves under intermittent cannon fire. The fort at Marabout surrendered, but news also arrived that the French intended to attack General Eyre Coote's forces to the west before he received the reinforcements he needed for his own attack. Hutchinson ordered another diversionary attack from the east, but this never materialised. Instead, it was acknowledged that an offensive from the west was more likely to be successful. Despite continued French bombardment, enemy outposts were attacked with the bayonet so that batteries could be established within four hundred yards of the Redoubt des Bains. On 26 August, four batteries opened fire against the eastern side of the town. There were also gunboats on the inundation, making the French position increasingly vulnerable. As a result, at half past four on the afternoon of the 26th an aide-de-camp of General Menou arrived with a letter requesting a three-day halt to hostilities in order to prepare for surrender. This request was granted by General Hutchinson but Menou proved difficult. Three days later and again on 30 August, the order was given to resume the bombardment. On each occasion the French general backed down. Finally, on 2 September, the British took possession of the French lines in accordance with the agreed terms of capitulation.

'The day was extremely fine, and the whole of the scene, heightened by the reflections, which must have arisen in every breast on the termination of a glorious campaign, was certainly one of the most pleasing and gratifying that a soldier can feel.

'This day crowned our efforts and gave us the entire possession of Egypt. The effusion of human blood now ceased; the torrent subsided; and the long hovering dove at length found a place for the sole of her foot. An enemy, who during the war had considered himself as invincible, was taught by this campaign, that British troops, meeting him on fair ground, will ever maintain a fair superiority. From it we hope will result some advantage to our country; and we trust it will not be easily forgotten, either by our enemies, or by our friends.'[26]

By October the 30th had left Egypt for Malta, but as a result of their part in the campaign 'Egypt' became one of their battle honours, inscribed on the emblem of the Sphinx. Forty-eight years later six officers and fifteen men claimed the General Service Medal with a bar for Egypt although by a quirk of fate most of the men who had taken part in the Egyptian campaign subsequently served with the first battalion in India, thus missing the honours of the Peninsula and Waterloo.

By the spring of 1802 the regiment was back in England, six companies marching to Sunderland, and four to Tyneside. Here they remained for the rest of the year, and the first half of 1803, the year which saw the formation of a second battalion to whom would fall the glory of the next twelve years.

Chapter 3

A Second Battalion

By 1802 the Revolutionary War had run its course. The French Revolution had become the rule of Napoleon Bonaparte; and Europe was exhausted by nearly a decade of conflict. The Peace of Amiens was negotiated by Addington's short-lived government before news of the British victories in Egypt reached London, and was signed in March 1802. It proved short-lived, however. Renewed military activity was evident on all sides even by the end of 1802. Napoleon was determined to tighten his grip on Germany, Italy, Holland and Switzerland. In response, Britain refused to leave Malta, arguing speciously that they would only do so when Europe was properly at peace. In January 1803 reports were received of a planned French expedition to the Levant and the peace was doomed. In April Addington pre-empted the French by sending an ultimatum, which was followed by an embargo on all French shipping in British ports. A month later this became a declaration of war.

The immediate effect on the 30th Regiment was an order to support the activities of the impress officers. Manpower was urgently needed for the ships which were the bulwark of British defence, and requiring the army to find men for the navy seemed a sensible policy. After the declaration of war on 22 May, however, there was a critical need to strengthen both military arms. The 30th, brought south to Ipswich, now recruited for their own purposes. Men were drawn from the traditional recruiting grounds: Sleaford, Lincoln, Nottingham, Wakefield and Doncaster; but also from new and scattered territory: Cambridge, Alcester, Glasgow, Perth, Armagh, Sligo and Tuam.

In June 1803 a royal order transformed the 30th into a two-battalion regiment, along with fifteen other regiments of the line. In theory, each battalion would comprise fifty sergeants, fifty corporals, twenty-two drummers and 1,000 privates, numbers which were never realised. Brevet Lieutenant Colonel Lockhart, in active command of the regiment, took to Chelmsford nearly 1,000 men, however, and a further 900 were available from the newly established Army of Reserve, Addington's response to Napoleon's renewed military activity. Men from the militia, who often developed a taste for military life, could already volunteer for the regular army, and their training meant they were absorbed more quickly than the raw material found by the recruiting parties. The Army of Reserve was similar to the militia in that men were conscripted by ballot and could not be forced to serve outside the United Kingdom, but they were also encouraged to volunteer into the line regiments. The Additional Forces Act, which set up the new county-based units, produced about 30,000 fit and effective men, although another 15,000 were lost through death and desertion, because they were unfit or were under age. Since two-thirds of the 30,000 eventually volunteered for regular service, Addington's innovation should have proved valuable to the army as a whole. There is a difference of opinion, however, as to the quality of the men thus obtained. Sir John Fortescue, in his *County Lieutenancies and the Army*, dismissed Addington's plan in his table of contents as 'Utter Failure of the Army of Reserve', producing figures to demonstrate that the yield of worthwhile man-power was too limited to justify the expense. A more judicious view suggests, however, that the army was strengthened at a crucial point in the war.

It is difficult to envisage how the 30th would have raised a second battalion without the Army of Reserve. More crucial, though, was the quality of the new men. One view damns them comprehensively. 'It looked as if Mr Addington's plan was a success, but the sickness and desertion were very great.'[27] This comment is supported by figures for the two months from the end of October to the end of December, which is to take a very short-term view. In this period fourteen men died and eighteen deserted. However, when comparison is made with non-Army of Reserve men a different picture emerges. For example, in the second battalion six men from the Army of Reserve deserted, as did five men already in the regiment. Similarly, four men against six died, figures compounded by an outbreak of smallpox. And a further point which must be noted is that 285 of the new men had volunteered for regular service by the end of 1803, thus distorting the figures. In fact, the biggest problem with the new men was their age; the reason that so many of them served such a short period was that they were often superannuated soldiers, experienced but well past their best. On the other hand, a good many of the newcomers saw service through to Waterloo and beyond.

There was an equal need for extra officers. Some transferred from other regiments, some from half-pay, while the ensigns were newly commissioned. Lieutenant Colonel Wilkinson had command of the first battalion, although junior at this rank. The senior lieutenant colonel, with the army rank of major general, Sir Charles Green, was returned as in Grenada. He never returned to the regiment, being promoted to the general list. Brevet Lieutenant Colonel Lockhart was appointed lieutenant colonel in the regiment with command of the second battalion, while Philip Vaumorel and Ralph Smythe, also from within the regiment, were the two second battalion majors. None of these three field officers stayed long with the second battalion. Smythe had already retired with the rank of captain before being gazetted major, and his appointment finally went to Major William Wright. Lockhart was transferred to the first battalion in 1804, and Vaumorel was returned as second major in the first battalion in January 1804.

There were departures as well as arrivals, so that it is not until the return of January 1804, the last return before the regiment transferred to the Irish establishment, that a full picture of the officer-strength of the two battalions emerges. According to this return, there were sixty-six officers serving with the 30th. Twenty-six had been with the regiment previous to July 1803. Fourteen were transfers from other regiments. Fourteen came in from half-pay. The remaining twelve, ten ensigns and two assistant surgeons, were newly commissioned.

Initially old and new, experienced and inexperienced, were divided between the two battalions, although some imbalance was inevitable. The first battalion had seventeen of the old officers, against nine in the second battalion, and eighteen of the new officers, against twenty-two. Amongst the company officers the division was reasonably even, nine old to eighteen new in the first battalion, nine to sixteen in the second, neither battalion having a full complement. Amongst the field and staff officers, however, the difference was marked. The first battalion took the existing staff, so that only the lieutenant colonel and adjutant of the second battalion were old officers. The majors had come in from half-pay, the quartermaster and surgeon had transferred from other regiments, and the two assistant surgeons were newly commissioned hospital mates. Since only one paymaster was allowed to the regiment at this time, this function was performed in the second battalion by Lieutenant Elias Malet, who had been with the regiment since 1795.

Bannatyne is of the opinion that 'few of the officers brought in played any part in the life of the regiment. Some seized the opportunity to realize their capital by selling out, others returned to half-pay. The fact is that as a class they were too old and their appointment was due to an effort of Government to reduce the non-effective charge.'[28] There is some justice in this view. Of the fifty officers appointed to the regiment in 1803 who can be traced in the army lists ten had quit by the end of the year never having physically joined the regiment, while another ten had moved on by the beginning of 1805. A further twenty-one stayed less than five years. This last number is less remarkable, however, since transferring between regiments to effect promotion was normal for the times.

There were some notable exceptions, however, and thirteen of the new officers served ten years or more. For example, Thomas Walker Chambers served with the 30th for twelve years and was killed at Waterloo, Robert Howard and Peter Ryves Hawker served twenty-three and fifteen years respectively, eight years of which they spent as prisoners in Verdun. Henry Cramer stayed twenty years, the quartermaster, John Foster Kingsley, twenty years, and the surgeon, Robert Pearse, twenty-five years. John Tongue, who came into the regiment as an ensign, served for forty years and retired as a major, a reminder of how promotion slowed down with the end of the Napoleonic Wars.

While a body of officers and non-commissioned officers travelled to Buckingham, High Wycombe and Aylesbury to collect the men assigned to the 30th from the Army of Reserve, the rest of the regiment marched to Chelmsford where the second battalion took shape under Lieutenant Colonel Lockhart. The official date for the muster of the two battalions was 6 October, but on 25 August David Glass, regimental sergeant major since the Egypt campaign, was appointed to the second battalion, which would indicate that its formation was already under way. To alleviate the inevitable inexperience of the new battalion, there was division between new and old, both NCOs and rank and file. Sergeant Robert Daniell, a long-serving soldier who was later commissioned, was appointed quartermaster sergeant, while two other veterans, Luke Pickering and Joseph Peale, became paymaster sergeant and armourer sergeant respectively.

To complete the staff, the new adjutant was Ensign William Stewart, who had joined the regiment in 1802 from the Londonderry Militia. Kingsley, as has already been mentioned, was the quartermaster. As for acting paymaster, Malet surrendered the position in 1804 to the newly joined Lieutenant Alexander McNabb, formerly an ensign on half-pay. He was an American of Scottish descent whose father had settled in Canada after the Loyalist defeat in the War of American Independence.

The two-battalion regiment was now sent to Ireland where, as a result of the rebellion, the army was required to adopt a higher profile than seems to have been the case in the eighteenth century. In December orders were received to march to Liverpool, whence the first battalion sailed to Dublin on 23 January 1804, with the second battalion following a day later. On 25 January, the regiment was transferred to the Irish command.

During their years in Ireland the two battalions readjusted their relationship, which could not be sustained on the presumption of experience equally shared. Instead of both existing as fighting-fit units, the second battalion became a depot for the first. The pay lists and muster rolls demonstrate the annual exchange. The first battalion discarded its unsatisfactory men into the second battalion, where their stay was often brief before discharge from the army as unfit to serve, although some proved their worth by remaining with the second battalion until disbandment in 1817. At the same time, men were transferred from the second to the first to strengthen the senior unit. It was now necessary for the first to shed men from the Army of Reserve (and the later Army of Defence) who had not volunteered for foreign service. The war was spreading and the senior battalion could expect to serve abroad.

By December 1804 the second battalion was demonstrably a feeder unit for the first. The senior battalion chose the best men from the junior battalion, while off-loading all their undesirables. Strangely enough, these best men included three recently demoted NCOs, a man released from regimental confinement, and several who were returned in the muster as sick, either in hospital or in quarters. On the other hand, the second battalion retained a body of men who would prove themselves in battle and would produce from among their number a cadre of excellent NCOs as well as several officers commissioned from the ranks. The junior battalion gained only a handful of men from the first battalion, the exchange favouring the senior battalion, whose strength was crucial to War Office plans. To make up their numbers, however, they received sixty-six men from the Army of Defence. In addition, many men who had been transferred into the second battalion because they were reluctant to serve abroad later volunteered for regular service.

Equally significant was the policy regarding officers. Initially, they were allocated to either the first or the second battalion on a fairly *ad hoc* basis without reference to seniority. Promotion, however, was strictly tied to seniority. In the autumn of 1804, therefore, it was decided that the senior officers of each rank would serve with the first battalion, the juniors with the second, an arrangement which worked while the two battalions were geographically close and which stressed the subordinate position of the second battalion. There were practical considerations too. An ensign could learn his business with the second before moving up the list and being transferred to the first, with the expectation of active service. Similarly, a new officer joining the regiment, who was always the junior of his rank, would become familiar with the ways of the corps in the less critically placed second battalion.

The policy was easy to implement once the initial confusion of the change-over had been completed by the beginning of 1805, and functioned smoothly while both battalions were in Ireland. For example, in the period between May 1805 and May 1806 eleven lieutenants and eight ensigns moved from the second to the first battalion. Once the first battalion had sailed to India, however, the physical distance between the two units meant that transfers were difficult to effect. The parallel monthly returns of the two battalions make this clear. In July 1812, for example, the month of the battle of Salamanca, there were twelve officers serving with the first battalion who should have been with the second battalion in Spain, and nine with the second battalion who should have been in India. A further complication was the time taken for official communications to travel from London to India, or for information to be transferred from one battalion to the other. Consequently, in July 1812 the first battalion was unaware that three of its officers, the newly promoted Major Leach, Captain Nunn, and Captain Richardson, who were returned at their previous rank, properly belonged to the second battalion, their promotion making them the juniors of their new rank. Similarly, the second battalion did not realise that Lieutenant Herring had been cashiered in India.

During the two years both battalions spent in Ireland they were engaged in similar activities. Most of the year the first battalion was quartered in Tullamore, King's County, while the second battalion had their headquarters at Moate, Westmeath, with detachments at Clara and Kilbeggan, but in July and August the two battalions were temporarily reunited in camp at the Curragh for drill. By all accounts, these camps were the military event of the year. For example, the camp of 1805, when the regiments of the regular army were joined by various militia units, opened spectacularly. 'On the first [of August] the troops destined to occupy this camp appeared on the ground in six divisions. The order to take up their positions being given by signal, the different points allotted to the several regiments were immediately occupied; and the command to pitch tents being announced by another signal, the whole camp was formed in little more than two minutes from the instant in which the signal was made.' Particularly impressive was the light infantry: 'the movements of these brigades to their posts to the sound of the bugle, the celerity of their manoeuvres, the brilliancy of their uniforms and the gay diversity of their various standards glancing across the hills – altogether produced a delightful effect.' The display continued. 'Great was the galloping hither and thither of staff officers of every grade and denomination for nearly an hour, until at one o'clock bang went the signal gun . . . when the columns poured into the magnificent plain, or rather downs of the Curragh by all the roads leading to it. Bands playing, colours flying, drums beating, bugles screaming and all the pomp, pride and circumstance of military display.'[29]

After these diversions, the two battalions returned to their previous stations, although the light company of each was on detached service with the Light Brigade in Dublin. Recruiting continued in both England and Ireland, and there were further drafts from the Army of Defence, although examination of the muster rolls suggests that by 1805 the newcomers were the scrapings of the barrel. The majority were rapidly lost to death, desertion, and discharge as unfit for service.

The Register of State Papers reveals the perceived state of Ireland at this time. With the memories of 1798 still hauntingly vivid, the greatest fear was another rebellion. Informers' letters constantly reiterated the message that a rising was imminent, that French spies lurked everywhere, while a French invasion could be expected at any time. There were doubts about the loyalty of the militia and the yeomanry regiments, which made the presence of the regular forces all the more important. Even if these fears were unjustified and the punctiliously reported rumours were nothing more than a means of keeping the informers in employment, there was violence enough to disturb the government: the activities of gangs like the infamous Corcoran gang; the regular robbing of post boys and the mail; and the administration of threshers' oaths. Any large gathering was suspect. As many as 3,000 people might assemble for a ball game or a hurling match and such an event was assumed to be a cover for subversive activities.

There is little direct evidence of the relationship between the regiment and the local population while the two battalions were stationed in the Irish Midlands, although contact must have been close since there were no barracks in Tullamore, or in Moate, Clara and Kilbeggan. As a result the men were billeted in inns and private houses, a possible recipe for friction. It may be assumed that the fracas between the first light battalion of the King's German Legion and various Irish militia light companies, which erupted in Tullamore in July 1806 after a bout of fisticuffs on a bridge, was not the only instance of such an affray. In this case, three officers and twenty-five men were wounded (one fatally) on the German side, while the militia suffered nine casualties, one of whom subsequently died. One of the wounded German officers was Colonel von Alten, who would later command the second battalion at Waterloo.

The reason given for the tension between the militia and the Germans was the faithlessness of some of the militia men's sweethearts, who transferred their favours to the Germans when they arrived in Tullamore. There is no doubt that some of the 30th also found wives and sweethearts in Ireland, as the list of women left behind when the second battalion sailed for Portugal makes clear.[30] The only known trouble of a domestic nature does not fit into this category, though. Edward Laughron was an Irishman with an Irish wife who joined the regiment in 1798. His merit was quickly appreciated by the second battalion, which he joined on its formation; he was appointed corporal in June 1804, and a month later had been raised to sergeant. The muster roll for 24 January 1805, however, records that Laughron had been 'given over to the civil powers charged with murder.' The next month he was returned as 'in Mullingar gaol on a charge of murder.' On 7 January 1805 seven NCOs and privates marched to Mullingar, presumably to escort Laughron to prison, which suggests that the murder must have occurred about that time. A local newspaper, *The Leinster Journal*, tersely reported the final details: 'On Thursday last, Edward Laughron, for the murder of his wife, was executed in front of Mullingar gaol.' Any further thoughts about this domestic tragedy can only be speculative; but some doubt about the fidelity of his wife is a possible motive.

This sad story, however, had a happier conclusion. On 21 January 1805, 10-year-old John Laughron, of Dunmore, County Tyrone, was enlisted into the regiment at Tullamore as a drummer, and was sent to the second battalion. Boys who enlisted as young as this were usually children of the regiment. There were no other Laughrons in the regiment at this time, suggesting that John was the motherless, and soon to be orphaned, son of Edward Laughron, a theory reinforced by an occasional tendency to record him as Edward rather than John. If so, he fulfilled what his father had briefly promised, eventually leaving the regiment in 1837 with the rank of colour sergeant.

After the exercises on the Curragh in the summer of 1805, the second battalion went to the Royal Barracks, Dublin, while the first marched to Limerick for a brief stay. Meanwhile there were plans under way for a British force to act with Swedish, Russian and Prussian forces and attack French interests from the north, taking Hanover and then invading Holland, while Austrian and other Russian forces attacked from the south. The latter campaign ended at Austerlitz on 2 December. The northern attack came to nothing when the lukewarm support of King Friedrich Wilhelm of Prussia collapsed after the shattering defeat of his allies.

The first battalion of the 30th was one of the units chosen to take part in the northern campaign, although *Faulkner's Dublin Journal* reported on 30 October that 'the 30th Regiment of Foot, quartered in Limerick, received route for Charleille and Deneraile; the first division marching on Thursday and the second on Friday, where they are to remain only a few days previous to their embarking for Cork, for foreign service.' In fact, the second battalion was still in Dublin, where they stayed for another six months.

The rendezvous for General Cathcart's expedition was the Downs off Dover, where the first battalion assembled with the 9th and 89th Regiments as part of Major General Rowland Hill's brigade. On 16 December the convoy was caught by storms, and many of the transports ran for shelter from the gales. One of the transports, the *Jenny*, number 365, was blown onto the French coast near Gravelines. Thanks to the intervention of the French National Guard eleven sailors, 115 soldiers, four officers, twelve women, five children, and a baby born during the night were safely brought to shore. They were accommodated in the local barracks for a couple of nights, and then marched off as prisoners of war. This was an inevitable fate, but it did not prevent the captain of the *Jenny* and the officers of the 30th writing to the mayor of Gravelines to thank the townspeople for their kindness.

As a result of this disaster, Captains Roberts and Hawker, Lieutenant Howard, and Ensign Sullivan, with five sergeants, two drummers, and 101 rank and file remained as prisoners of war until 1814. All the officers survived, but not all the men were so lucky. Only eighty were returned as having rejoined the regiment in 1814 after a general exchange of prisoners. At least two escaped and one volunteered for an Irish regiment in the French army. We shall hear more of them later. Some of the survivors, including Howard, fought at Waterloo, possibly feeling that there were debts to be settled.

Three other companies were driven back into Kentish ports by the storms which so disastrously blew the *Jenny* off course. Another transport, the *Adventure*, was wrecked near Yarmouth and the men on board were mistakenly returned as lost. As for the companies that survived the storms, Cathcart's force eventually reached the mouth of the Weser at the end of December. By February, and the break-up of the Third Coalition, it was obvious that the original plan had to be abandoned, and Cathcart brought his dispirited army back to England. The five companies returned to Ramsgate, and were reunited with the rest of the battalion at Canterbury. By April they were in Portsmouth, where they received orders to proceed to India on East India Company ships. They received seven subalterns and 400 men from the second battalion, although fifty of the men were rejected. The rest embarked with the first battalion on 6 May, for a period of service in India which lasted until 1829.

A digest of an inspection carried out on 23 April, while the battalion was waiting to embark but before it had been joined by the reinforcements from the second battalion, gives an impression of the corps. The overall assessment described the unit as a body of healthy, well-drilled and well-equipped men, with active and intelligent officers and NCOs. Regimental and company accounting was regular, and regimental courts martial were infrequent.

Of the thirty-three officers who sailed to India, only three, Lieutenants Richardson, Fettes and Chambers, ever saw service with the second battalion, although many of them subsequently belonged to it 'on paper'. One other officer who should have sailed to India, Lieutenant John Lorraine White, on command when the embarkation papers arrived, remained with the second battalion until he transferred to the 14th Foot in 1814. He was one of the handful who survived until 1848 and was able to claim the General Service Medal, with bars for Ciudad Rodrigo, Badajoz and Salamanca. There was a stronger flow of officers in the opposite direction, however, since the second battalion continued to serve as a training ground for young officers, as well as a depot for NCOs and other ranks. Consequently, there were times during its service in the Peninsula when the unit was seriously under-officered because the needs of the first battalion remained paramount. At no time did the senior unit suffer the dearth of captains, for example, which frequently characterised the second battalion.

In 1805, after a seven-month sojourn in the Royal Barracks, Dublin, the second battalion moved to Strabane. The Royal Barracks, conceived in a grandiose style in the reign of William III and only completed in 1767, were badly built, so the transfer to Ulster was probably a relief. The corps was depleted, lacking the seven officers and large contingent of men who had marched off to join the first battalion in Portsmouth, en route for India, but steps were taken which resulted in the second battalion being fit for active service abroad. There still remained in the ranks a large number of men from the Armies of Reserve and Defence who had not volunteered for general service, and others who were considered too old for active service. In November and December 1806 those who were unwilling to serve abroad or considered incapable of doing so were transferred to the 9th Garrison Battalion, depriving the battalion of 246 men, including three sergeants and nine corporals. The rest of the survivors from the Armies of Reserve and Defence volunteered for general service, which explains why so many men of English origin enlisted, according to their discharge papers, in Ulster.

A handful of men from the Army of Reserve later changed their minds, however, and returned to the regiment from the Garrison Battalion. For example, William Cleveley, a tailor from Northampton, returned to the regiment in May 1808, in time to serve abroad. Four years later he was posted missing on the retreat from Burgos.

At the same time that men were leaving the battalion for garrison service, newcomers were arriving from the Irish Militia regiments, particularly from Westmeath and Longford, by a process known as disposability, which made annual volunteering possible. Battalions stationed in Ireland were initially able to send officers and NCOs every autumn to designated militia regiments for recruiting purposes. They had fourteen days to effect this before the 'season' finished, and alcohol seems to have been a popular inducement if the testimony of militia officers is to be believed. Eventually, though, the volunteering was conducted by the militia regiments themselves, with other constraints on time, and on the men, being introduced. Since the militias were now better trained and more effective military units than those which had conducted themselves so poorly during the crisis of 1798, the arrival of men who had already received basic military training was welcome. It is probably no coincidence that many of the men promoted to NCO over the next few years were former militia men.

More problematic was the number of lads and boys brought into the ranks, while old soldiers were encouraged to enlist for second, or even third terms of service. Thus the battalion became an old-young unit, which led to its initial rejection as an active service corps by Sir Arthur Wellesley in 1809. And there was another constraint brought about by short service enlistment. Men could sign up for seven years, although without the promise of a pension. Many of the men who accompanied the battalion to the Peninsula left the regiment in 1814, at the end of their seven-year period, although others enlisted for a further term and found themselves fighting at Waterloo.

Peninsula service lay in the future, however. For the present, the battalion remained in the north of Ireland, employed on a variety of military and quasi-civil tasks, soldiers frequently being called upon by magistrates to uphold some aspect of civilian law. As a writer of the time explained: 'outside the towns all the police duties had to be performed by the troops; mail coaches had to be escorted, the coastguard work had to be done, bailiffs had to be protected – in short all the work ordinarily delegated to the civil authorities was the everyday business of the troops.'[31] One of their constant duties was the suppression of illegal stills in Omagh. There was still the annual drill and training at the Curragh, and then further postings in different parts of Ireland, such as Athlone and Longford in 1808.

Just how dangerous this peacetime policing might be is brought out by the details in two sets of discharge papers. Charles Adams, aged just twenty, was discharged in 1808 after only two years' service as a consequence of being 'houghed' between White Rock and Longford. Presumably, this was a political gesture against the presence of the army. The attack on John Maloney in the same year was probably motivated by simple greed. Maloney had been four years with the regiment. He was aged forty-four, a reminder that not all men enlisted in their youth. He was 'assaulted at his post at the Commissariat stores at Athlone between the hours of nine and ten o'clock by four ruffians, unknown, who after maltreating him in a most inhuman manner left him on the high road in a state of insensibility, and with his arm fractured in several places so as to endanger his life, since which his arm has been amputated.' Lieutenant Colonel Minet, writing his testimonial, continued, 'I have to add that the said John Maloney is a man of most excellent character.'[32]

Crucially, though, the battalion was now considered fit for foreign service. A hundred NCOs and men who were on their way to join the first battalion in India were recalled. They had set off for Cork at the beginning of August 1808, but were then re-routed at Fermoy to return to the second battalion, stationed at Athlone. In January 1809 the whole battalion marched from Athlone to Dublin, and then to Kinsale, arriving in early March. On 11 March, under

Lieutenant Colonel Minet, who had commanded since Lockhart's transfer to the first battalion, they embarked for Portugal. As the *Historical Records* of the regiment noted: 'The commencement of the second phase of the Peninsular War, however, put a stop to home service, and, while the flower of the British army was being wasted at Walcheren, a number of second battalions, whom five years had failed to make into respectable troops, were hurried out to join Sir Arthur Wellesley in Portugal.'[33] This harsh opinion would seem to reflect Sir Arthur's own when he finally set eyes on the second battalion of the 30th Regiment.

Chapter 4
Active Service

The action fought at Corunna on 16 January 1809 ensured the safe embarkation of a retreating British army but the death of General Sir John Moore and the shocking state of the returning troops led to calls to abandon the Iberian Peninsula. The British government, however, was already preparing a fresh campaign under the command of Sir Arthur Wellesley, victorious against the French at Roliça and Vimeiro, and now cleared of guilt by association which the Convention of Cintra had visited upon him. Two thirds of his British battalions, however, were unpromising second battalions of which the 30th was amongst the least impressive. They landed at Lisbon, some on 7 April, some rather later, after a voyage of considerable excitement according to the adjutant, William Stewart. He later recorded in his journal for 1811, while he was on a visit to Lisbon: 'Saw the ship *Susan* and went on board her. This was the transport in which we had so many miraculous escapes coming out from Ireland in 1809.'[34]

Sir Arthur was not impressed by the new arrivals, who mustered (present) thirty-nine sergeants, and 611 other ranks. Lieutenant Colonel Minet was in command, with Majors Hamilton and Grey and a complement of staff which lacked only one of the assistant surgeons, still at Kinsale. There were, however, only eleven company officers present in Lisbon. Two others were on staff duty elsewhere; one, recently appointed, was still with his regiment in Martinique; three were at the depot in Kinsale; one was recruiting; and eleven were on command with the first battalion in India. This deficiency was a persistent problem. At best, companies could boast two officers, but all too often a company had only one officer, and he a youth of junior rank with limited experience. For example, in the monthly return for June 1812, three weeks before Salamanca, only nineteen officers were with the battalion, and five of those were staff officers.

When Wellesley moved north to confront the French under Marshal Soult at Oporto he left the 30th as an unattached battalion in garrison in Lisbon, occupying quarters in the castle. Initially they were to be engaged in frontier duties, but in May 1809 they were sent to Gibraltar, along with the 2/29th, to replace the 1/48th and 1/61st Regiments, units that were acclimatised to the harsh conditions of the Peninsula.

Once the focus of Spanish military ambition, Gibraltar was now little more than a backwater. Thomas Walsh visited in 1800, on his way to Egypt, and noted: 'A very good road, skirted with trees, and parallel to which runs the aqueduct, reaches from South Port to the part of Gibraltar called "the South", where there are barracks and an extensive naval hospital. These, with several other buildings, form what may be termed a second town. The garrison and inhabitants were very much distressed for water, owing to the want of rain the preceding season, and perhaps to the great quantity consumed by the ships of the expedition, many of which were allowed to water here. It is also said, that the grand parade, the sand of which is beaten down and levelled, is very prejudicial to the aqueduct; as the rain, which filters and oozes through the loose red sand, cannot penetrate through so hardened a surface. Gibraltar is wholly furnished with water from cisterns, which are filled in this manner by the rain.' Water may have been scarce, but wine was 'in such abundance, and so cheap, that in no part of the world exists such repeated scenes of intoxication. It is indeed distressing to see whole bands of soldiers and sailors literally lying in the streets in the most degrading state of inebriety. Drunkenness is no crime in the garrison, except in those who are on duty; and every man coming off a working party is ordered to be paid eightpence on the spot, which he immediately proceeds to spend on a kind of bad wine, called black-strap. Houses for the sale of this pernicious liquor are found at every step, and furnish no small part of the revenue.

'The situation of the officers here, especially in time of war, is very melancholy; cooped up in a prison, from which it is impossible to stir, and with no other amusement or resource, but what they can find among themselves [and the garrison library, which Walsh praised] ... In time of peace, the garrison is more fertile in amusement, an intercourse being permitted with the Spanish territories. Hence, too, the forces are amply and cheaply furnished with every thing they can want ... In the event of war on the one side, and pestilence on the other (the Barbary Coast), it often happens, as was the case when I was there, that the garrison is compelled to live entirely on salt provision; not having even the advantage or comfort of vegetables; which are scarce, and very dear.

'During the summer, the climate is excessively hot, and the reflection of the sun from the rock is dreadful, and very distressing to the eyes. In winter, the weather is often very cold, and the damp from the heavy rains so great, as to render fire necessary for two or three months of the year. Notwithstanding these inconveniences, the climate is far from being unhealthy.'[35]

In a time of peace (and alliance) with the Spanish Gibraltar was an ideal location for a weak battalion to learn its business in the field, and to adapt to the climate. Probably the most exciting incident during this period of garrison duty was a duel, and subsequent court martial involving an officer of the battalion. Duelling was against the Articles of War, and carried the death sentence. Consequently, Lieutenant Richard Heaviside's situation was perilous when he stood trial on 20 December, accused of murdering Lieutenant Montford of the 47th five days previously. The court proceedings were extremely brief, although it is possible to surmise, from the evidence of Lieutenant Eades of the 30th, that Montford had used some very harsh, presumably insulting, words against Heaviside while both men were on duty at the Landport guard. The accused was acquitted after he declined to offer any defence, stating instead that he meant to abide by his plea of not guilty. His second, Lieutenant George Rumley, and Montford's (Lieutenant Scott of the 47th) also refused to answer any questions, and the only other witnesses heard in court were the surgeons. They were both remarkably evasive. John Hennen, of the 30th, agreed that Montford had died as a result of being shot, but claimed not to know how he had received the wound. When asked if Heaviside had been on the scene, Hennen replied that he had, but added that he could not remember what he was doing. Perhaps not surprisingly, when the court papers arrived in England the Adjutant General expressed some concern about the outcome, which nevertheless was allowed to stand.

This was not the only court martial involving the 30th, but a rather sordid case of breaking and entering, in order to steal a miscellaneous collection of merchant goods, was unlikely to have attracted the same attention. John Simpson and William Woodhouse were charged with stealing forty-five pairs of black stockings and two bundles of shawls, while Brian Farrell was accused of conniving in the robbery while posted sentry on the main guard. All three were found guilty, and were sentenced to be transported for seven years to wherever the King chose to send them, which undoubtedly meant Australia.

While the battalion was in Gibraltar, several officers were detached for staff duties. At the beginning of 1810 Captains Thomas Williamson and Henry Craig were on the staff in Portugal, Captain Richard Machell, who had just joined from Martinique, was brigade major to General Bowes, and Captain Alexander McNabb was town major in Gibraltar. For all these men there would have been an increase in salary and the hope that a staff position would accelerate their promotion.

In April 1810 a detachment was sent to Tarifa, although the purpose of this expedition is somewhat puzzling. In a letter to Wellington, however, General Graham, who commanded in Cadiz, made the following comment in his summary of the situation there. 'Unless by some means a diversion were made in the rear of the enemy, it would be great imprudence to risk the loss of so advantageous a position by a battle in the field, where hitherto the Spaniards have so seldom behaved tolerably. General Campbell has sent a small party to Tarifa, and talks of augmenting it; but it is scarcely to be expected that anything material can be effected by such a diversion unless the country people can be organized and give great assistance.'[36] The five companies sent to Tarifa presumably constituted that 'small party', but it is unlikely they saw any action. A month later this detachment accompanied the rest of the battalion to Cadiz, where the French threat was more immediate. The town, which was the only safe location for the Spanish government, had been under siege since February.

As the French were learning, Cadiz was a hard nut to crack, given the range of even the heaviest artillery of the period. Situated at one end of an elongated peninsula, or sand spit, which turned south and west from the Isla de Leon, it was virtually impregnable against land attack. The Isla itself was separated from the mainland of Andalusia by the Rio Santi Petri, an arm of the sea

The Siege of Cadiz, 1810

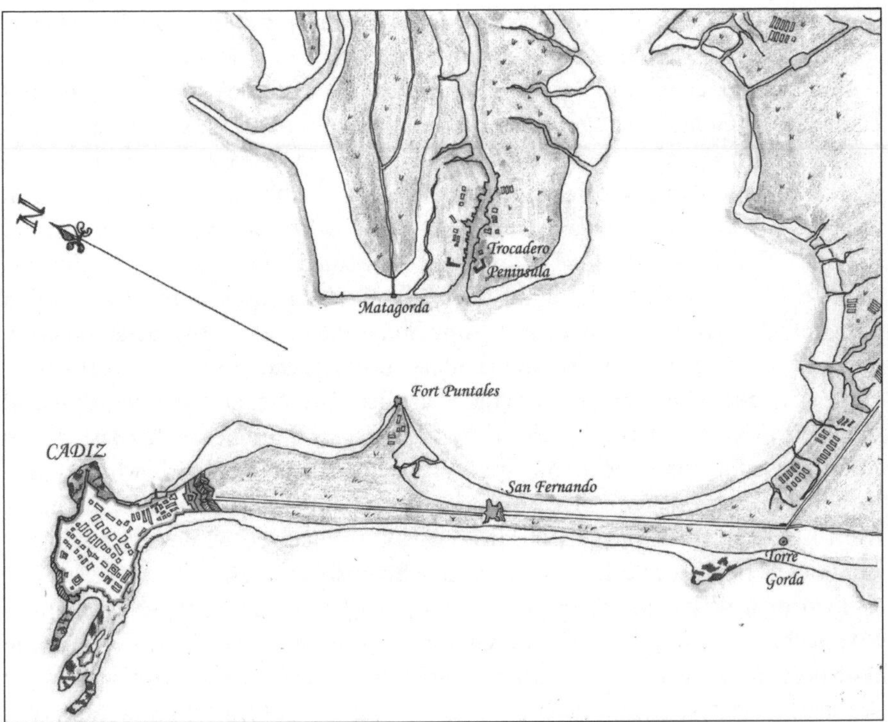

flowing through brackish marshland. It was so strongly fortified that only an attack by sea had much chance of success; and this was unlikely when it was protected by British and Spanish naval vessels. The sand spit, four miles long, had an entrenchment at the halfway point, and there was a further line of defences in front of Cadiz itself. The most vulnerable approach was from the east, and three forts had been built to defend the inner harbour, which lay on this side: San Jose and San Luis, and lying to the front of them, situated on a mud flat in the marches, Matagorda. Were the French to take these three forts, they would be able to attack Puntales Castle, which was crucial to the defence of the town. For that reason, the forts were blown up, although Matagorda was later reoccupied by Spanish and British troops.

On the French side, the attack was under the command of Marshal Victor, who was able to observe and blockade but could not prevent the arrival of reinforcements and supplies into Cadiz from the sea. By May when the 30th arrived there were 18,000 Spanish and 8,000 British and Portuguese troops engaged in the defence of Cadiz. Victor's first objective was Matagorda, which he was able to take with the other two disabled forts. He could now fire into the inner harbour, which sent the ships to the outer harbour or the shelter of the Isla de Leon, an inconvenience more than a serious strategic blow. His guns did little damage to Puntales, however, which makes it ironic that the 30th should have taken their only casualties in the castle.

Graham, in command of the Anglo-Portuguese forces under the overall command of General La Pena, had placed the larger part of his force in the Isla de Leon, with a garrison inside the town, to guard the land front by the principal gate. It is not known for sure where the 30th served, although as part of General Houghton's brigade they were probably close to the town. Accommodation may have been a problem. As Graham commented, the people of Cadiz had never experienced the billeting of troops, and their houses were also crowded with refugees from elsewhere in Spain. Some members of the battalion were attached to the engineers and the artillery, one sergeant and seven privates as carpenters and artificers, six privates as artillery drivers, and one sergeant and nineteen privates on the 'Great Gun Exercise' at Puntales. This last group would probably have been the specially trained artillery cadre which every battalion possessed. One of them, Private William Page, a framework knitter from Leicester, died on 19 June from a wound received while serving in the Puntales battery, a fate he shared with a Spanish general.

Two men of particular interest arrived with a detachment in September. Private James Waters and Drummer John Winterflood had both been on the transport *Jenny* when it was driven onto the French coast, and were subsequently registered as prisoners of war. Having escaped from French captivity, they rejoined the regiment at the depot and now came in a detachment commanded by Captain Thomas Chambers. This officer had left India in April. He had signed a resignation after some regimental unpleasantness in Madras. Far from activating it, however, he joined the detachment of two sergeants and eighty-two men marching from Wakefield to Portsmouth. Since he properly belonged to the second battalion, he naturally assumed command over the only accompanying officer, Ensign Neville. There is no mention of him in the depot returns, which suggests that he was acting on his own initiative.

However he may have employed them, Graham, like Wellesley (as he then was) before him, was not particularly impressed by the newly arrived battalion. Indeed, General Houghton reported to Graham that although their general appearance was clean, and they were steady in the ranks, they could not perform field manoeuvres accurately. The inspection might be satisfactory in all other respects, but the inability to manoeuvre correctly meant that the battalion was still of little use to Wellington. Graham might also have noted the mismatch of old and young, long-service and raw soldiers in the ranks. The statistics speak for themselves: fifty-six privates had seen more than twelve years' service, while only forty-two had served between seven and twelve years, and 662 had less than seven years' service. Similarly, 467 were under 30, including nearly half the sergeants.

The cause of this situation was, of course, the relationship between the two battalions. Even in December 1809 the junior battalion was still sending men home so that they could be transferred to the first battalion: two sergeants, a drummer, and fourteen rank and file. At the same time, two lieutenants, an ensign, a drummer, and seven corporals were detached to join the depot in England, which consisted of two companies and had been established to supervise recruiting activities. By August 1810 headquarters were at Wakefield, where the commanding officer was Brevet Major James Spawforth. Also at headquarters were two sergeants and thirty-six other ranks. The rest of the two companies were dispersed around the various recruiting grounds which (with the exception of Edinburgh) preserved the familiar Ireland-East Midlands pattern. As for the recruiting officers, there was an equal number (four) from each battalion.

It is not clear whether General Graham eventually reported more favourably on the battalion or whether the recently ennobled Lord Wellington presumed that acclimatisation in Gibraltar and Cadiz would have hardened the unsatisfactory troops he had seen in Lisbon. In September 1810, however, the 30th, along with the 2/44th, were transferred to Portugal. Cadiz had seen, incidentally, the resumption of a close relationship between the two units which began in Egypt and continued until the Flanders expedition of 1814.

Upon their departure from Cadiz, Hamilton and Malet were each given a particular commendation by General Graham, who wrote to Wellington: 'I take this opportunity of mentioning two officers of the 30th highly deserving of notice whom I have long known and served with on various occasions; Major Hamilton, who has often distinguished himself by his gallantry, and. Captain Malet, a most intelligent and attentive officer. He filled a situation here in the Quarter-Master General's department, so as to make his loss now greatly lamented by Lieut.-Colonel Cathcart.'[37] This compliment to Malet's abilities may explain why he was subsequently detached for staff duties in the Spanish service.

The two battalions embarked on 25 September, and enjoyed a fair wind during the day, although it weakened in the evening, for what amounted to an uneventful voyage. The adjutant Stewart, however, who was on the *Princess Royal* with the battalion headquarters, recorded in his journal a disturbing moment when a chisel dropped from the mizzen mast and just missed his head. Not surprisingly, this led him to reflect upon his own mortality. Land was sighted on 30 September, and the next day they were off Cape St Vincent, sailing past the towering cliffs which mark the south-west corner of Portugal. These were the waters where some of the regiment, serving as marines, had been with Admiral Jervis when he beat the Spanish in 1797, and they may have reflected on the strange turn of events which had made allies of these former enemies.

Four days later the little fleet was becalmed, but on the following day they reached the mouth of the Tagus. On 6 October the ships weighed anchor at 4.00 a.m. and then stood up the river for Belem where they arrived at midday. Two hours later they disembarked in good order and marched for the Castle. They stayed in Lisbon only briefly, however, before marching to the Lines of Torres Vedras, the defensive system which Wellington had devised a year before in anticipation of a French invasion of Portugal. Since the battle of Buçaco on 27 September the Anglo-Portuguese army had been in steady retreat, pursued by the French under Marshal Massena. The Lines brought this pursuit to an abrupt halt. Their existence was not previously suspected by Massena, and although he sat his army down in front of the outer line, his hopes of driving the British leopard into the sea were effectively baffled. As William Gomm, attached to the fifth division, wrote: 'He does not appear at all inclined to attack us. What with hills and men and redoubts, I believe we puzzle him, and we shall have the wet season at our backs very shortly. He must do something very soon, and I believe we are equally prepared to receive him or to follow him. I suspect we shall take the latter step, although with a good deal of caution.'[38]

On 16 October the 30th advanced and encamped on the mountains fronting Sobral. The Great Redoubt was essentially an earthwork which exploited the terrain and consisted of ditches and ramparts built from the spoil. The finished redoubt had twenty-three fronts, a practical response to the lie of the land. It was also protected on both fronts by other defensive positions, this being a crucial feature of the Lines.

Stewart noted how they now found themselves in the company of the battalions of fifth division. The division consisted of the usual three brigades. The first, commanded by Major General Andrew Hay, comprised the third battalion, the Royals (1st Regiment of Foot), the 2/9th, and the 2/38th. The second brigade, which was commanded by Major General Dunlop from November 1810, consisted of the 1/4th, the 2/30th and 2/44th. Following the usual pattern, the third brigade, commanded by Major General Spry, was made up of Portuguese regiments, the 3rd and 5th of the line, and the 8th Caçadores, a light infantry unit. The two British brigades acquired detached companies of Brunswick Oels Jägers early in 1811, but otherwise the composition of the division remained unchanged during the period the 30th served with it. In command was General James Leith, a man who seems to have commanded considerable respect. At the end of the year Stewart recorded the general dismay when Leith, whose health was not good, left them for a period of recuperation in Lisbon; and on 4 January he commented upon everyone's satisfaction when he returned. This may have been compounded by the unpopularity of General Dunlop, who took overall command in Leith's absence.

The battalion now settled in for an extended period behind the Lines. As at Cadiz, they were required to hold a virtually impregnable position. To a French army accustomed to living off the land, the situation was critical because Wellington had ordered a scorched earth policy during the retreat to the Lines. The French, however, held their position longer than might have been anticipated in conditions of increasing privation. Yet any direct attack on an army securely ensconced behind strong defensive lines, with provisions and reinforcements to hand, and heavy guns in position, had little chance of success. Massena's best hope was to retire to Santarem, where the people had ignored their government's command to remove themselves and their possessions to Lisbon, and there await his own reinforcements. He delayed this withdrawal for as long as possible. Since none of his fellow commanders in the Peninsula could (or would) move without a direct order from Napoleon, and the time taken for messages to travel to Paris and back was protracted, the risk of eventual starvation remained very real, even to soldiers as skilled in foraging as the French.

Crucial to the whole allied defensive system was Mount Agraça. It lay four miles in front of Wellington's headquarters, in the middle of the highly fortified section of the outer line. Here were concentrated six Anglo-Portuguese divisions, of which two were in support as flanking divisions. The fifth division was positioned on the reverse of the heights, directly behind the defensive works. Andrew Leith Hay, aide-de-camp to his uncle, General Leith, wrote of the period on Mount Agraça that 'the French army continuing in the immediate front of the lines, the allies were invariably under arms every morning long before daybreak. Frequently in the course of the first ten days dense fogs prevailed, rendering objects at any distance imperceptible, until the mist dispelled, which it usually did, gradually, after sunrise. On these occasions, Lord Wellington remained in the redoubt on Mount Agraça receiving the reports of the night, by sound alone enabled to judge whether the enemy was moving in advance. The few musketry shots sometimes heard early in the morning, proceeding from the French piquets feeling their way in the mist, occasioned some degree of anxiety to ascertain whether the firing continued, or assumed a more serious noise. This never was the case; nor was there the slightest attempt made to assail any of the works, or an endeavour to penetrate the line during the wide extent of its range.'[39]

While the 30th were encamped on Mount Agraça they spent a miserably wet period in tents, doing duty as required in manning the fortifications of the Great Redoubt or serving with the working parties which were engaged in strengthen ing the position. One of their number, Sergeant Charles Watson, suffered a particularly unhappy fate. William Stewart recorded for 5 November that Sergeant Watson was murdered the previous night, supposedly by some Portuguese with whom he had been drinking. As a result, orders were given that a sergeant's guard should visit the booths at sunset and send the soldiers back to their units.

On 14 November Massena finally retired northwards on Santarem, but not before a steady stream of deserters had crossed to the allied positions with stories of extreme privation. Leith Hay saw Massena's obstinacy as a mistake. 'On arriving in front of the position, of the natural or artificial strength of which he was probably in perfect ignorance, he must have at once become convinced of the defensive intentions of Lord Wellington, and the means he possessed of carrying them into terrible effect. Having ascertained this fact, no satisfactory reason can be assigned for bivouacking in the months of October and November, close to an army which he very properly had not the temerity to attack.'[40]

For the men of the 30th, the marshal's strategic thinking would have been of little interest, but it must have been a relief to find themselves on the move after a month in rain-soaked tents. William Stewart noted for 16 November that the division marched from their encampment at short notice, leaving their tents on the ground. He was more moved by what he subsequently witnessed. 'I found a good stable with plenty of sweet straw and our mess contrived to get a middling room for our accommodation. It had however one very great fault, namely that the doors and windows were surrounded with dead bodies not buried more than a few inches under the ground. The Enemy must have lost great numbers in this place, as every garden contained heaps of their dead and even amongst the rubbish in the houses many unfortunate wretches were found by our soldiers in the same state.'[41]

This may explain a general order of the same day, issued by the Adjutant General's Office, that commanding officers were to make sure any quarters previously occupied by the French were thoroughly cleaned. Fires were to be lit, although care was to be taken not to burn down the houses. Such measures were thought to contribute to the health of the men.

The following day, in weather conditions which were boisterous and inclement, the battalion was sent from Sobral to Oeiras, a small, pleasantly situated village. Here they were criticised for not cooking their day's provisions in advance. This oversight may be explained by their lack of experience of active service conditions; despite the few old hands who had been in Egypt, the battalion was essentially young in practice, but they were undoubtedly learning fast.

Another concern of the Commander of the Forces was that every soldier should have a blanket to accommodate him against the cold, and several general orders were issued requesting officers commanding regiments to attend to this matter. Colonel Minet, however, declined to apply for extra blankets for the battalion so that each man would have one, believing that the extra load would overburden the men. Stewart does not record what the men themselves thought of this.

On 18 November, 'After a march of about five leagues over a most barren country (generally) and such a road as we had never seen before in point of badness, and after being thoroughly drenched and soaked with heavy rain, we at length arrived at about two o'clock p.m. at that most beautiful and romantic village called Alenquer. I certainly was so disgusted with the horrid sights I had this day seen on our line of march that I was not exactly in humour to receive the pleasing impression which I otherwise should have felt in viewing the beauties of this place. Bodies of men, horses, asses, mules, bullocks etc lay so thickly strewed along the road as really even this cold day to contaminate in a high degree the air we breathed.'[42] Stewart's view is supported by Leith Hay, who ascribed the destruction in Alenquer to a spirit of pure wantonness, which he blamed on the lack of discipline in the French army. This was in contrast to the general orders coming from allied headquarters which stressed the importance of not offending the local population. Those who did so suffered severe punishment, although there is no record of any member of the 30th transgressing in this way.

Azambuja, reached the next day, was found to be in a similar state of ruin. From there the division was ordered forward to Cartaxo, where an action was anticipated. There was no encounter with the French, however. Instead, the allies were ordered into quarters, the tenure of which, as Stewart somewhat ruefully recorded, might prove uncertain. When General Leith turned Colonel Minet out of his quarters, the colonel then deprived Stewart and his mess-mates, Hamilton and Bamford, of theirs, with the result that they finished up 'roosting' in a cock loft. 'It now rained most severely, and the dirty streets were everywhere up nearly to your knee and here and there stacked up with dead horses as well as several houses with dead and dying soldiers left by the enemy.' Stewart himself was required to attend to regimental business until the early hours of the morning. Then he 'returned and found all my chums in the arms of Morpheus. After having shown orders to the field officers and eat some beef stew, as well as change once more my boots, I threw myself on the floor and was soon as comfortable as my companions, which (as the rain came plentifully thro' our roof) did not admit of high degree of comparison.'[43]

At daybreak on 20 November the division marched out with Wellington, nearly to Santarem. General Hay's brigade were to ford the Rio Maior above the town, so that they could turn the enemy's right flank, while the other two brigades, with the first division, crossed the causeway which led into Santarem. Unfortunately, the river was flooded and Hay's brigade was supplied neither with pontoons nor with bridge-building equipment. Furthermore, it was found impossible to take the causeway without the certainty of heavy losses. As a result, they were stranded on a common, exposed to heavy and continuous rain. In the evening they returned to Cartaxo.

Three days later their hopes of action were raised again when they advanced to Aveiras de Baixa, where they stayed the night. The following afternoon they reached Alcoentre, where the 30th, still inexperienced, were harangued by General Dunlop on correct conduct when in touch with the enemy.

Alcoentre was their base for the next three weeks, near enough to Santerem should the French venture out. Massena made no such move, though, and on the 15 December the fifth division marched in the usual deluge back to Torres Vedras. The whole division was suffering severely from sickness, which may explain why it was moved from the front line. The November return for the 30th listed ten sergeants and 155 other ranks sick present, out of a total strength of 740 given as present, while four officers were also sick present. For the next two months the division manned Fort San Vincente, the largest of the fortifications in the Lines (actually three forts in one), in weather that varied only between rain, thunder and lightning, and the largest hailstones Stewart had ever seen.

There is no record of how the men passed the time, other than at drill (presumably learning to conduct themselves on the march in a manner that satisfied General Dunlop) or manning the fortifications, although some of them at least seem to have engaged in cheating the locals of their goats. There were some diversions for the officers, though. Entertaining officers from other units was one way of relieving the tedium. On 5 January, Lieutenant Colonel Belsdin of the 3rd Portuguese Regiment and Ensign H dined with Stewart and his messmates. After an animated evening Hamilton had a bad fall down his own stairs. On 17 January there was some good racing on the Drill Ground. Stewart also refers to a 'leaping match' won by Captain Machell of the 30th, and he seems, like several of his fellow officers, to have taken pleasure in walking the countryside, while shooting expeditions were a regular amusement. On a quieter note, he was probably not the only one teaching himself Portuguese.

On 3 February the battalion had a rather different experience, an earthquake, the second they had suffered since coming to Torres Vedras. 'The inhabitants all quitted their houses both in Torres Vedras and Vera Toghe but the English soldiers tho' rocked out of their beds in many instances scorned to fly from their barracks, and happily no accidents took place.'[44]

Furthermore, Torres Vedras was near enough to Lisbon for officers fortunate enough to be granted leave to enjoy its diversions – while being appalled by the general filth which virtually every diarist commented upon. Interestingly, Stewart, who was granted four days' public leave by General Dunlop, makes no mention of this. Instead, he saw all the sights, including the churches (which his Irish Protestantism did not prevent him from admiring), and visited brother officers, including the dying Lieutenant George Rumley, to whose condition he made melancholy reference. He also took the opportunity to equip himself for the forthcoming campaign. He did mention in passing, however, that the quartermaster, Kingsley, who had taken himself to Lisbon on his own initiative, having neither public nor private leave, had no difficulty in obtaining rations. Stewart, on public leave, was not permitted to draw rations, and he came to the conclusion that quartermasters were a law unto themselves. This did not prevent him from spending an evening with his fellow Irishman when, by his own account, he ended up 'most ridiculously merry.'

As a new campaign became imminent, the battalion found themselves depleted of officers. In addition to three officers lost through illness (Lieutenant Rumley,

Ensign Crawford and Assistant Surgeon Irwin), staff duties had claimed several more. Captain Malet, attached to the Spanish forces as a deputy assistant quartermaster general, had witnessed the recent rout of the Spanish near Badajoz by a French army under Marshal Soult, sending an account of the affair to the 30th. Captain McNabb was Commandant at Figueras, with Lieutenant Daniell as acting quartermaster. Captain Machell was brigade major in the fifth division. Captain Henry Craig was serving with the Adjutant General's Department, while Lieutenant Adamson was at Belem, although in what capacity is not clear. Perhaps the most notable absentee, however, was Lieutenant Colonel Minet, who had commanded the second battalion since 1804. He was on staff duty in Lisbon, and never returned to the battalion. Instead, after serving as president of a court martial in Lisbon, he remained on detached duty until promoted major general in June. As a result, the battalion was now effectively under Hamilton's command.

Meanwhile, Massena continued to sit in Santarem, taking advantage of the failure of its inhabitants to retreat behind the Lines, but supplies were not inexhaustible and the news that French foraging parties were having to ride as far as Obidos in search of food must have given hope to those who were fretting for action. Everything, however, depended upon the stoicism and endurance of the enemy which, through the winter and into February, showed no sign of weakening.

Chapter 5

Over the Hills . . .

The French retreat from Santarem happened without warning. On 6 March 1811 Stewart received orders to have the battalion ready to march at the shortest notice. This so excited him that in his haste to publicise it he sprained his ankle, which left him wondering whether he would be able to undertake the march, even though as adjutant he was entitled to ride. The next day, however, he accompanied the battalion to Cadaval. Here he was impressed by two Portuguese he encountered, a gentlemanlike priest (again no sign of Protestant bigotry) and a Padrone who despite his own sad situation gave time and money to the care of the poor and sick in his village. From the impression one gains of Stewart in his journal, this was one humane man meeting another.

On 8 March the battalion was at Rio Maior, where only the poorest accommodation was available. Two days later they had reached Leiria. Retreat was not an experience the French were used to at this stage of the war and with the tacit consent of their commanders the men vented their anger on the inhabitants of the places they passed through. The result was dead bodies in burnt-out houses.

The pace of the advance was accelerating as the Anglo-Portuguese forces pursued the retreating French with the enthusiasm of men released from the frustrations of a stalemate situation. On 11 March the fifth division marched with the third towards Pombal. They set up camp on a common above the town and from this position witnessed skirmishing between the light division and the French rearguard under Marshal Ney. The next day took them through Pombal, which like Leiria had been fired by the French, and then on to Redinha, where they camped above the town. The following day Stewart wrote in his journal: 'The enemy left in and near Pombal a great number of their killed and wounded and it was disturbing to see in the streets of this dirty town the mangled remains of our fellow creatures bruised and blended with the mud by the trampling of horses and mules as well as the passage of guns, waggons etc over them, until those once valiant heroes could no longer be distinguished from the filth of the road.'[45]

That night they halted near Condeixa, on the rock-strewn slopes of a mountain. The following morning they entered the town while an action was taking place nearby, their arrival coinciding with the retreat of the enemy from their final position. Again they spent the night encamped on a virtual mountain-side some distance from the action.

So far the advance had proceeded relatively smoothly, but the next day demonstrated to Stewart just how complicated following a route could become in a country where accurate maps were a rarity. The morning started mistily, and the march was delayed until eleven o'clock. They passed through Podentes, which was in flames and where he saw both dead French soldiers and murdered peasants. In one house which was on fire he encountered a woman of about seventy whose arm had been broken by a French soldier. She pointed to an inner room where Stewart found the woman's husband, who had been hanged. All he could do was send some soldiers to cut the unfortunate man down and take the old woman to a surgeon. While marching from Miranda do Corvo, the next town after Podentes, 'Thro' an error in the usual manner, our Division was conducted through a vineyard instead of continuing to pursue the road, which tho' not very good, was nevertheless passable. This gross want of knowledge of the country was the means of retarding our march at least two hours! during which time Col. Offley of the Lusitanian Legion and myself waited in the road and saw the troops pass in true Indian file, for they could not be made to march otherwise.

'Such as the mounted officers who were with the column had very narrow escapes from breaking their necks over its walls and stumps of vines etc. Our march now lay considerably to the right of the Ponte de Maracalla road, and over mountains and by rocks. This circumstance joined with the unpleasantness of a long and most tedious night march rendered our sufferings by no means trifling, indeed, many of the officers and men actually were sleeping at intervals as they walked, and for my own part I nearly fell off my horse seven or eight times.'[46]

Two days later they were near Foz de Arouce, having crossed the river Ceira and passed through Povoa and Ceira dos Albas. Provisions, particularly biscuit, were now very scarce as the commissariat struggled to keep up with the advance. Nor was there any opportunity to celebrate St Patrick's Day except in the heavy dews of the night. Stewart was probably not the only one to lament a St Patrick's Day without appropriate liquor, since its celebration was an annual feature of battalion life, an occasion when even the English and Scots (to say nothing of one young Portuguese) were happy to adopt an Irish identity.

Passing over the heights of the Estrella range, they reached Celorico on 18 March, and were near Alva on the following day. Provisions were still a problem. Stewart and a fellow officer had to satisfy themselves with half a carton of chocolate and some stale biscuit which he found at the bottom of his haversack. Another two days brought them to Venda do Valle, where they halted in some woods for four days, a welcome respite from the constant marching and long enough to build huts. By 29 March they had reached Vila Pouca on the Mondego where they bivouacked for a further three days. On 2 April though, the relentless advance was resumed in heavy rain. They crossed the Mondego by the stone bridge at Porto de Carne [sic] and then passed through Guarda, which Stewart described as a large but filthy place, although he conceded that they were seeing it at a disadvantage. He also recorded that the cathedral and the bishop's palace were thought to be worth seeing, and that it was supposed to be the highest habitable city in Europe. Presumably, he was not the only officer to combine the passing thoughts of a tourist with the business of soldiering.

As Massena continued his retreat, he decided to march south, across the mountains to the Tagus valley and then on to Estremadura, where he could combine with Soult. If this had proved successful, it would have enabled him to threaten Portugal once again. Despite the protests of his corps commanders, the loudest from Ney, who was relieved of his command as a consequence, this route was initially followed. Such was the suffering of the starving French troops, however, as they found themselves exposed to the extreme cold of the mountains, that Massena had to accept the practical impossibility of his strategy. Instead, he redirected his retreat upon Almeida and Ciudad Rodrigo.

Having spent the night at Vila do Touro, four leagues beyond Guarda, the fifth division arrived at Sabugal on 3 April. Reynier's II Corp, in the rear of the French forces, had taken up a defensive position and Wellington decided upon an engagement. The fifth division on the left of the allied force was to storm the town by way of its bridge while to their right the light and third divisions would attack Reynier's forces directly. 'Morning fine,' Stewart wrote. 'March'd forward to attack the Enemy in their position on the right bank of the Coa at Sabugal. Placed our picquets quite close to theirs, and lay down to rest and refresh whilst Lord W. was reconnoitring and making his arrangements. All being ready, the Light Division posted considerably above the town and were engaged immediately. The third under M. Genl Picton were sent to support them, but in the mean time they had beaten off the Enemy, taken a howitzer and destroy'd about a squadron of cavalry who had the temerity to charge them where they had retired to, behind a low stone wall – the 43rd Lt Infantry particularly distinguished themselves. The other Divisions having crossed the Enemy retired towards Nave and we accepted his ground for the night.'[47] In fact, the fifth division under Dunlop crossed the bridge at a critical moment in the attack, drove the French right from the heights and were able to occupy Sabugal without loss, even enjoying the meal which the French had been forced to abandon. But once again they had found themselves on the fringes of the action.

As Massena fell back on Salamanca, the principal purpose of the advance had been achieved. The French had been driven out of Portugal for what proved to be the last time, although they still had possession of the border fortress of Almeida which had fallen into their hands, somewhat fortuitously, eight months before. This was the next allied objective, and a concentration of Anglo-Portuguese divisions signalled to Massena where Wellington would focus his attack. The fifth division was brought up to the Spanish border as part of the blockading force. Sir William Gomm wrote in a letter home: 'We have invested Almeida with a garrison of a few hundred men, and the whole of the French army are gone off to Salamanca. Almeida must fall immediately. This is the whole of my news. We are in a delightful Spanish village,'[48] Aldea del Obispo, where the 30th were also posted, although probably not in such comfortable quarters as a staff officer like Gomm.

The somewhat leisurely march from Sabugal had taken six days during which Stewart and his messmate, Bamford, had even found time to go fowling, a favourite pursuit of many British officers, and a way of varying the diet of beef and biscuit. Nevertheless, the French were not far away and on 7 April several men were captured while foraging.

Aldea del Obispo was reasonably comfortable, and a welcome change from marching and bivouacking. It was also the nearest village to Fort Concepcion, situated on the Spanish side of the border as a counterpart to Portuguese Almeida. Although it was in a ruinous state, having been blown up by the light division in a previous campaign, the fifth division was required to man this outpost in order to secure the Dos Casas river from enemy passage.

The next month was relatively peaceful for the battalion, although life could still be made uncomfortable by commanding officers. On the day of their arrival at Aldea del Obispo General Dunlop kept them standing in heavy snow while quarters were allocated in 150 houses for twenty-three officers and 482 NCOs and other ranks, which suggests considerable overcrowding. On 14 April they marched to Almeida, setting off at three in the morning so that they were within reach of the French guns by sunrise. For the rest of the day they remained in support of the picquets. Then on 16 April, having risen at two in the morning, they advanced to Gallegos where they missed a French convoy going into Ciudad Rodrigo, Almeida's Spanish twin which the French had taken the year before. The same day they returned to Aldea del Obispo.

On 2 May there was news of a French advance. Having reached Salamanca three weeks before, Massena had lost no time in strengthening his decimated forces. (Their losses since September 1810 have been calculated at 25,000 men.)

With some rather grudging reinforcement from the Army of the North, commanded by Marshal Bessières, Massena intended to relieve Almeida, first overcoming the allied army at Fuentes d'Oñoro. There followed three days of intermittent fighting and manoeuvring. Stewart reported that 3 May was a 'Remarkably fine day, the Enemy came on in high style, driving our Cavalry and Lt Division; the skirmishing as one party advanced and the other retired was one of the finest sights possible. In the course of this day the Enemy was occupied in taking up his ground in our front and endeavoured frequently to possess himself of Fuentes D Honor but could not. Towards evening both armies placed their picquets and we were not much disturbed during the night.'[49] This is a somewhat laconic account of the fierce fighting which took place in the narrow streets of the village, but Stewart, on the far left of the allied position, would have learnt about it at second hand.

The following day the two forces 'Engag'd smartly on the right, and several new attempts made to turn our right at Nave d'Aver.' Finally, on 5 May, 'Our Army engaged the entire of this Day, more especially on the right. A most incessant cannonade kept up upon both sides which did great execution. The superiority of the Enemies' cavalry and the openness of the ground on our right enabled him to oblige the Light and 7th Division on our right to retire from Pozo Velha and form en potence. Our line was now formed into two sides of a triangle; from Fort Concepcion to Fuentes d'Onor being the base and from there to Villa Formosa the perpendicular. Behind these angles lay Almeida at the distance of one and a half leagues. The Enemy having now possessed himself of Nave d'Aver and Pozo Velha commanded the road leading to the bridge and fords of the Coa at Sabugal which Lord Wellington had hoped to keep open.

'The action continued with various successes on each side, (but chiefly on ours) during the day and the brilliant conduct of many of our regts could not be surpassed. Our cavalry consisted of about 900 whilst the Enemy brought into action more than 4,000!! our infantry however ably assisted in bringing down a fear of the Enemy by well directed volleys and none more so than the Chasseurs Britannique. At night all firing ceased.'[50]

The fifth division played only a minor role in the battle of Fuentes d'Oñoro. Commanded by Sir William Erskine, their position on the extreme left of the allied position, at Fort Concepcion, kept them relatively inactive. The ravine through which flowed the Dos Casas river, wide and deep at this point, offered protection from a frontal attack. They were flanked on their left by a 300-strong unit of Portuguese cavalry, while to the right were the sixth division. From Fort Concepcion to Fuentes d'Oñoro, where the bulk of the allied forces were concentrated, is a distance of five miles, which gives some idea of how thinly the two divisions were stretched in their strong position. Opposite the fifth division was Reynier's II Corps. On 3 May, while Massena was making a frontal attack on Fuentes d'Oñoro, Reynier merely demonstrated against his opponents. At one point Wellington sent the light division to support his left but it soon became obvious that they were not needed.

4 May saw some light skirmishing in Fuentes d'Oñoro. The following day's action, however, engaged all but two of the allied divisions in fierce fighting as Massena successfully turned the allied right and gained temporary possession of the village. Once again he instructed Reynier to demonstrate against the allied left but only to launch an all-out attack if he detected any weaknesses or if the allied centre collapsed. Consequently the fifth division remained in the same position all day. Reynier employed the 31^{ieme} Légère, supported by two guns, against the light troops of the fifth division across the ravine but could do little else. He was opposed by forces roughly equal to his own, so that a frontal attack would have resulted in heavy losses. If he moved closer to Fuentes d'Oñoro to support his own centre the fifth division could cross the river and launch a flank attack. The result was desultory fighting, as the casualty figures make clear. The 31^{ieme} Légère lost four officers and forty-eight sergeants, with a corresponding number of men. The light troops of the fifth division, made up of the light companies of the 3/1st, 1/9th, 2/30th, 2/44th, the 8th Caçadores and two detached companies of the Black Brunswickers lost twenty-seven men in total. The 30th suffered a sergeant and three rank and file wounded, according to Wellington's dispatch. These wounds could not have been serious, however, since there is no record of them in the muster roll. Similarly, Hamilton, in command, made light of the wound he received. On the other hand, there is reference to a certain William Mason who 'went to the enemy 3 May'.

Because they were not engaged in a sustained musketry contest, the regiments of the fifth division do not bear Fuentes d'Oñoro as a battle honour, although the 30th certainly thought of it as such. Those who later claimed the GSM in 1847, however, earned a bar for this engagement, a total of eight officers and thirty-one men. Their numbers include Stewart, and Mr James Poyntz, a volunteer with the battalion. Poyntz, the son of the first battalion's quartermaster, had remained with the junior battalion when his father and two teenaged brothers sailed for India. Now, as a thirteen-year-old volunteer, he served with the light company, who alone of the battalion saw some action. A year later he was enrolled as a cadet at the Royal Military Academy, subsequently being commissioned into the 30th and eventually rising to the rank of major. Also significant in the GSM list is Captain Robert Lynch; in

1848 he was the only surviving 30th officer who could claim bars for both Egypt and the Peninsula.

By 8 May the French were in retreat, leaving their cavalry as a defensive screen. Having repulsed the enemy attack, the allies could now concentrate upon Almeida. The 30th, though, returned to Aldea del Obispo. 'Our padrone and his family were rejoiced to see my messmate and myself back again. About 11 o'clock this night the Enemy in Almeida blew up the works and strange to say escaped through the piquets to the bridge of Barba del Parco, which post had been ordered to be occupied by the 4th Regt from our Brigade, but unfortunately that Corps lost its way and instead of being at the spot to prevent the Enemy passing, it was only enabled to come up with them in conjunction with the 36th and some lt companies of our Division whilst they were in the act of crossing the bridge. The result was, however, better than might have been expected under all the circumstances of this truly unfortunate affair.'[51]

Stewart's journal ends after just one more entry, so there is no further explanation of the 'unfortunate affair', and no record of its final tragedy. The exact circumstances of what went wrong on the night of 10 May will probably never be known. *The Royal Military Chronicle* for February 1812, in a continuing account of Wellington's Peninsular campaigns, suggested the following scenario. 'Though Massena had failed in his attempt to relieve the garrison of Almeida, he got a letter conveyed to General Brenier [sic], which informed him of the bad success, and which, I believe, determined this officer to attempt what fortunately for him succeeded. General Brenier saw that he was left to his fate: if he remained in his garrison his troops must starve, or become prisoners of war; if he quitted the garrison in a dark night, they could only be taken, but some might escape: – in the one case there was a chance of his escaping, in the other there was none; he therefore determined on quitting Almeida with his troops, and accordingly left it at about one o'clock on the morning of the 13th May. For several nights previous to the 11th, Brenier had employed his troops in the destruction of the ordnance, which he did by firing one piece into the mouth of another, so that our picquets, being accustomed to the reports of artillery, did not pay so much attention to the blowing up of the mines as they might otherwise have done. On leaving the gate, he moved forward in two columns, which, however, kept close together, and coming in contact with a picquet of the sixteenth Portuguese regiment, it was immediately overpowered and bayoneted on the spot.

'The sixth division, which after the retreat of Massena was ordered to resume its station before Almeida, had only come into its position that afternoon; and General Pack's brigade, which had continued the blockade during the absence of the sixth brigade, had been moved to its former quarters late that evening, which circumstances were much in Brenier's favour. Brigadier-gen Pack, who was at Malpartido, being immediately informed of what had happened, collected about one hundred of his brigade and attacked the rest of the column; and threw them into considerable confusion. By throwing away their baggage, and casting loose their horses and mules, the French distracted the attention of the pursuers, so that General Pack's party, engaged in securing the plunder, was soon diminished. Major-gen Campbell and a party of the thirty-sixth, also joined in the pursuit. The loss of the enemy was immense; but the fourth regiment unfortunately missing its road, did not arrive at Barba del Puerco as soon as was expected, so that General Brenier and a few did escape, but that number was very small.'[52]

The 36th were strengthened by the light companies of the 30th and the 44th and together these troops pursued the French to Barba del Puerco, where the bridge across the chasm was very narrow. As a result, at least 300 of the French were taken prisoner while others were driven over the precipice into the stream below. A few saved themselves by clinging to the rocks, whereupon the senior officer on the spot, Captain Jessop of the 44th, allowed French troops on the other side of the chasm to rescue them.

The crucial point in the account printed in *The Royal Military Chronicle* was the failure of the 4th to find their road to the bridge at Barba del Puerco. There seems to have been a breakdown in communication in the division, which may have been the fault of Sir William Erskine, to whom Wellington sent the original order, or of Colonel Bevan of the 4th, or even of the messenger who carried the message from one to the other. Whoever was responsible, the result was that General Brennier and his forces were indeed able to break out of the town shortly before midnight, and too many of them for Wellington's liking made their escape. The tragic result of this debacle was the suicide two months later of Colonel Bevan. Possessed of a somewhat depressive temperament, he could not cope with being blamed, wrongly he felt, for the sorry affair. In a show of their own opinion on the matter, every officer of the fifth division attended his funeral.

Lieutenant William Tomkinson of the 16th Light Dragoons, reflecting on the affair from a more neutral standpoint, wrote: 'Col. Bevan of the 4th Regiment was so much hurt at the expression in Lord Wellington's dispatch, viz.: "that the garrison escaped through the 4th Regiment losing its way," that at Portabayre, on the route down to Badajos, he put an end to his existence, though certainly no blame was attached to him. With his regiment he was ordered to watch the passes over the Agueda to the right of Barba del Puerco, where he was the day previous to the escape of the garrison. On the morning they got away, he heard the firing, and had his men under arms to march of his own accord to the point, and that instant the order arrived for him to move to Barba del Puerco; but it was too late, as on his arrival the enemy were passing. The order reached Sir Wm. Erskine at 2 p.m. the preceding day; he put it in his pocket, and did not dispatch the letter to Colonel Bevan before midnight, and to cover himself, he said that the 4th Regiment unfortunately missed its way, which was not the case.'[53] Tomkinson does not give the source for this story, but it seems to have been retold and widely believed throughout the army.

Wellingon's attention was now diverted southwards to the crucial Spanish border town of Badajoz, which had surrendered to the French (not without some suspicion of treachery) on 19 March. Four divisions were engaged in besieging the place, having beaten off a relieving force under Soult at the bloody battle of Albuera. The fifth division, with the first and sixth, were placed under the command of General Sir Brent Spencer to guard the line of the Agueda. The 30th were sent to Nave de Haver where they were quartered in the village or in huts quickly constructed from the boughs of trees. At the beginning of June the activities of Massena's successor, Marshal Marmont, caused the allies to withdraw to Sabugal. By 7 June Marmont's intentions had become clearer. He passed on the right of the allied position, which suggested that his objective was Estremadura, where he could combine with Soult to raise the siege of Badajoz. In response, Spencer made for Vila Velha and the all-important boat-bridge over the Tagus which he had to cross in order to join up with Wellington before the two French forces united. Marching via Castelo Branco, the fifth division crossed the Tagus on 18 and 19 June. Four days later they were close to Arronches, where they were joined by the rest of the allied force, the siege of Badajoz having been abandoned on 10 June.

An action seemed possible between the 54,000 allied troops and the 60,000 French opposed to them on the other side of the Guardiana until disturbances in Andalusia at the end of June sent Soult back to that province, which was his principal sphere of interest. He left a detachment with Marmont which gave the French 50,000 men but numbers were of little consequence when Marmont's problem was not men but supplies. Despite scouring the countryside the French coerced only meagre provisions from the unwilling population and on 15 July Marmont retired to Merida.

At this point the activities of the fifth division can be followed through a journal kept by J.A. (Ensign John Anderson) of the Royals, which he sent to *The Royal Military Chronicle* at regular intervals. Although the Royals were in the first brigade, much of what Anderson reported applied equally to the second brigade.

The country around the Guardiana was notoriously malarial, and as soon as the French no longer posed an immediate threat the fifth division were sent back to Portalegre, two marches away. They spent two weeks in the town before going into hutted cantonments. Then, on 20 July, they moved to the Sierra d'Arronches, in the neighbourhood of Quinta de Alamira, where they bivouacked in a wood and built huts. They called this place Vauxhall because of the woodland setting and the music of the regimental bands.

This peaceful interlude was brief. Wellington already had Ciudad Rodrigo in his sights. The long-requested siege train was at Oporto, which made taking the border town a realistic option. Leaving the second division and a Portuguese force at Elvas to cover Badajoz, he took the rest of the army northwards. On 29 July the fifth division marched to Castelo de Vide, along a barren, mountainous road, while the tops of the mountains appeared like ruined fortifications. Anderson took the opportunity to explore the ramparts and fort of Castelo de Vide and was entertained by the playing of the band of the 4th Regiment in the evening. Even on campaign the civilities of life could be maintained. After a day's rest in Castelo de Vide orders were received for a seven-day march. On 31 July the division advanced three leagues to Nisa, across mountainous country, bivouacking in a wood for the night. The next day they descended to the Tagus at Vila Velha. This was even rougher country. The road ran over broken rocks and precipices and the steepness of the terrain, combined with the high summer heat, made for hard marching. On 2 August, at Sarnadas, they heard news of a French concentration on the Tagus. Wellington responded by bringing five of his divisions together near Castelo Branco, the fifth division arriving on 3 August. The next day they reached Atalaya and easier marching country, 'more cultivated, and a considerable quantity of oak, chestnut, and cork trees. The heaths were covered with a species of Erica, the gum cystus, and broom. There is an abundance of game, rabbits etc.'[54] This was an excellent opportunity to supplement one's diet.

The hard marching continued. A day had been missed when the division halted at Atalaya, so two marches were completed in a day, over unforgiving country. The five leagues traversed on 7 August killed off many of the transport animals and the experience was made worse by the stench of the rotting remains of other transport animals which had been lost by the divisions ahead of them. There was some expectation of battle, however, which always raised the spirits of the British soldier and his Portuguese ally. The number of local people fleeing in the opposite direction could only mean that the French were advancing. When the division reached Sabugal on 8 August they discovered that the town had been completely ransacked by the French. Again, they remained in bivouac, and Anderson was particularly struck by the large number of snakes and the size of the grasshoppers.

On 10 August they passed Alfayates, which had also been pillaged by the French, and then crossed into Spain. They settled around the small town of Navas Frejas, high in the Sierra de Malcata, where they remained for several weeks, watching for any attempt by Marmont to raise the blockade of Ciudad Rodrigo which was already in place. The advance watch was kept by the light companies, including the Portuguese Caçadores and the two companies of Brunswick Jägers attached to the division. One or other of the battalions would be in support, hutted against the bitter cold at night (although the days were pleasant enough). The rest of the division remained in Navas Frejas and Peñaparda, where the 30th had their headquarters. The advance forces were turned around week by week, and the light companies prided themselves on the speed with which they could effect the changeover. By running the distance of twelve miles they could reach Valverde in two hours, no mean feat when both the terrain and the weight of their equipment are taken into consideration but no doubt there was regimental pride at stake.

Time passed slowly. One of the few diversions was hunting the wolves which haunted this wild country and even invaded the bivouacs. On 16 August, however, there was a brief promise of action when the French surprised an outpost of the King's German Legion, and took sixty commissariat mules, loaded with stores. The light companies, hurrying up in support, almost took the enemy at San Martino. The French got off, but not before they had killed several of the villagers who were coming out of church, as well as causing twenty KGL casualties. By 18 August, though, it was known that the French had pushed on to Ciudad Rodrigo, taking with them the chance of action.

Another officer J.P. (Lieutenant Jonathan Parker) of the Royals, writing from Navas Frejas early in September, equated the sickness in the division with the paucity of spirits available. 'At present the allowance is too small, and it frequently happens that they have but half an allowance. In the marshy parts of England, where the ague is most prevalent, it affects those the least who live the best, and the most necessitous are obliged to purchase their safety at the expense of a small quantity of spirits before going out in the morning: smoking is also a good preventative. I regret to say, that there is here a great number of sick; which, I am confident, would not be the case if the men had a sufficient allowance of spirits. To this subject I would seriously implore the attention of the government. And this is the more wanted at present, when the men are constantly eating fruit of different kinds, which generally produce dysentery; nor does the wine of the country appear to prevent its effects . . . If the men had half a pint of good West India rum, one half in the morning and the other in the evening, you would hear very little of sickness.' Parker was at pains to stress

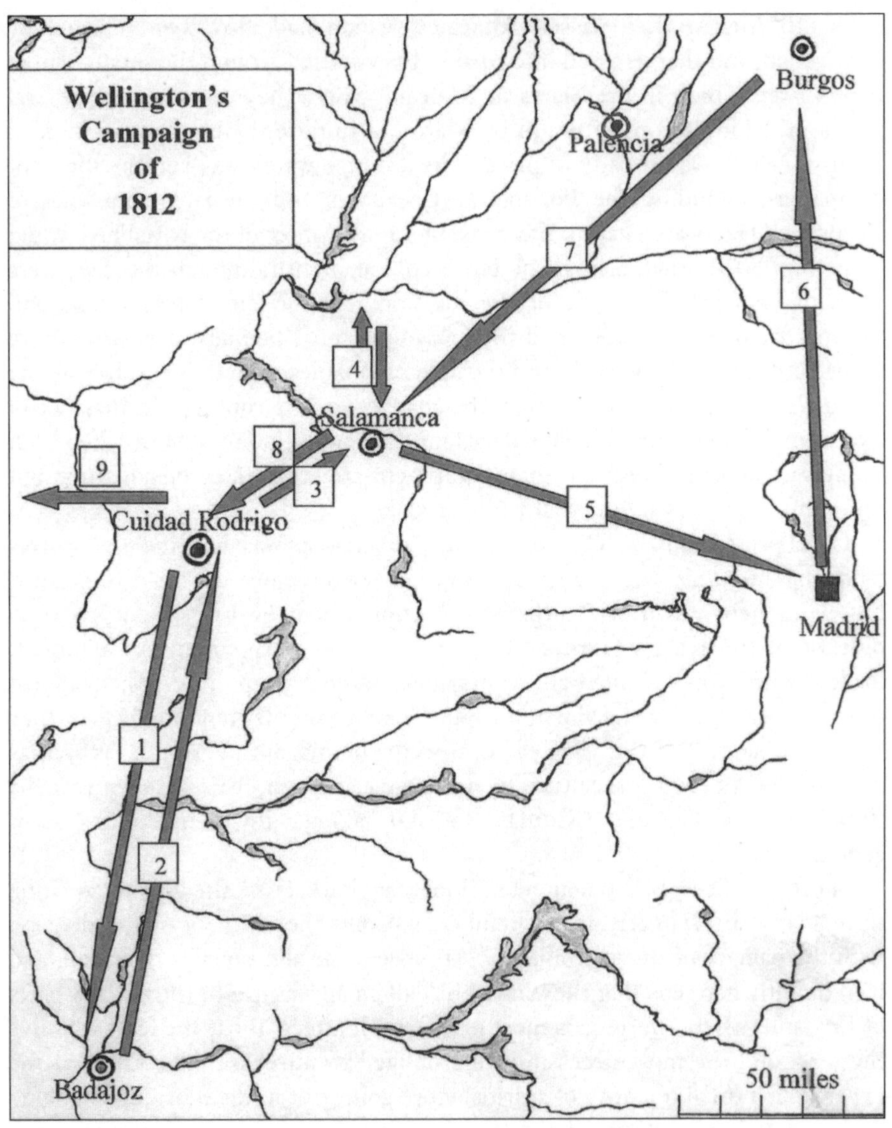

that 'in suggesting this for consideration, I have no motive independent of the good of the service.'[55]

At first sight, the numbers of sick returned by the 30th in August (twelve sergeants, six drummers and 227 rank and file), seem to support Parker's contention. Of these, however, only twelve were with the regiment. The others were in Lisbon, and many of them may well have been there since before the spring advance which drove Massena out of Portugal. Nonetheless, bad wine and spirits, which the Portuguese themselves were reluctant to drink, and a propensity to eat fresh fruit, caused ongoing health problems for the British soldiers.

At the beginning of September the weather broke. Bitterly cold during the day, the temperature dropped even further during the night. Provisions were scarce and expensive, so that the temptation to steal overwhelmed many of the soldiers. Potatoes were their favourite booty. Then on 11 September there was 'a most tremendous storm of thunder and lightning, which seemed to shake the basis of the mountains; the lightning was incessant, and "stream'd like a meteor to the troubled air"; the rain fell in torrents, which rolled in cataracts down the sides of the mountains with great velocity; while the loud-warning peal, communicating their arrival at the bottom, lingered on the ear.' From this point the situation deteriorated even further. Anderson reported on 17 September: 'The weather very wet and cold, and our huts as wretched and miserable as a grave. We have had neither wine or spirits for the last ten days.'[56]

At the same time that he was sending his journal to *The Royal Military Chronicle*, he was also composing poetry to reflect his experiences. One example of his output was published as 'The Subaltern's Complaint: on picquet to Peña Perda, a very lofty mountain, one of the passes of the Sierra de Gata, in Spain.' The following verses give the substance of his feelings:

> Bleak was the wind, and dreary was the night,
> When posted at the pass of Gato's Height
> A luckless sub, with cold and hunger pressed,
> Look'd on the Moon, and thus his grief expressed.
>
> Ah! Fatal hour, when first I left the 'Town' –
> The shadow of vain glory to pursue,
> Now every pleasure, every comfort flown;
> In vain my distant friends, I think of you . . .
>
> E'en now, alas, how sadly changed the scene!
> My haversack, my only store contains,
> Nought there but crumbs of mouldy biscuit seen,
> A knife – a horn, and salt – some few dear grains . . .
>
> No bed, no blanket here our bones defends
> From cold, or damp, diseases, aches and stitches,
> Pale shivering ague with her train attends,
> No lining here to regimental breeches!!! . . .

My once gay coat in tatters hangs about,
With many vary coloured pieces patch'd,
From ghosts of shoes, my wounded feet peep out,
Thro' threadbare gaiters, how my legs are scratched ...

At morn, before the break of cheerful day,
Rous'd by the bugle's brisk and brazen sound,
Almost asleep, we stagger on our way,
By dust half choak'd, or rain completely drown'd.[57]

Chapter 6

The Long Road to Badajoz

The fifth division were finally relieved of outpost duty when Marmont launched a joint action to relieve Ciudad Rodrigo with General Dorsenne, in command of the Army of the North. To disguise his intentions Marmont instructed General Foy to feint an attack on the fifth division through the passes of the Sierra de Gata. This move caused eager anticipation of action. Four days later Marmont and Dorsenne combined their forces at Tamames, to the east of Ciudad Rodrigo. The French considerably outnumbered the widely dispersed allied forces but Wellington nevertheless interpreted this manoeuvring as an attempt to get supplies into Ciudad Rodrigo. The action at El Boden on 25 September, however, when the third division had to fight a fierce retreat convinced him that the threat was serious. That evening he withdrew his forces to Alfayates, leaving camp fires burning to deceive the enemy.

The fifth division heard the heavy firing coming from the direction of Ciudad Rodrigo and subsequently learnt of the attack on Wellington's head-quarters at Fuenteguinaldo, which led to the action at El Boden. The next day General Dunlop, who was temporarily in charge during Leith's absence, put the division under arms from 4.00 a.m. as a precaution. Meanwhile, the distant firing continued. On 27 September the division marched to Aldea de Ponte where they halted. Unfortunately, 'when just in the midst of our cookery the alarm was given that the French were approaching, in great force, on the other side of the town, and which was confirmed by an instantaneous discharge of cannon and musquetry. The beef and soup were thrown in every direction, and we stood to our arms ... The attention of the enemy was, however, called off by a division to the left of ours, and General Dunlop thought it advisable to remove to a more advantageous position, and more protected from cavalry.'[58] They were now merely spectators, although according to Douglas of the Royals, 'the men, though tired and hungry, and lacking even wine and spirits, wanted to fight, and were hammering their flints, and making all the usual preparations.' He was particularly amused by some Irish lads whose conversation was truly laughable. But the French attack petered out before the fifth division could become involved.

All the Anglo-Portuguese divisions were now pulled back across the Coa. On 28 September the fifth division marched through Coito and on towards Sabugal, 'as bad a march as, I think, was ever undertaken, extremely dark, and the road broken, craggy, and rocky; such a road as I had never witnessed, through a perfect valley of stones. I really could not have rode, if anyone would have given me the best horse in our division. The road is, however, very good on reaching Coito, and from thence by Sabugal ... A very heavy rain, during which we halted for three hours, and afterwards slept in a wood. On the 25th all our baggage had been ordered to the river, so that not one in ten had even a great coat – nothing but their uniform. Spent another miserable night, without any other covering than my regimental coat; no great-coat or blanket.'[59]

The next day the division reached Vila do Touro, where they hoped to find their baggage, but were disappointed to discover that it had been sent on to Guarda. By this time many of the officers, with mustachios and whiskers, and smoky complexions, were beginning to resemble the Portuguese who marched alongside them because there had been no opportunity to wash or shave. On 30 September, however, they were finally reunited with their possessions at Guarda. Stewart had previously described the city as large but filthy. Now, in Anderson's opinion, it was slowly recovering from the damage the French had inflicted. He was probably not the only one to look forward to a period of rest so that the men could recover from their exertions in the mountains. Despite divisional field days, which were ordered twice a week, and an inspection by General Graham, there was a pleasant mixture of duty and merriment. Indeed, the only disadvantage of Guarda was its mountainous location and wet, foggy weather; it was not unusual to see cloud below the town, or to be engulfed by cloud while knowing that the sun was shining in the valleys below.

The division remained in Guarda until 23 November, when they received a sudden order to march at five in the morning. That day they reached Marmeleiro, and the following day, Alfayates. From here, one British brigade covered the Coa while the other, which included the 30th, suffered cramped quarters in Vila do Touro for five days until Wellington satisfied himself that there was no threat of a French attack. Then the allied forces were once more dispersed. The fifth division returned to Guarda and then retired to the Mondego valley: 'On the immediate bank of the river stands the village of Miserella, I think the sweetest romantic seclusion I ever beheld; a valley of prodigious extent on either side, bounded by mountains, and abounding in every luxury:– The oak, chestnut, and most of the other forest trees which are known in Britain; and the orange, the pine, the arbutus, and an infinity of others, in full foliage and luxuriancy of fruit. It was really extreme winter on the tops of the mountains, and midsummer in this valley.'[60] The division stayed only briefly in this land of milk and honey and eventually the different battalions were quartered in the villages around Coimbra, on the lower reaches of the Mondego. The 30th were at Medais where time allowed for drill and an occasional field day. There were also woodcock in abundance, which provided some of the officers with regular sport.

Commissariat supplies could be supplemented, although nothing was cheap. It cost four shillings to acquire notepaper and pens for letters home. Cheese, bacon and butter, the latter coming from England or Ireland, cost at least three shillings a pound, against a daily income of 4/8d for a lieutenant. Tea, a favourite beverage, was fifteen shillings a pound. Those who drank it excited the curiosity of the Portuguese, who thought it must be grog. More affordable, though, was the local produce such as oranges, olives and chestnuts.

With the end of the year's campaigning the 30th could take stock of their losses, not in action, but to disease. In total, 101 members of the battalion had perished: five sergeants, two drummers, ninety-one rank and file; and the three officers, Rumley, Crawford and Irwin, who had all died earlier in the year. A further 258 men had been invalided home.

There had been some additions to the strength of the battalion, however, because their requirements were now taking precedence. The senior battalion received no reinforcements in 1811 while in June the depot at Wakefield received authorisation to send fifty men to Portugal, but actually sent fifty-nine. Transferred from recruiting duties were two sergeants, a drummer and five rank and file, while eleven rank and file, presumably recovered invalids from India, were transferred from the first battalion. A further thirty-eight of the newcomers were recruits, while two were specifically described as returning invalids, and one was a transfer from another unit. They marched in July, and reached Lisbon in October. Then, in November, two sergeants and thirty-three rank and file were marched from the depot but did not arrive until 1812. Overall, though, the Peninsular campaign was taking its toll on what was still the weaker of the two battalions.

There had been seven desertions during the year, although four of these subsequently returned, which suggests that some form of incapacity, probably drunkenness, had caused their absence. As already noted, one man was taken prisoner, joining the ninety-nine men from the *Jenny* still recorded as on the strength of the second battalion. Of interest is a man recorded as 'returned', in March 1811. Daniel McCarthy had been a prisoner of the French, a claim supported by the records, since he was on the ill-fated *Jenny*. As an Irishman, from Galway, he was offered the chance to enlist into an Irish regiment in French service, an offer which was made to all Irish prisoners of war. He accepted in the hope of being able to make his escape. On rejoining the regiment, he gave his sworn word that at no time had he raised a weapon against a British soldier. Finding himself within reach of British cavalry in Estremadura, he deserted from the French and was sent back to the 30th. Such was the tale he told, and it was believed. Indeed, he continued to serve with the battalion until 1817. Upon reduction, his nineteen years' service was rewarded with a pension, plus two extra years for Waterloo. Furthermore, his conduct was described as 'good'.

The most upsetting change for the battalion, however, was the near loss of Major Hamilton, who had been the acting commanding officer since Colonel Minet's departure late in 1810. In June Hamilton was appointed lieutenant colonel in the West India Rangers, without purchase, an unenviable promotion to a notoriously unhealthy station. Lieutenant Colonel Charles Turner of the West India Rangers, but attached to the Portuguese service, was appointed to the 30th vice Lieutenant Colonel Minet, who had been placed on the general list. News of these appointments reached the second battalion in September and Hamilton returned to England on four months' leave preparatory to taking up his new appointment, leaving Major George Grey in command. Turner, however, had been seriously wounded while in command of his Portuguese regiment at the first siege of Badajoz. In 1812 he was awarded a pension of £300 per annum for the loss of an arm, suggesting that he was not fit for an active service command. Both his and Hamilton's appointments were cancelled, and Hamilton was now appointed lieutenant colonel in the 30th. This must have given particular satisfaction to Hamilton but there is a neatness about the manoeuvring which provokes some suspicion.

In the last monthly return of 1811 the strength of the battalion at head-quarters and fit for duty was: one field officer, fifteen company officers, three staff officers, twenty-nine sergeants, fourteen drummers, and 363 rank and file. Although some of the men returned as sick or on command subsequently rejoined, this was not an impressive force to play an active part in a new year's offensive campaign.

The Portuguese side of the frontier, guarded by Almeida and Elvas, was securely in allied hands but no advance into Spain could be risked while the French held the two Spanish strongholds of Ciudad Rodrigo and Badajoz. The former, Wellington's immediate objective, was already under blockade by the end of 1811 but as 1812 dawned the weather prevented the commencement of a siege. Heavy snow fell on the first day of the new year and again on the third. The next day there was a violent gale, making it impossible to bring up the fascines, gabions and entrenching tools. Not until 8 January was the ground finally broken.

Such inclement weather meant that conditions for the besieging army were particularly unpleasant. In his instructions to general officers commanding divisions, dated 8 January, Wellington recognised this by deciding that operations should be carried out by the different divisions on a twenty-four hour alternating basis. He further instructed that enough men should be left behind to cook provisions for when the division was relieved, an attention to detail which was typical of him as he nursed his army through its campaigns. The fifth division received orders on 2 or 3 January to advance to the line of the Agueda, a short march from the villages around Almeida which they had occupied since the end of December. They, like the other divisions similarly summoned, were in position by 5 January. A general order also invited officers from all regiments to volunteer for engineering duties. Lieutenants Andrew Baillie, Parke Percy Neville, John Lorraine White and Ensign Robert Smith subsequently claimed Ciudad Rodrigo as a bar to their GSMs, but eleven officers from the 30th actually undertook this dangerous work, making themselves prime targets for enemy marksmen.

The battalion was not involved in the actual assault, which took place on 19 January, earlier than Wellington had intended when the approach of a French relieving force under Marmont forced his hand. The third and light divisions provided the storming troops while Pack's Portuguese brigade made a false attack as a diversionary tactic, and the town was taken with relative ease. Thirty-six years later, when the GSM was finally granted to those surviving Peninsular veterans who claimed it, in addition to the four officers already mentioned, eight men also received the bar for Ciudad Rodrigo. These men were probably the survivors of a larger group of volunteers who joined the working parties which dug the trenches. It might be supposed that they were men with specific skills, miners, carpenters and masons whose expertise was considered particularly valuable during a siege. Their discharge papers, however, reveal that five of them were labourers, while a sixth was either a labourer or a brickmaker, depending upon which of the two John Hills in the battalion (both of whom survived to claim the GSM) received a bar for Ciudad Rodrigo. Unfortunately, there are no records for the other two men but five or six out of eight suggests that the response to a call for volunteers was motivated by something more than the chance to utilise civilian skills.

The most interesting of the eight is Anthony Callinan, who had enlisted in 1807 when only twelve. He must have fancied being involved in some action, rather than being able to offer the skills required, because (not surprisingly considering his age on enlistment) his occupation is given as labourer. He continued to serve until the disbandment of the second battalion in 1817, fighting at Quatre Bras and Waterloo, but then disgracing himself by deserting while stationed in the Bois de Boulogne during the occupation of Paris. He returned soon afterwards but, not surprisingly, his discharge papers describe his conduct as 'bad'. Obviously, the efforts he made at Ciudad Rodrigo had long been forgotten. He was a great survivor, however, still alive in 1874 when the pension he was awarded despite his bad conduct was transferred to Tralee.

Although one other officer of the fifth division, Lieutenant Peacocke of the 44th, claimed a bar for Ciudad Rodrigo, no man from any of the other five regiments in the division was awarded this particular bar. Indeed, a claim made by a former soldier in the 4th was actually disallowed. This does not mean that the 30th alone provided volunteers for the working parties but it does suggest that they supplied the highest number, assuming chances of survival until 1848 were equal in all regiments.

The day after the fall of the town, which was accompanied by outrages that were to be repeated even more grotesquely at Badajoz, the fifth division were marched in to escort the drunken troops back to their encampments, and generally restore order. Then they were put into quarters and given the task of repairing the damaged defences against the possibility of a French counter-attack. In this role they formed a silent witness to the final journey of General Robert Crauford, who had died of wounds received during the assault. They lined the route taken by the funeral cortège to the lesser breach, where Wellington himself had ordered that his brilliant but unpredictable subordinate should be buried. They came to attention with reversed arms as the general's body was carried past them, escorted by the light division he had commanded with such erratic distinction.

Ensign Anderson, coming to the town soon after the successful assault, was struck by how little the place had suffered. 'Rodrigo, though not at any vast extent, has an air of magnificence, nor does it look as if it had so lately sustained a siege. Passed the Coa [Agueda], on which it is situated, on a neat bridge of seven arches, and halted my men at the draw bridge, and after arranging them as well as I could, had the pleasure of marching into the Plaza Mayor . . . The internal appearance of Rodrigo fully justified my expectations. The houses are generally well built, and the churches very magnificent. The principal church, although extremely close to the greater breach, has suffered very little; some few balls have grazed it, but it has experienced no serious injury . . . About the greater breach seems to have been the great "tug of war"; and especially near the magazine which was blown up, and which occasioned the death of General M'kinnon, and so many of our countrymen. Here had indeed been hot work, as the blood and mangled remains of bodies sufficiently evinced.'[61] The battle scars on the cathedral noticed by Anderson are still visible today.

Private (later Sergeant) James Hale of the 9th Regiment recorded his impressions of the state of Ciudad Rodrigo in his journal. 'When our division arrived, not having had a share in the grand attack, we were put into possession of the garrison ...

'When we entered the garrison, it was a most miserable place to behold, for the enemy's dead were lying about in all directions, and the buildings beat to pieces by our cannon shot in a frightful manner, and several houses were then on fire, in consequence of which, we were immediately set to work to extinguish the fire, and fortunately, by great exertion, we got the upper hand of it in a short time. The next thing that was thought necessary for us to do, was to put the dead bodies under ground and clear the streets, that the market people might be able to come in with their goods as soon as possible: for at that time there was not a thing of any description to be got in the town, except a few bags of French biscuits, and those our commissary seized: therefore we were very busily employed the first day, and not only the first, but every day except Sunday; for we were all hands put to work as soon as possible, repairing the walls and ramparts round the garrison, for fear the enemy should advance and attack us in the ruins: but however, that did not happen to be the case.'[62]

At the beginning of the year clothing worn out during the previous year's campaigning was replaced and the fifth division found themselves holding the allied position at Ciudad Rodrigo while the regiments of the other divisions were told off to receive their new uniforms. Finally, the regiments of the fifth division did likewise, the 30th marching to Penacova to collect their uniforms, which would have been made up in a rough and ready fashion, and then 'finished' by any tailors in the battalion. Fortunately, there were many such men. Similarly, shoemakers and cordwainers could use their skills to make good the condition of shoes, usually the first casualties of hard marching. Re-equipped, the division then followed the rest of the allied army to Estremadura, to the area dominated by French-held Badajoz. It was a sign of Wellington's confidence that he left Ciudad Rodrigo under the protection of Spanish regular and Portuguese militia troops.

When the fifth division arrived late on the scene they found the third, fourth and light divisions already in position for the investment of Badajoz. The first, sixth and seventh divisions were with General Graham at Llerena watching Soult in the south, while Soult himself was watching the Spanish general, Ballesteros. If Soult were to advance on Badajoz as he had in 1811, Ballesteros could disrupt the French lines in front of Cadiz. As for Marmont, he was still in the Salamanca area, held there by Napoleon's misreading of the situation. According to the Emperor's mistaken scenario, a move towards Ciudad Rodrigo would draw Wellington away from Badajoz.

Time was a crucial factor. Should Soult deal successfully with Ballesteros and Marmont start manoeuvring south, the combined French forces would be a serious threat to the allied position. Nor was Badajoz likely to fall as easily as Ciudad Rodrigo. Two failed attempts were testimony to its strength and to the determination of the French to retain the stronghold they had taken only a year before.

The investment of the town began on St Patrick's Day. A week later all the battalions of the fifth division were reunited at Campo Maior, fourteen miles

The assault of Badajoz, 1812

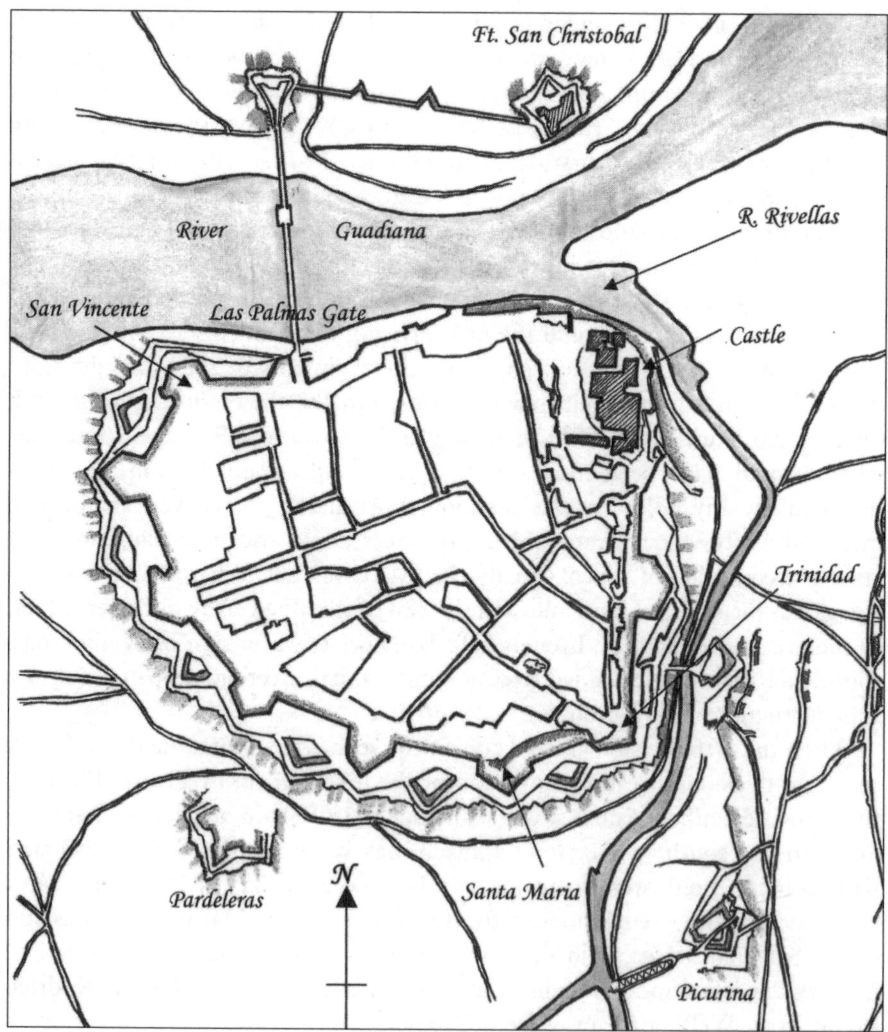

from Badajoz. Nevertheless, they had a clear view of the place, although the town itself was almost hidden by the smoke of the French guns which were aimed at the allied working parties and causing heavy losses. By 22 March the division was on the right bank of the Guadiana, unable to cross because the pontoon bridge had been swept away by a sudden flood. Two days later though, the flood subsided and the bridge was successfully repaired, allowing the division to reach the left bank. They then invested Fort San Christobal, a crucial outwork of the town's defences.

Badajoz, with its sophisticated defences, was a much more formidable obstacle than Ciudad Rodrigo. Sir John Jones described it with an engineer's eye as a large, fortified town on the left bank of the Guadiana. The river, from 300 to 500 yards wide, flowed close to a considerable stretch of the defences, making attack difficult. These defences consisted of a weak, flanked rampart with an exposed revetment. The rest of the defences were stronger; eight well-built bastions each having a good counter-scarp, covered-way, and glacis, although the ravelins had not been completed. Jones estimated the scarp of the bastions as more than thirty feet in height, while the curtain varied from twenty-three to twenty-six feet. There were also two detached works, the Pardeleras and the Picurina. To the north-east where the river Rivillas flowed into the Guadiana was an old Moorish castle. As a further defence, a mined glacis lay along the western front.

On the right or northern bank of the Guadiana the Christobal heights, which matched the elevation of the castle, were fortified to overlook Badajoz itself and to prevent a besieger from attacking the town.[63] There had been two previous attempts to take Badajoz. In May 1811 Marshal Beresford had blockaded the town but had been forced to raise the siege when Marshal Soult advanced from Andalusia. On 16 May Beresford had defended his position at Albuera. Wellington himself directed the reinvestment of the town and in June launched two assaults on San Christobal. Both ended in failure. In 1812 a new, rapidly implemented strategy was needed. Marmont and Soult might not pose an immediate threat but the eventual advance of one or both was inevitable.

Since the events of 1811 the French had been strengthening the defences of the place under the command of the determined governor, Baron Armand Philippon. They concentrated on the castle, which they had heavily fortified with guns, and the rear of San Christobal. More significantly for a plan which ignored San Christobal and concentrated on the actual walls of the town, 'They had well enclosed the gorge of the Pardeleras outwork, and had connected it with the place by intermediate works; and had erected very powerful batteries looking into the rear of it. They had also countermined the three right fronts. On the east side they had built up the arch of the bridge over the Rivillas in rear of the lunette St Roque, so as to impede the flow of the current, and had by that means formed an impassable inundation, spreading along the foot of the glacis to the breadth of 200 yards.'[64] This inundation presented an obstacle to any attack on the Santa Maria and Trinidad bastions. Wellington's strategy was first to take the Picurina fort, and then breach the wall between the Santa Maria and Trinidad bastions, which would be the focus of the main assault.

The Picurina fort was taken on the night of 25/26 March by a force of 500 men drawn from the third and light divisions under the command of Major General Kempt. Now the guns could be concentrated on the two chosen bastions. On 30 March the fifth division were withdrawn from their watching brief on the heights of San Christobal and brought into the front line in response to Soult's advance from the south. By 4 April Soult, having seen off Ballesteros, was at Llerena and Wellington was faced with the choice of either abandoning the siege or risking an immediate assault. He opted for the latter. On 5 April the fifth division joined the besieging force as a support force to the imminent assault.

The final 'Arrangements for the assault of the breaches', planned for 6 April, delayed the time of the attack to 10.00 p.m., allowing the defenders two and a half hours to litter the breaches with harrows and crows' feet, and barb the summit with a *chevaux-de-frise* of sword blades. The 'Arrangements' also identified the points of attack as the castle (third division), La Trinidad (fourth division), and Santa Maria (light division), the first by escalade and the two bastions by storming the breaches. Numbers 26 and 27 of the 28 items read that 'The 5th division must be formed, one brigade on the ground occupied by the 48th Regiment; one brigade on the Sierra del Viento; and one brigade in the low ground extending to the Guadiana, now occupied by the pickets of the light division. The pickets of the brigades on the Sierra del Viento, and that in the low grounds towards the Guadiana, should endeavour to alarm the enemy during the attack by firing at the Pardeleras, and at the men in the covered way of the works towards the Guadiana.' There is an added note. 'A plan has been settled with Lieut. General Leith for an attempt to be made to escalade the bastion of San Vincente, or the curtain between the bastion and the bridge, if the circumstance should permit.'[65]

This may have been the intention, that the division should operate as a back-up force, but events were to give them a very different role, and they were about to experience 'one of the most arduous undertakings on which troops can be employed – an undertaking in which fatigue, hardships, and personal risk, are the greatest – one in which the prize can only be gained by complete victory, and where failure is usually attended with severe loss or dire disaster.'[66]

Chapter 7

'No nation ever sent forth braver troops ...'

The story of the storming of Badajoz is well-known: the sustained but increasingly hopeless attacks by the fourth and light divisions on the breaches between La Trinidad and Santa Maria; the third division's successful escalade of the castle; and, often merely a footnote, the fifth division's assault on the San Vincente bastion. Andrew Leith Hay, however, recorded his observations somewhat differently: '*four* divisions of the allied army were destined to mount the walls of Badajos, and triumphantly to accomplish a service, only to have been achieved by the best soldiers and the bravest men.'[67] Leith Hay paid generous tribute to the other divisions but any account that omits what actually happened after the fifth division scaled the walls leaves several questions unanswered. For example, how did the fourth and light divisions ever get into the town? And how could the third division, penned in the castle, be said to have taken Badajoz, even if they would have done so at daybreak?

The most succinct account of the part played by the 30th comes in a hand-written digest based on earlier reports. This notes how the second battalion 'lost half its number in escalading the Bastion of St Vincent, which it gained, and held against a superior force; and succeeded in opening the principal gate of the City called "Las Palmas".' This bald statement, however, does justice neither to the events of the night nor to the rest of the fifth division.

Crucially, the division was late in launching its attack while the third division under Picton was early, two mishaps which help to explain the heavy allied casualties. Once the advance of the third division had been discovered the escalade had to be attempted, necessitating in turn the assault on the breaches. From then on the carnage was inevitable. The evidence of Colonel Jones, and of Colonel Lamare, the chief engineer of the garrison, establishes that the fifth division were still in bivouac at eleven o'clock, when the other divisions were taking heavy casualties. According to Jones, the officer guiding the ladder party lost his way, thus delaying the division, to the mortification of General Leith. Although the 8th Caçadores successfully distracted the enemy with a false attack on the Pardeleras outwork, San Vincente was not finally escaladed until midnight, just after three of the companies holding it were transferred to the defence of the castle, according to Lamare. Some time before midnight, however, the third division was ordered to remain in the castle until morning while the fourth and light divisions were withdrawn from the breaches.

Jones identified the escalade of San Vincente 'as marking what it is possible for brave men to effect. The bastion of San Vincente, which Major-General Walker's brigade [the second brigade] escaladed, had an escarpe 31 feet 6 inches in height, flanked by four guns at the ordinary distance, the palisades of the covered-way were entire, the counterscarp wall 11 feet 9 inches deep, and in the ditch a cunette had been excavated 5 feet 6 inches deep, and 6 feet 6 inches broad ... There were only twelve ladders supplied from the engineers' park for this escalade, and two or three of that number were never reared: the loss of the assailants, above 600 in killed and wounded, shows that the garrison behaved well, and it is believed that no one gave way until overpowered.'[68] He later corrected the height to twenty feet but in his opinion this did not detract from an escalade undertaken with ladders which were too short.

The glacis had been mined while the defenders each had three loaded muskets. Some 1,600 men held the defences between San Vincente and Santa Maria, the eventual objective of Walker's brigade. This figure does not allow for the three companies which had been drawn off (if Lamare is to be believed) but neither does it include a 'battalion of administration', a motley collection of clerks, sutlers and other army followers who were, nonetheless, ready to defend Badajoz. There were also some Hessians, part of a reserve unit drawn into the counter-movement once the allied assault began. Walker's brigade was numerically stronger, over 2,000 men, but during an escalade the initial advantage was with the defenders.

It was a cloudy night with intervals of bright moonlight, during one of which 'The troops were discovered by the garrison when on the glacis, and a heavy fire opened upon them before they had forced the barrier gate; but nothing could check the progress of General Walker and the battalions under his orders, until they reached the lofty wall, at the summit of which the enemy, aware of their intentions, and fully prepared, were extended, deliberately and obstinately to resist men ascending singly, and on ladders of upwards of thirty feet high. This does not appear the description of [a] situation where defence could be difficult, or entrance practicable to ordinary men. At first, few of the ladders could be placed. Some of them, after being reared, were thrown from the walls back into the ditch, others, constructed of green wood, opened and separated, or were not of sufficient length, consequently the troops forced in by means of three or four only of the number originally appropriated for the service; but force in they did, and General Walker formed his brigade on the ramparts. He had been instructed to move forward, and by making a circuit of the interior of the works, to come in rear of the enemy's troops defending the breaches.

'There are no means of destruction more alarming in contemplation of mankind than mines, nor any warlike engine or preparation calculated to have the same appalling ideal effect on the minds of the soldiery. There is also the darkness of the night, and the treading of hostile ground, supposed to have been prepared for every species of obstruction, something so uncertain, that it is neither to be wondered at, nor considered inconsistent with their general bearing, that, under such circumstances, the bravest troops should be seized with irresolution from the most trivial causes. The flame of a port-fire struck a momentary terror into the minds of men, that artillery, musketry, walls, and the bayonets of French infantry, had failed to daunt. Part of General Walker's brigade, mistaking this appearance for the forerunner to the explosion of a mine, broke, and were bayoneted back to the spot where they had previously surmounted difficulties which there could have been no discredit in failing to overcome. Fortunately, General Leith had advanced part of the right [first] brigade of the division in support of that already in the town. The second battalion of the 38th Regiment, under Colonel Nugent, had ascended, and were formed on the ramparts. When the circumstance above detailed occurred, that corps, being prepared, received the pursuing enemy with a volley and bayonet charge that speedily terminated all contest. In the course of this short reverse, General Walker was dangerously wounded, and Lieutenant-Colonel Grey, of the 30th Regiment, a very gallant officer, died in consequence of profuse bleeding, before assistance could be procured.

'General Walker's brigade having been formed, the other regiments of the division ascended the ladders, and the whole marched on the troops defending the breaches. General Leith narrowly escaped being precipitated into a ditch by the fall of a soldier, shot dead at the upper part of the ladder he was mounting. Having succeeded in penetrating, and dispersing his opponents, he sent an officer to report to Lord Wellington that the 5th division was in the town. His bugle sounded the advance in all directions, distracting the enemy's attention, and inducing him to believe that he was to be assailed from all quarters. Whether it proceeded from a knowledge that the castle was in possession of the allies, or an impression that further resistance was in vain, the efforts of the garrison relaxed, the 5th division drove every thing before it, and having opened the communication with the bastions of La Trinidad and Santa Maria, the 4th and light divisions, which had previously been withdrawn, again advanced, and marched into the town by the breaches.' After considering all that had happened, Leith Hay concluded: 'Had the attack by General Picton failed, still the success of the 5th division ensured the fall of the place. It was consequently the escalade of the bastion of San Vincente that occasioned the immediate reduction of the fortress.'[69]

Other participants offered different interpretations. Captain McCarthy, assistant engineer to the third division, believed that taking the castle enabled the other divisions to enter the town. He acknowledged, however, how 'General Walker, having found it advantageous, made a *real attack*, and himself leading with extraordinary gallantry, – which could not be exceeded, – his Brigade descended into the ditch, and as stated, escaladed the face of the bastion of St Vincent, and gained the ramparts, although the ladders (conducted by a party under Major Faunce, 4th Regiment) being too short, did not reach the top of the wall, and the men were obliged to push and pull each other up; but an embrasure, without a gun was discovered in the curtain of the wall, by which many officers and men entered ...

'The Brigade was ordered to man the ramparts, and the struggle was severe; when as General Walker was bravely leading his Brigade towards the interior of the breaches, to drive the enemy from thence, he received a most dangerous wound from a ball which struck him on the right side, breaking several ribs and driving in a part of the watch he carried in a small pocket in the breast of his coat. The Brigade continued its progress along the rampart, and the General was alone on the ground.'[70] Robbed of his epaulettes, and with his pockets rifled, Walker gave himself up for dead when another French soldier began to load his musket. This soldier, however, stayed with him, and when an English soldier arrived, the two of them, English and French, carried the General to safety. Since McCarthy spent time with Walker while recovering from his own wounds, he undoubtedly received this account from the General himself. (There is another version of the story which adds the significant detail that both Walker and the French soldier were freemasons.)

Lamare, from the French perspective, also suggests that it was the third division's successful escalade of the castle which served as a turning point for the defenders, shaking their courage and leading to disorder. Indeed, he ascribes Wellington's 'extraordinary success' to General Picton's boldness. In his account, 'The crown-work Pardeleras was attacked at the same time as the breaches by another division [the 8th Caçadores]; the Garrison of this Fort vigorously received the assailants and obliged them to retire, leaving both the glacis and the ditches strewed with dead and wounded; they did not surrender until the morning. More than 28,000 men [a gross exaggeration] (the half of the English Army) were employed at the assaults and escalades on the different sides of the Town. It was midnight when a last attack was made on bastion No. 1 [San Vincente]. One of the columns, the 5th division, under the orders of

Lieutenant-General Leith and Major-General Walker, planted their ladders and escaladed; which was no difficult matter after the detachment, which guarded that part, had been weakened by more than 5-sixths, in order to retake the Castle . . . Nevertheless, this detachment did not yield until the last extremity, and the loss to the enemy in this quarter amounted to more than 600 men. From thence he extended himself into the Town, formed a junction with the 3rd division, and then all was lost. In this state of things the Governor could no longer communicate with his troops. Doubt and dismay took possession of their minds; they fled about the streets and fired in disorder. Cries of Victory! And frightful groans were heard; confusion was at its height. Notwithstanding this extreme disorder, such as imagination can hardly paint, the Governor and General Veiland assembled about 50 men with a few of the Cavalry, with whom he proceeded to the square of Las Palmas. It was only by this means and favoured by darkness that he succeeded, with the greater part of the Officers of the Staff, to retire by the bridge of San Christobal. It was then one o'clock in the morning.'[71]

Much of this is disingenuous. If it was so easy to escalade San Vincente, then the 600 casualties remain a mystery. Similarly, who were the people overcome by doubt and dismay once the allies were in the town? Lamare claimed that the castle's defenders were all put to the sword, and implied a similar fate for the defenders of San Vincente. He also maintained that the defenders at the breaches held their position until after the governor's flight to San Christobal, although according to a tradition in the 4th Regiment the first men into the town found themselves in eerily silent and deserted streets. Implicitly, though, Lamare's account recognises the significance of the fifth division's success. They did not link up with the 3rd division as he claimed, but their presence in the town may have convinced the governor, Philippon, that the situation was lost.

In contrast, while Jones recognised that the third division's possession of the castle made resistance ultimately useless, he believed that the successful escalade of San Vincente 'was the more immediate cause of the fall of the place; for though General Picton's escalade of the castle placed the garrison at the mercy of the besiegers, still the third division remaining formed in the castle without further movement their success produced no instant effect upon the defence and the fifth division met with the same opposition as if the castle had not been escaladed.'[72]

Although the losses of the fifth division, killed and wounded, were not quite as high as the 600 mooted by both Leith Hay and Lamare, they were still considerable, comprising thirty-nine officers and 471 men. The 9th took no losses, and the Royals, two officers, presumably volunteers with the engineers.

Otherwise, the casualty rate reflects the order in which the battalions ascended the ladders: the 4th, seventeen officers and 213 men; the 30th, six officers and 126 men; the 44th, nine officers and ninety-five men; and the 38th, five officers and thirty-seven men. Furthermore, of the two officers and thirty-three men returned as casualties by the Brunswick Oels regiment, a considerable number must have been with the two companies serving with the fifth division. The Portuguese were acting as ladder bearers but took casualties at the Pardeleras. These numbers in total are similar to the third division (580), but do not approach the carnage suffered by the fourth (829) and light (927) divisions.

To focus on the 30th, the storming party, under the command of Lieutenant Colonel Brooke of the 4th, consisted of the light companies of all three second brigade battalions plus the light company of the 38th. The light company of the 30th was commanded by Captain Chambers. The first casualty was the engineering officer guiding the brigade. He was killed as the storming party was ascending the glacis. It was a cloudy night but, as already noted, the moon suddenly came out and illuminated the attack. A French challenge was immediately followed by a hail of bullets. The first casualties in the 30th came soon afterwards. As the light companies tried to place the ladders in position, a mine was sprung and logs and live shells were dropped on top of the assault force, while artillery rained down grape. It was probably at this point that Chambers was seriously wounded.

The accounts of Major Piper and Captain Ellers Hopkins, both of the 4th, describe how part of the brigade was detached from the assault on the sequence of bastions from San Vincente to Santa Maria in order to nullify some French fire. If there were any of the 30th in this detachment, they would have been among the first into the town and may well have opened the Las Palmas gates.

Once the fifth division came upon the defenders from within, the town was at the mercy of a rampaging mob of allied soldiers ready to seize any reward – wine, women or loot – after three hours of bloody struggle. Leith Hay is silent on this but Napier's account vividly recreates 'that wild and desperate wickedness, which tarnished the lustre of the soldier's heroism. All indeed were not alike, for hundreds risked and many lost their lives in striving to stop the violence, but the madness generally prevailed, and as the worst men were the leaders here, all the dreadful passions of human nature were displayed. Shameless rapacity, brutal intemperance, savage lust, cruelty, and murder, shrieks and piteous lamentations, groans, shouts, imprecations, the hissing of fires bursting from the houses, the crashing of doors and windows, and the reports of muskets used in violence, resounded for two days and two nights in the streets of Badajos!'[73]

Corporal (later Sergeant) John Douglas of the Royals laments that being in Wellington's guard cost his battalion their share in the glory of the assault before describing what the battalion encountered the following morning when they were ordered into the town. 'The sight, even to the soldier, was horrible. The instruments of death had been successfully applied on both sides; fragments of men torn to atoms met your view in every direction. The bridge leading to the main guard or entrance had been sprung and our poor fellows found their mistake in the dark, tumbled in and were irrevocably lost, numbers of whom were floating. We piled arms in the main square. To attempt anything in the hope of a description of the scene that was going on would be a task not easily performed, and even could it be delineated no one (unless an eyewitness) could credit the tale. But rather than leave you altogether in the dark I shall relate a few passages. Fancy so many thousand soldiers let loose, unrestrained by any authority, mad after such slaughter, and I might say doubly so with brandy and rum. The excesses committed were horrible, nor could it be avoided, as any officer who would recall them to a sense of their duty ran the hazard of his life. An officer of the 30th Regiment lost his life in attempting to save a young woman from violation. But the principal scene of drunkenness took place in the bread and rum store, which appeared to be a vault. Here the soldiers of all regiments were making themselves at home, sitting on the bent baskets which contained the biscuits . . . They were roaring and singing while others were employed in drawing up rum in casks from an underground store. Those below not being well versed in slinging them dropped them when the casks were perhaps within a few feet of the surface; down they went and got staved. In this manner the floor of the vault became a sea of wine, and those who went down perfectly sober got drunk without drinking . . .

'I was selected by the colonel to go round to the mean break [main breach] and order the servants to bring in the horses. Such a sense of destruction as was here presented to the view baffles description. The very rungs (or steps of the ladders) by which the troops descended into the ditch were literally shot to atoms with musket balls, while underneath the dead and dying lay in heaps; some calling for a drink for God's sake while their drunken comrades were selling their booty without taking the least notice.'[74]

Douglas's reference to an officer of the 30th is puzzling since the only officer to die at Badajoz was Major Grey. He seems to have heard, or misheard, a rather romantic tale concerning Ensign Purefoy Lockwood, a nineteen-year-old Sir Galahad. According to family tradition, the young officer was accosted by a distressed nun, who implored him to protect her. This Lockwood managed so successfully that he was able to return her, unharmed, to her family. Any chance of a reward, however, was prevented by the insistent call of duty, in this case the sounding of bugles.

Just who in the 30th ascended the ladders at Badajoz is a point of some contention. Because of staff appointments, officers on leave, like Hamilton, and the ongoing complications of transfers between the two battalions, there were only seventeen combatant officers present. Normal practice would have kept the (acting) quartermaster, and the officer commanding the guard in the bivouac. If the three staff officers (Grey, Bamford and Garland) and the two ensigns who carried the colours are subtracted from the remainder, there were only seven officers for the command of ten companies. Furthermore, the muster rolls for March and April indicate widespread sickness. In the fourth company, for example, only twelve men reported fit for duty on 24 March. These fit men took part in the assault because seven of them later claimed a bar for Badajoz on their GSMs. They could not have functioned as a company, so some ad hoc arrangement between companies seems the most feasible explanation of how so few officers effectively led the battalion into action.

A combination of the pay-list, muster roll and casualty returns for April gives the following figures for the battalion: two sergeants, three corporals, and twenty-four privates killed in action, while another five subsequently died of their wounds, the last of these in June. A further ninety-four survived their wounds. The effects of Badajoz might be long-term, however. Daniel Rohan, eighteen at the time of the assault, was one of those who fell off the scaling ladders. He was not returned as wounded but his commanding officer, Lieutenant Heaviside, later testified that he had received a contusion on the head, the effects of which were very often troublesome to him. Nevertheless, he continued to serve with the battalion through to Waterloo and was discharged in 1817 upon reduction. He then returned to his previous employment as a servant but within two years applied to Kilmainham for a pension because he was unable to work as a result of the wound to his head. His application was supported not only by Heaviside but by his current employers who described him as honest and sober but subject to attacks (fits, perhaps) which made active work impossible. As a result, he belatedly received a pension for his service with the 30th.

The death of Major (brevet Lieutenant Colonel) Grey was reported in the *London Gazette*: 'Severely wounded, since dead, storming of Badajoz, 6th April 1812.' Wellington, in his dispatch of 7 April, wrote: 'Lieut. General Leith's arrangements for the false attack upon the Pardeleras, and that under Major General Walker, were likewise most judicious; and he availed himself of the circumstances of the moment, to push forward and support the attack under Major General Walker, in a manner highly creditable to him. The gallantry of

Major General Walker, who was also wounded, and that of the officers and troops under his command, were conspicuous ... In the 5th division I must mention Major Hill of the 9th Caçadores, who directed the false attack upon the fort Pardeleras. It was impossible for any men to behave better than these did. I must likewise mention Lieut. Colonel Brooke of the 4th Regiment, and Lieut. Colonel the Hon. G. Carleton of the 44th, and Lieut. Colonel Grey of the 30th, who was unfortunately killed.'[75]

Grey had served with the regiment for thirteen years, having joined from the 6th Dragoons in March 1799 as Captain Lieutenant. He was present at the capture of Malta in 1800, and saw action in Egypt a year later, being mentioned in dispatches. He was promoted to major in 1804, and lieutenant colonel in the army the following year. He sailed with the 2nd battalion to Portugal in 1809 and, apart from six months' leave while the 30th were in Gibraltar (probably to get married), he remained with the battalion throughout, being present at both Fuentes de Oñoro and Ciudad Rodrigo. He posthumously received a gold Peninsular medal for Badajoz. A commentator on his death wrote: 'It is painful for me to state that this brave officer, who had been in 32 general engagements, without having received the slightest wound, was subsequently killed at the storming of Badajoz, in the act of entering the breach at the head of his regiment, being the Lieut.-Colonel commanding the 30th.' According to the same writer, Grey had expressed the wish that, should he die in battle, he hoped it would be of a wound similar to that suffered at Corunna by Sir John Moore, who had been his close friend, 'and singular to relate, it was precisely such a wound he received.'[76]

There is a certain irony in Grey's death. His wife had begged him always to take a tourniquet into action. On the night of 6 April he neglected to do so. He lay among the dead and wounded for nine hours, bleeding to death. Mrs Grey was in Lisbon at the time, heavily pregnant. She heard the news of the storming of Badajoz being shouted in the street, and also learnt of her husband's death, the shock of which sent her into premature labour. She gave birth to a son who later became Governor of the Cape of Good Hope, and of New Zealand. Grey himself was thirty-three at the time of his death, according to a memorial which was erected at Newtown, Fairtullagh, Co. Meath.

Of the six wounded officers, Captains Chambers, of the light company, Hitchen, of the grenadiers, former colleagues from the 17th, and Ensign Pratt were out of action for three months. They were sent to Lisbon to recuperate. Lieutenants Baillie and Neville, both returned as slightly wounded, were back with the battalion by the end of April. Neville, according to his service return of 1829, suffered a severe head wound while employed as an assistant engineer.

He had already volunteered for service with the engineers at Ciudad Rodrigo and was to do so again at Burgos.

One other officer of the 30th was wounded at Badajoz, although not generally included in the battalion's losses. Captain Richard Machell was General Walker's brigade major. His narrow escape from death was described in a letter written by Captain Charles Levyns Barnard of the 38th to his mother. 'I was the first to mount the ladders, we supported Genl Walker's Brigade the 4th, 30th & 44th. The remainder of our Brigade the 1st & the 9th had nothing at all to do indeed never fired a shot. An Offr & two or three men of my Company came up just in time to save Machell three men had got hold of him & were going to bayonet him altho' he was shot thro' the neck. It was the most bloody thing ever known.'

When the 30th, with the rest of the fifth division, finally marched back to Portugal they left behind not only their dead and their severely wounded comrades but also one of their assistant surgeons. Because of the heavy casualties taken by the allies, John Evans was placed in charge of the wounded from all units and did not return to the battalion until June.

No other account of the taking of Badajoz matches Napier's evocation of the horrors of the assault, which remind us of what was actually achieved on the night of 6 April. 'Let any man picture to himself this frightful carnage taking place in a space of less than a hundred square yards. Let him consider that the slain died not all suddenly, nor by one manner of death; that some perished by steel, some by shot, some by water, that some were crushed and mangled by heavy weights, some trampled upon, some dashed to atoms by the fiery explosions; that for hours this destruction was endured without shrinking, and that the town was won at last, let any man consider this and he must admit that a British army bears with it an awful power. And false would it be to say that the French were feeble men, for the garrison stood and fought manfully and with good discipline behaving worthily. Shame there was none on any side. Yet who shall do justice to the bravery of the soldiers? the noble emulation of the officers? . . . many and signal were the other examples of unbounded devotion, some known, some that will never be known; for in such a tumult much passed unobserved, and often the observers fell themselves ere they could bear testimony to what they saw; but no age, no nation ever sent forth braver troops than those who stormed Badajos.'[77]

Chapter 8
Stalemate

The fall of Badajoz was followed by an extended period of manoeuvring. The timing of the assault had been occasioned by the news of Marshal Soult's advance northwards but the loss of the town sent him into precipitous retreat. He could not be pursued into Andalusia because Marmont, with the now misnamed Army of Portugal, was still threatening Ciudad Rodrigo and Almeida. To deter a French attack on either place the fifth division was sent towards the Agueda. The 30th, under the temporary command of their senior captain, Bamford, marched with the other battalions by way of Portalegre, Nisa and Vila Velha, retracing the route which had brought them south to Badajoz in March. The second brigade was now under the command of Major General Pringle, Walker having been sent to England for the recovery of his wounds.

A general advance sent Marmont back across the Agueda. The different divisions were then dispersed while their transport was used to carry provisions into Ciudad Rodrigo and Almeida, a sensible precaution against the possibility of renewed French interest in those two places. The fifth division found themselves quartered around Lamego, near the Douro. The May monthly return came from Taliora [sic], and they remained there in cantonments until the beginning of June, by which time they were once more under the command of Lieutenant Colonel Hamilton. He had returned to Portugal in mid-April, too late for Badajoz.

Wellington's next objective was Salamanca, a move anticipated by Marmont, who seems to have exaggerated the allied strength in his imagination. According to Leith Hay, he was demanding immediate reinforcements because his Army of Portugal, although still formidable, was not strong enough either to resist the anticipated attack or to manoeuvre effectively against the allied army. Leith Hay noted further that Marmont's forces comprised eight infantry divisions, numerous cavalry, and a hundred pieces of artillery. In addition, Caffarelli's Army of the North was 16,000 strong, the Army of the Centre, 13,000 and the Army of Aragon, 10,000, while in the south Soult had command of a further 55,000 men. Together they constituted an enormous threat to the Anglo-Portuguese forces. However, their control of the various parts of Spain was too insecure to permit any consolidation, while the marshals themselves were mutually jealous, disinclined to co-operate, and united only in their contempt for the unfortunate Joseph Bonaparte, *soi-disant* King of Spain.

The fifth division left their cantonments on 5 June, advancing through Trancosa and Freixedas until they reached Castel Mendo, a town perched high above the Coa, which itself ran through a wild and picturesque landscape. This was a hard march, and it must have been a relief to reach Poço Velha where the country was kinder and shaded by trees. The advance then continued through Espeja and Carpio to the Agueda where the fifth division was united with the fourth division. Reinforced by two brigades of cavalry, these two divisions formed the centre of the allied army.

The mood was optimistic. Leith Hay commented: 'Upon no occasion had the allied army taken the field in a more efficient state; every description of force composing it was serviceable and well appointed. The cavalry had recovered their condition. Experience taught the practical minutiae of active warfare. The weather was beautiful. Confidence in their leader and themselves occupied the minds of the troops; while presages of success and anticipated variety of scene imparted gaiety and buoyancy of spirit.'[78]

On 12 June the division halted near Ciudad Rodrigo. The next day they rested at Tenebron, before moving on to San Muñoz, a beautifully wooded area, replete with water and trees to shade the encampment from the sun. So far there had been no sign of the enemy, but on 16 June, about two leagues from Salamanca, allied cavalry encountered French cavalry. Various running fights broke out, and the French were driven back to within two miles of Salamanca. The fifth division, meanwhile, were encamped on the bank of the Valmusa, but the next morning they broke camp and continued the march towards Salamanca.

Apart from the garrisons in the forts they had constructed, the French had abandoned the city, although without destroying the bridge over the Tormes. As a result, Wellington was able to ride into Salamanca where he received a rapturous welcome. His mind, however, was already on the need to take the 'forts', ruined convents which the French had been strengthening since 1810 at the cost of the buildings round about, thirteen other convents and twenty-two university buildings. Leith Hay accompanied Wellington into the city and was overwhelmed by the welcome the allied army received: 'the streets were crowded to excess; signals of enthusiasm and friendship waved from the balconies; the entrance to the plaza was similar to a triumph; every window and balcony was filled with persons welcoming the distinguished officer to whom they looked up for liberation and permanent relief . . . It is impossible to describe the electric effect produced under these circumstances by the music; as the bands of the regiments burst in full tones on the ear of the people, a shout of enthusiastic feeling burst from the crowd, all ranks seeming perfectly inebriated with exultation.'[79]

It took the sixth division, who were given the task despite being inexperienced in siege and assault, ten days to reduce the forts. The fifth division, along with the rest of the allied forces (except Sir Rowland Hill's corps in Spanish Estremadura), remained encamped outside the city. A French advance led to a realignment of the covering allied forces on 20 June, bringing them onto the Heights of San Christobal, from the Tormes on the right to Aldeaseca de Alba on the left, where the fifth division spent the night. The next day, the division was pulled back to cover Salamanca itself and the whole army stood to arms. Despite some sporadic bickering between the two armies the French held their ground and it looked increasingly as if a battle was inevitable. To relieve the forts Marmont needed to break through the allied lines. Similarly, if the forts were to be taken, and this was proving difficult without the requisite heavy artillery, the French had to be held off. At this point, the relative positions of the two armies 'presented a singular contrast: the allies on high and commanding ground, from whence the slightest movement of the enemy was perceptible; the French, on the plain directly below, just sufficiently distant to be out of the range of the artillery, were not in sight of the town, or of those garrisons which it was their object to communicate with, and succour.'[80]

Marmont continued to probe the allied position. Early on 22 June there was a slight affair which cost the French 100 men. Later in the day Marmont himself, accompanied by his staff, rode to Aldeaseca de Alba to discover the deployment of the allied left and was nearly taken. The next day there was yet more French movement, which was construed as an attempt to cross the Tormes. This was frustrated by the counter-movement of the first and seventh divisions. Meanwhile, the forts remained untaken. An attempted escalade on 24 June failed with heavy losses but by 26 June fresh supplies of ammunition had been received and a renewed bombardment with heated shot produced the desired result. Already on fire, the forts were taken the very next day. His purpose frustrated, Marmont retreated along the Valladolid and Toro roads, while the fall of the forts and his departure were celebrated with a *Te Deum* in the cathedral.

At 3.30 a.m. on 29 June, the allies commenced a pursuit of Marmont's retreating forces. The fifth division were still in the centre with the first and seventh divisions and Le Marchant's brigade of dragoons. Once again, Leith Hay felt compelled to comment upon the fine weather, good spirits of the allies and the general cheerfulness.

By 30 June the centre column was at Fuente la Peña, which the French had occupied only the preceding day. Reaching Aleajos the following day, the allies learnt that they were now within very close reach of Marmont, who had left the town at 2.00 a.m. From Aleajos the centre advanced to Torrecilla de la Orden as Marmont crossed the Duero and established himself at Tordesillas. His outposts lined the Duero to guard the fords by which he expected the allies to cross the river. Wellington, however, was content to hold his position for five days during which period the fifth and sixth divisions were encamped on the right bank of the Zapardiel, on gently rising ground. It was a pleasant interlude. The weather continued fine and the soldiers of the two armies spent time bathing on their separate sides of the river, while engaging in light-hearted banter. Since rations and wine were both plentiful, there was little cause for complaint.

This period of rest came to an end when Marmont finally decided to take the initiative. At first, the only sign of French activity had been a determined effort to repair the bridge at Toro, on the extreme right of their position. This suggested that Marmont planned a return to Salamanca since Toro lay on the most direct route to the city and Wellington responded by realigning his forces.

On 9 July the fifth division was moved to Nava del Rey, where they bivouacked in heat so intense that the men took to lying in the fields by night, and retreating to what cover they could find during the day in order to avoid the burning sun. This realignment extended the allied left, thus covering Toro. During the week spent in this new encampment the men were kept in a state of readiness. 'Some part of the night we were allowed to wrap ourselves up in our blankets and lie down, but not to take off our accoutrements on any pretence whatever, and should we be allowed to lie still for four or five hours (as by chance we were sometimes), our blankets would be almost as wet outside, merely with the dews of the night, as if it had been a storm of rain.'[81] On 16 July the first French reinforcements, under the command of General Bonnet, arrived from the Asturias. They crossed the Duero by the repaired bridge at Toro. This, however, was a feint to deceive Wellington, because Bonnet then returned to the right bank of the river and rejoined the main French force as it marched out of Tordesillas. The intention seems to have been to persuade Wellington to deploy his troops so that Marmont could turn the allied flank and cut all communication with Salamanca.

Wellington reacted swiftly. By the evening of 17 July the allies were again on the move, the fifth division marching to Canizal. The next day they advanced on Torrecilla de la Orden, to shield the fourth and light divisions as they retreated before the French advance. Hearing a heavy cannonade directly ahead, Leith Hay rode forward to investigate and witnessed a struggle between allied cavalry, and French cavalry supported by infantry and artillery. Not surprisingly, the allies were getting the worst of it, so Wellington ordered a retreat to the heights of Canizal. This was not an easy manoeuvre. The French advance on Aleajos had turned the allied left flank, while their determined pursuit of the retreating columns threatened any retrograde movement. The manoeuvre was completed in perfect order, however, even though the light division had to abandon the road and retire by way of footpaths.

For the fifth division, the moment proved rather more perilous. Out of sight of the encounter between the French forces and the allied cavalry, they were unaware of the danger and had stopped to fill their water bottles from a river. The heat was oppressive and made worse by the amount of dust which covered the men from head to foot, so that the water was more than welcome. The first intimation of their danger was the sound of cannon fire. General Leith immediately decided upon a retreat, in open order and as quickly as possible. According to Douglas, there had been 'the usual examination of arms; not looking for burnished pieces, but blew down the barrel to see if the touchhole was clear, flints fast and all's well.

'Our position retarded their progress for some time, until they had examined our strength. We retired again and halted on the side of a gentle declivity with a small rivulet in front and formed line, from line into square, for the purpose of keeping their cavalry in due bounds. Our squares were scarcely formed when Arthur and all his staff came galloping down the hill, his head going like a weather cock while the French 9 pounders whizzed about fiercely. We could see, by the clouds of dust, the march of the enemy, when just in our front a French officer rode to the top of the hill which his Lordship had just descended, and fired a pistol. We were pretty well aware of the signal, for in the space of 5 minutes 7 artillery pieces opened fire upon us. 'Twas lucky that Leith had deployed us into line so that the round shot could not do the execution, which it would have done had they caught us in square ... After remaining about half an hour under this fire without returning the compliment, the guns ceased, and on came the cavalry. Each regiment now formed into square double quick.' The division remained in chequerboard formation of squares, which Douglas retrospectively likened to Waterloo, until the other divisions had reached safety. Then the fifth division was able to retire 'in ordinary time; their guns playing on us as long as a shot could reach us. We retired all that day in column of companies, wheeling distance apart, marching over every obstacle that came in our way, fields of wheat, vines, etc which, with the heat of the day, and no water, rendered this as fatiguing a day's march as ever I remember.'[82] Only a few casualties were taken, none of them from the 30th, and the division was able to reach the relative safety of the Heights of Canizal where, Hale recorded, 'we formed our camp in the evening, as convenient to wood and water as possible, in the usual manner, near Hornillos, but not without throwing out stronger piquets to watch the enemy's movements, should there be any. Therefore, after a little refreshment, we laid ourselves down, but without any hopes of getting much rest, for we were not allowed to unroll our blankets, neither take off our accoutrements.'[83]

There was one more attempt to turn the allied left but this ended in the discomfiture of the French, including the capture of a general. Wellington seemed content to stand his ground, leaving it to the French to initiate an attack. Fieldworks were constructed to cover the infantry and working parties from the fifth division laboured on these during the night. There followed yet another day's stalemate. Then towards evening Marmont began a march to the left. In response the light and fifth divisions were put under arms, the latter following the former with the fourth division between them as they moved in parallel with the French. The change of position continued all night, so that by the next morning both the French and the allies occupied the plain of Vallesa. There were hopes of a general action but these were disappointed when Marmont continued his flank movement, which now threatened the allied position and necessitated an advance by the right. There followed a strange spectacle which seems to have caught the imagination of many of the participants.

Douglas remembered how 'On the 19th the enemy kept on our left flank, we in the same order – our companies at wheeling distance – marching over everything that came in their way, while the guns were not slack in taking all advantages that the ground would admit of and the cavalry sporting between the 2 armies.'[84] Hale similarly recalled how 'The enemy took to the mountains which led towards Salamanca, and our army took the valleys, across hedge and ditch, fields of corn, vineyards, etc just alongside of the enemy, some times so near together, that they would give us a few cannon shot off the mountains. Our cavalry took their route between the two armies, by which a little skirmishing took place with them and the enemy's cavalry several times in the day, but nothing further.'[85] Presumably by mountains Hale meant the higher undulations, since there are no mountains in the region of Salamanca.

Leith Hay's account, viewed through a staff officer's eyes, presents the situation more explicitly. 'When the two armies were thus put in motion, they were within cannon-shot of each other; the French occupying higher ground than the allies; but the space between them was lower than either of the routes, and nothing intervened to obstruct a view of the columns of the enemies, that thus continued to pursue their course without the least obstacle to prevent their coming into instantaneous contact; for the slightest divergement from either line of march towards each other, would have brought them within musketry distance. I have always considered this day's march as a very extraordinary scene, only to have occurred from the generals opposed commanding highly disciplined armies, at the same time pursuing an object from which he was not for an instant to be abstracted by minor circumstances: the French marshal pushing forward to arrive first at the Tormes; Lord Wellington following his motions, and steadily adhering to the defensive, until substantial reasons appeared to demand a deviation of the course, and the adoption of a more decided conduct. During the day of the 20th, which exceeded in heat those that had preceded it, the British infantry, encumbered with the enormous weight they then carried, had to perform a very long and fatiguing march.'[86]

There was some minor skirmishing caused by a shared desire to pillage and also by some allied straggling. It was only when some enemy voltigeurs took possession of a village which lay between the two armies that definite offensive action was taken. The fifth division was brought to a halt and the 8th Caçadores were sent down to drive out the voltigeurs. This was quickly achieved and the march continued until the allies were in position at San Christobal, the same position they had occupied on 28 June. The French were across the Tormes, as far forward as Calvarrasa de Arriba, out of sight of the fifth division, who now settled down near the village of Pitiegua in expectation of a quiet night. Almost at once, though, there was a rumour of a French cavalry attack. The enemy turned out to be Portuguese cavalry of D'Urban's brigade, but their identity was not established until a cannonade from the third division had killed several men and horses. Peace restored, nothing else occurred to disturb the night.

The next morning the allies ascended the heights of San Christobal, and then marched down to the Tormes. The enemy were downstream by the fords at Huerta but at the end of the day Marmont brought his forces across the river and moved towards the Ciudad Rodrigo road. Wellington's response was immediate. Leaving the third division, D'Urban's Portuguese cavalry and a Spanish force under Don Carlos d'España on the Salamanca side of the Tormes, he brought the rest of his army back to the higher ground which lay behind Calvarrasa de Arriba. The fifth division were in bivouac behind a stretch of woodland on a plateau which extended from the ford of Santa Marta on the left to the village of Arapiles on the right. It proved a memorable night: 'the appearance of the air bespoke an approaching storm. The rain soon fell in torrents, accompanied by vivid flashes of lightning, and succeeded by instantaneous peals of thunder. A more violent crash of the elements has seldom been witnessed; its effects were soon apparent. General Le Marchant's brigade of cavalry had halted to our left; the men, dismounted, were either seated or lying on the ground, holding their horses, who, alarmed by the thunder, started with violence, and many of them, breaking loose, galloped across the country in all directions. This dispersion, and the frightened horses passing without riders in a state of wildness, added to the awful effect of the tempest.'[87]

For Douglas and the other soldiers the terrified horses were even more of a danger. 'The thunder rolled in awful peals, the glare of the broad sheets of lightning, with the rain that fell in torrents, seemed as if the angry heavens were making their displeasure felt at the scene about to take place. The 5th (or Green Horse) were lying on our right. The awfulness of the night caused numbers of their horses to break from their picketing and run through our ranks as we lay drenched to the skin but unwilling to rise lest we should lose our berth in the ranks and miss a comfortable nap.'[88]

On the morning of 22 July a battle was still not a certainty, although greatly desired by the allied soldiers. Wellington was aware that he commanded a force which must be carefully husbanded (since there was none to replace it) and which could not be squandered upon risky adventures. A retreat upon Ciudad Rodrigo was the sensible option – unless Marmont committed some

The Battlefield at Salamanca, shown with surrounding area

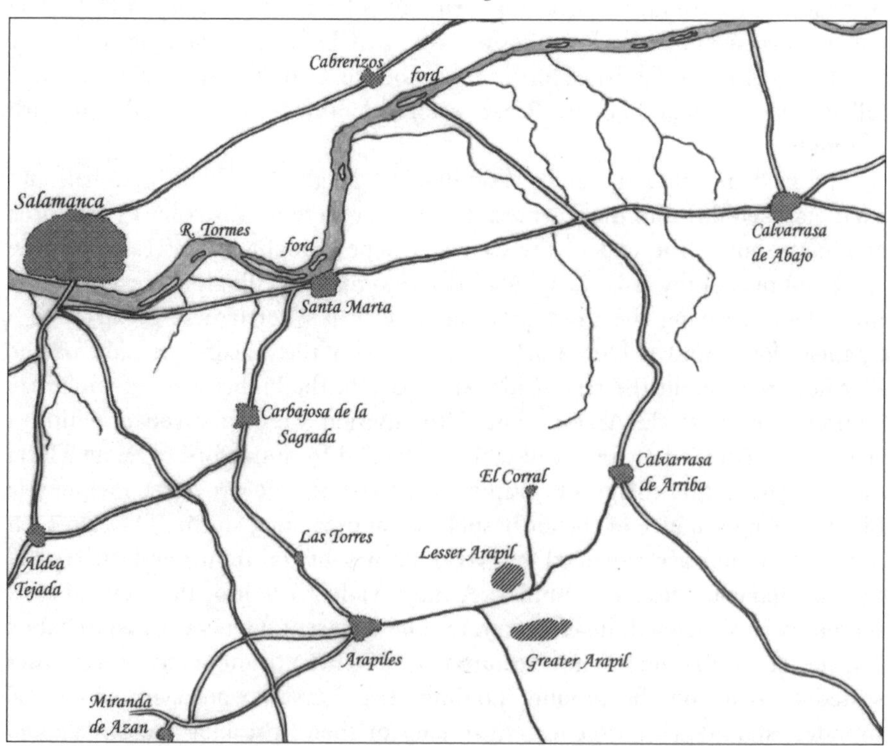

crass error of military judgement, which he had shown no signs of doing in the campaign so far.

The pivotal points of what would become the battlefield of Salamanca were the two hills, the greater and lesser Arapils. Leith Hay described the situation on the morning of 22 July which, even before daybreak, had begun with a musketry tiraillade between the French and some of the seventh division, supported by Victor Alten's cavalry, near Calvarrasa de Arriba. 'The nearest of the Arapiles, which, although considerably higher, is connected with the ridge on which we now stood, had been occupied by the allies on the preceding night; the other hill of that name, of greater altitude, more isolated, and rising from the plain at the angular point formed by the receding of the heights, had not been considered as important. Early in the morning, however, troops were sent to take possession of it; but the enemy had anticipated this movement, and part of the brigade of General Maucune already crowned the summit, no effort being made to dislodge him.'[89] Once they had possession of the Greater Arapil, the French were able to extend to the left. General Leith, observing this movement, and considering the enemy to be within reach of the fifth division's artillery, ordered his gunners forward. Captain Lawson opened fire, causing the French to retreat in some disorder. They promptly retaliated by bringing their own guns forward, and several men and horses were killed before the allied guns were withdrawn. The enemy continued to harass the fifth division with artillery fire, however.

The weather, in contrast to the night before, was fine and dry; 'the sun shone bright – nor was there any atmospheric obstruction to prevent a clear view of passing events: no haze withheld a distinct observation to the very extremity of the plains upon which the enemy was in movement. Occasional smoke from the firing, and dust, alone created a temporary uncertainty in the view of any movements of either army.'[90] This was as well, for Marmont spent most of the morning manoeuvring his forces.

About noon, a force which Leith Hay estimated as 10,000 strong was placed near the Arapiles, opposite the fifth division, which was the strongest division in the allied army, 6,700 men in eleven battalions, five of them Portuguese. Accompanied by artillery, these newcomers bore the appearance of an attacking force. Leith Hay was sent by his uncle to inform Wellington of this development, and Wellington then rode back with Leith Hay to see for himself what was happening. He found the fifth division under arms, ready to receive an attack, but the French were showing no inclination to advance. Convinced that nothing would happen in this part of the field, Wellington returned to his previous position.

He was prepared to play a waiting game for as long as was needed. Yet he was also manoeuvring his forces as necessary. Marmont clearly intended to threaten the Ciudad Rodrigo road and thus the allied line of retreat. In response, Wellington extended his line to the right, and occupied the village of Arapiles. Leith Hay gives the disposition of the allied force at this point. 'The 4th division, and General Pack's brigade of Portuguese infantry, had already arrived to our right of the nearest Arapiles. The 5th division soon after received orders to march in that direction; in executing which we passed close to the rear of the 4th division, taking up ground to its right, and on the same line. At some distance, in the rear of the 5th, was stationed the 7th division, under General Hope, while the 6th, commanded by General Henry Clinton, was in line to support the 4th. The 1st and light divisions continued between the Tormes and the Arapiles heights. General Pakenham, with the 3rd division, General D'Urban's cavalry, two squadrons of the 14th light dragoons, and Spanish infantry, were posted near Aldea Tejada; while General Bradford's brigade, and the heavy cavalry of General Le Marchant, were immediately on the right of the 5th division, but considerably to its rear: such was the disposition of the allied army at two o'clock in the afternoon of the 22nd.'[91] Yet Marmont had still to make a mistake.

Chapter 9

40,000 Men Defeated in 40 Minutes

As 22 July wore on into the afternoon Marmont finally committed himself to decisive action. On the rising ground to the south of the allied forces the French army was on the march. Marmont had taken the precaution of strengthening his line between the Greater Arapil and Calvarrasa de Arriba, which marked the right of his position, but the divisions of Brennier and Sarrut were still out of position when he fatally misread the situation. Possibly, he mistook the dust of the allied baggage train on its way to Ciudad Rodrigo for a general allied retreat, which was certainly what he wanted to see. Furthermore, even from his position on the Greater Arapil he could have no precise impression of the allied deployment because of the undulations of the ground. Whatever the cause of his misinterpretation, the result was an order to Maucune to extend along the French-held ridge. This, in turn, enabled Wellington 'to defeat forty thousand men in forty minutes', as a French officer termed it. In fact, the battle was considerably more protracted, but the opening forty minutes gave the allies an advantage which they could only lose through serious miscalculation.

In extended line, their left out of contact with their centre, and the rear divisions further detached, the French became vulnerable to a series of allied attacks: from the third division out at Aldea Tejada; from the heavy cavalry under Le Marchant; and from Leith's fifth division. It was Wellington's chosen moment. He is said to have exclaimed, as he threw away the chicken leg that was his lunch, 'By God! That will do!' To his Spanish liaison officer, General Alava, he then added, 'Mon cher Alava, Marmont est perdu.'

Wellington himself rode to alert the third division, still concealed at Aldea Tejada, to launch an attack against the French which would drive everything before the 'Fighting Division'. He then rode back to Leith to apprise him that the time had come for an advance. At once, the light companies of Pringle's (second) brigade extended to the right to close the gap between the third division and their own position. Once the advance began, however, these companies had to deploy to the left, not only because the line followed by the two divisions was converging, but also to allow the heavy cavalry to manoeuvre between them.

Leith Hay recorded that 'At about three o'clock, a force of not less than twenty pieces of artillery were assembled by the enemy on the heights directly opposite the 5th division. The ground upon which the division stood was flat, and the troops without any means of shelter. It became consequently advisable to make the regiments recline on the field, and, by so doing, avoid in some measure the effects of what was obviously to become a very heavy cannonade. For at least an hour did these brave soldiers immovably support the efforts made to annihilate them by the showers of shot and howitzer shells that were either passing over or ricocheting through the ranks.

'General Leith, on horseback, passed repeatedly along the front of his division, speaking to and animating the men, who earnestly expressed an anxious desire for permission to attack the enemy.'[92] This encouragement obviously had the desired effect. 'General Leith rode up about two o'clock. The cannonading at this time was terrible. Addressing the Regiment he says, "Royals," on which we all sprang up. "Lie down men," said he, though he sat on horse-back, exposed to the fire as calm as possible. "This shall be a glorious day for Old England, if these bragadocian rascals dare but stand their ground, we will display the point of the British bayonet, and where it is properly displayed no power is able to withstand it. All I request of you is to be steady and obey your officers. Stand up men!" '[93] Even if Douglas recorded only the gist of Leith's words, they still convey clearly the sentiments which could animate the British soldier. Leith addressed each battalion in turn and there can be little doubt that the 30th responded as enthusiastically as the Royals, for at long last they were going into action, not by ascending ladders into the chaotic hell of an assault but by marching face to face against the enemy.

Meanwhile, the light troops of the two armies were engaged in fierce skirmishing. The village of Arapiles was stoutly defended by the Guards and two fusilier companies to keep the enemy out. The fifth division, in support, was particularly strong in light troops, and gave a good account of itself, such that their French opponents eventually withdrew. This also led to the withdrawal of the guns which had been giving the division such an uncomfortable time.

'At length the welcome intelligence was imparted, that we were no longer to be cannonaded with impunity. Lord Wellington arrived from the right, and communicated to General Leith his intentions of immediately attacking the enemy.

'It is impossible to describe the energetic exultation with which the soldiers sprung [sic] to their feet; if ever primary impulse gained a battle, that of Salamanca was won before the troops moved forward! General Packenham [sic] commenced the action by advancing in four columns, coming direct upon the enemy's left flank, which he vigorously attacked, and drove back in disorder.

'General Leith was directed to form his division in two lines, the first of which was composed of the Royal, 9th, and 38th Regiments, with part of the 4th Regiment from General Pringle's brigade, necessarily brought forward for the purpose of equalizing the lines, of which the second was formed by the remainder of General Pringle's, and the whole of General Spry's Portuguese infantry.

'When General Bradford's brigade came up, the division was to appui itself on his left, march directly up the heights, and attack the enemy columns. Lord Wellington on this, as on all occasions, gave his orders in a clear, concise, and spirited manner; there was no appearance of contemplating a doubtful result; all he directed was to time and formation, and his instructions concluded with the command that the enemy should be overthrown, and driven from the field. He then proceeded towards the 4th division. The 5th, formed as he had directed, with its general in front of the centre of the front line, impatiently awaited the arrival of General Bradford; the moment he was in line, General Leith gave the signal, and the whole advanced in the most perfect order.' Leith had already sent his aides-de-camp to various points of the line, in order to restrain any over-enthusiasm which might disrupt the planned simultaneous attack. The light infantry who had been skirmishing with the enemy were also withdrawn so that they would not impede the line of march, and even the guns were sent to the rear, so that 'every obstruction to the regular advance of the line had vanished. Occasionally every soldier was visible, the sun shining brightly upon their arms, while at intervals all were enveloped in a dense cloud of dust, from whence, at times issued the animating cheer of British infantry.

'The confident presence of the enemy was now exchanged for the quiet formation proceeding in his ranks, as preparations for resisting the evidently approaching shock. His columns, retired to the crest of the height, were formed in squares, about fifty yards removed from the ground, on which, when arrived, the British regiments would become visible. The French artillery, although placed more to the rear, still poured its fire on the advancing troops.' At this point Leith Hay lost his horse. Taking another from an orderly dragoon, he rode beside General Leith 'in front of the colours of the 1st battalion of the 38th Regiment. The corps, numerous and effective, had joined the army on the previous day [replacing its junior battalion], and being the junior regiment, formed the centre of the first line: its commanding officer Colonel Greville, having charge of the brigade in the absence of General Hay.

'The second line of the division was about a hundred yards in the rear of the first; and between these, during the march towards the enemy, Lord Wellington at one time was, observing the progress of the attack.

'We were now near the summit of the ridge. The men marched with the same orderly steadiness as at first: no advance in line at a review was ever more correctly executed: the dressing was admirable, and spaces were no sooner formed by casualties than closed up with the most perfect regularity, and without the slightest deviation from the order of march.' Leith and his staff, being mounted, were the first to see the disposition of the enemy. 'He was drawn up in contiguous squares, the front rank kneeling, and prepared to fire when the drum beat for its commencement. All was still and quiet in these squares; – not a musket was discharged until the whole opened. Nearly at the same moment General Leith ordered the line to fire, and charge: the roll of musketry was succeeded by that proud cheer that has become habitual to the British soldier on similar occasions – that to an enemy tremendous sound, which may without exaggeration be termed the note of victory. At this moment, the last thing I saw through the smoke was the plunge of Colonel Greville's horse, who, shot through the head, reared, and fell back on his rider. In an instant every individual present was enveloped in smoke and obscurity. No struggle for ascendancy took place: the French squares were penetrated, broken and discomfited; the victorious division pressed forward, not against troops opposed, but a mass of disorganized men, flying in all directions. General Le Marchant's brigade of the heavy cavalry dashed forward on the right flank of the 5th division, while General Packenham, having overthrown every thing before him, added an immense number to the mass of fugitives escaping from this brilliant attack.

'Thus in the short space of less than an hour the battle was decided; the defeat of the French army became inevitable. Other divisions and corps of troops participated in the glory of the day, suffered seriously, and nobly upheld the reputation they had previously acquired; but the battle of Salamanca was in reality won by the 3rd and 5th divisions, General Bradford's Portuguese brigade, the squadron of the 14th dragoons, and the heavy cavalry. By the combined attacks of these troops, one-fourth of the French army was defeated, and driven in confusion on its centre; and ten thousand of the allies, regularly formed, flushed with success, and supported by a large body of cavalry, were on the flank of the enemy's army, every step they advanced adding to the discomfiture, driving him rapidly from height to height, and forcing back an additional crowd of fugitives to annoy and confound their still undefeated comrades. It will easily be conceived that, in such a state of affairs, the battle was irretrievably lost to the enemy.'[94]

Leith Hay subsequently qualified this claim by alluding briefly to the subsequent course of events, to which he was not a witness. Like General Leith, he was wounded during the attack on the French squares.

A full account of this devastating first stage of the battle, however, needs to consider what had been happening to their right while the fifth division were marching towards the French. Pakenham, in accordance with Wellington's orders, had advanced his brigade and cavalry support in four columns for more than two miles, hidden by the undulations of the terrain. This brought them into contact with the leading French division of Thomières. The first shock for the French was a flank cavalry attack; then even as they were recoiling from this onslaught they found themselves confronted by the tough men of the 'Fighting' third. The advance was unstoppable, despite Thomières' recourse to artillery fire, and the French division collapsed upon itself, Thomières being one of the first fatalities.

The survivors fled back to the following division, Maucune's, just as the fifth division launched their attack upon the French squares. Add to that the horror of Le Marchant's cavalry, cutting the fleeing troops with their heavy 1796-pattern swords, and it is no wonder that the result was a rout which soon enveloped the next French divisions, Brennier's.

For the man in the ranks this was a moment of justified exultation. 'A few paces brought us to the crest of the hill when we became exposed to the fire of all the guns they could bring to bear on us. I think the advance of the British at Salamanca never was exceeded in any field. Captain Stewart, of our company, stepping out of the ranks to the front, lays hold of Captain Glover and cries, "Glover did you ever see such a line?" I am pretty confident that in the Regiments which composed our lines there was not a man 6 inches out of his place. The French seemed to be taken by surprise as the 1st Royal Dragoons, the 5th Green Horse and a regiment of heavy Germans advanced with us on our right. Some of the Greens sung out, "Now boys, lather them and we'll shave them." As we approached the enemy their skirmishers retired, by ours and the Portuguese to within a few yards of their lines for seeing the British advancing through the tempest of balls, they (the Portuguese) kept advancing in like manner to within a few yards of the enemy's pieces, crying out, "Fogo ma felias" or "away my sons" . . .

'It was with a great deal of difficulty that the skirmishers could be made to retire, that the lines might open their fire. The enemy, as I before observed, seemed to be rather in confusion. The cavalry on our right was to them a puzzle. The enemy seemed to have formed parts of squares, and parts of lines, and before they could recover from their panic, our murderous fire opened, which swept all before it. The first line we fairly ran over, and saw our men jumping over huge grenadiers, who lay down exhausted through heat and fatigue, unhurt, in the hope of escaping. Of course we left them uninjured, but they did not behave honourably, for as soon as they found us at a little distance they resumed the posture of the enemy and commenced to fire on our rear; but nearly the whole of them paid the price of their treachery with their lives.

'The first line of the enemy being broken and falling back in confusion, the 2nd lined the side of a deep trench cut by the torrents of water which roll down from the hills near the village of Arapiles, and so deep and broad that it took a good spring to leap over it. Here the 2nd line kept up a heavy fire of musketry, which checked our centre for a few minutes, while our poor fellows fell fast. To remain long in this way was too much to be borne. The cheer was raised for the charge, a general bound was made at the chasm, and over we went like so many beagles, while the enemy gave way in confusion. The cavalry now came in for their share and cut them down in great number.'[95]

The only hope for the French was to launch a series of counter-attacks on the as yet unengaged allied divisions. Their difficulties were compounded by the fate of their leaders. Both Marmont and the third-in-command, General Bonnet, had suffered disabling wounds and overall command passed to the second-in-command, General Clausel, who had also been temporarily disabled by a wound to his heel. He was initially helped by the division of General Sarrut, which stood firm against the combined force of the third and fifth divisions until finally overwhelmed by the sheer impetus of the allied attack. It was a vital breathing space, however, which enabled Clausel's division to get into the action, with Bonnet, Ferey and Foy's divisions at least within reach. The allied fourth division, having launched an attack on Clausel's division, found itself dangerously exposed when Pack's Portuguese failed to take the Greater Arapil. At this point the fifth division also began to feel the force of the determined French counter-attack. 'Our poor fellows, having to bear up against the united fire of cannon and musketry, had their ranks equally thinned ere they commenced to ascend the hill. So determined were the enemy to maintain this post that one brigade of our division [the first] was cut off. Fortunately, our work was settled on the right as the enemy were falling back in confusion.'[96]

Douglas identified the 'poor fellows' as belonging to the sixth division, although what he actually witnessed was the confusion of the fourth division as Clausel made a last, desperate effort to turn defeat into victory. In the fifth division, Greville's brigade was put under such pressure that Pringle had to advance his brigade in support. Pringle himself was now in command of the division in place of the wounded Leith, and Lieutenant Colonel Brooke of the 4th had command of the second brigade.

For a moment everything was in the balance but Wellington had reserves in hand. He brought forward the sixth division while the fifth were re-forming, and their arrival destroyed any French hopes of victory. As the sixth confronted Ferey's division from the front in a fierce musketry fight, the fifth advanced, successfully outflanked the enemy, and delivered a *coup de grâce* which effectively brought the battle to an end. Ferey himself was killed but his division functioned as a rearguard while Foy's division effected a safe departure, never having got into the action. (The following day they were to be severely cut up at Garcia Hernandez.) Thus the French made their escape under cover of darkness, badly mauled and leaving behind many casualties and prisoners, but still maintaining some sort of order as they approached the Tormes. At this point they should have been halted by a Spanish force which was supposedly holding the bridge at Alba de Tormes. Unbeknown to Wellington, however, Carlos d'España had withdrawn his troops two days before. Consequently, while Wellington was searching the fords at Huerta, the French retreated unhindered. One version of what happened has d'Espana (actually a Frenchman) asking Wellington whether he should abandon the position and being so taken back by Wellington's vehement refusal that he did not have the resolution to tell him that Alba de Tormes had already been vacated by his troops.

Eventually, Wellington accepted that the French had escaped, and allowed the exhausted troops to collapse where they were. As Hale's journal recalls, their first concern was food. 'It plainly appeared to us this day, that the enemy were supplied with a lot of provisions for a long advance, just as if they were certain of driving us back into Portugal again; for in several places where they had been closely pursued by our army, they left a great quantity behind, which fell into our hands: however, in the course of this day most of us got loaded with what they left behind; for some found small bags of biscuits, about ten or twelve pounds weight; some small bags of flour, about the same weight; and some joints of mutton and goat's flesh; all of which we found very acceptable, for at that time we were rather short of provisions.

'So when our camp was formed, and our picquets posted, the remaining part were very soon busily employed in providing for the belly; some making hard dumplings with the flour we had found, some getting wood, and others searching for water for our cooking, which by chance was found at about one mile distant from our camp. Therefore towards the middle of the night, we enjoyed ourselves over a most able supper, and after a little conversation over what had passed during the day, we wrapped ourselves up in our blankets, with accoutrements on, and lay down in the hopes of getting a few hours' good rest, for we were then getting very much fatigued for want of sleep.'[97]

Douglas similarly remembered how they 'halted for the night on the ground occupied by the enemy during the morning (or during the action) and sent out parties for water, having nearly 5 miles to travel before it was found, and then it was as green as the water you may have seen during the heat of summer in a stagnant pond. However, it went down with a fine relish. The only piece of plunder either I or my comrade had got happened to be a leg of mutton off a Frenchman's knapsack, which I put in a kettle to boil, having made a fire of French firelocks.'[98]

Although they were spared the effort of harrying the enemy on the night of the battle, by 4.00 a.m. the fifth division were on the move in pursuit of the retreating French. 23 and 24 July proved days of hard marching for those who were fit enough to undertake it. In fact, considering their part in the battle (although admittedly in the second line for the advance across the plain), the 30th were not overburdened with casualties. Only two men were killed, and a sergeant and twenty-two rank and file were wounded, of whom two later died of their wounds. One man was taken prisoner, among the seven posted missing from Pringle's brigade. The only officer casualty was Lieutenant John Garvey, who was wounded. The battalion strength was about 300 (the monthly return for July gives twenty-two sergeants, fourteen drummers and 287 other ranks present), which indicates a casualty rate of around one in twelve, moderate compared with the losses at Badajoz. The casualties overall were 629 for the two British brigades and Spry's Portuguese brigade, although this number, as at Badajoz, does not include the two Brunswick companies. Of these overall casualties, seven officers and 103 men were killed in action, which again emphasises that the losses of the 30th were relatively light. The battalions that formed the front line during the initial advance took the heavier losses, suggesting that the division suffered most during that first stage of the battle.

A postscript to Salamanca concerns the vexed subject of imperial eagles, those iconic trophies treasured by any regiment that was fortunate enough to take one. The first eagle to fall into allied hands was seized at Talavera, while a second was gained at Barossa. Two more were claimed at Salamanca. The question of who actually took them, though, surfaced as a dispute in 1844 after it was initially asserted in the *Naval and Military Gazette* that the 44th had seized two eagles during the battle. There is no argument about the first, taken by Lieutenant Pearce and later identified as belonging to the 62nd Regiment. But who took the second? Crucial testimony was provided by Lieutenant John Garland, who was adjutant of the 30th at Salamanca. He wrote from Paris on the 22nd June, 1844: 'Seeing in your *Gazette* of the 15th instant a letter from one of Colonel Greville's brigade assuring you that only one Eagle was taken or picked up at the Battle of Salamanca by the 44th is quite correct, but I beg also to inform you that (to the best of my recollection, so long a period having now elapsed) another Eagle came into the possession of an Officer of the 30th in the same Brigade and who accompanied the Officer of the 44th to Head Quarters of the British army where the Eagles were deposited. The Officers' names are Lieut.-Colonel Wm Pearce, K.H., late Lieut. 44th, and Major John Pratt, now deceased.' It seems unlikely that even from a distance of thirty-two years Garland could have confused an eagle with the fannion which it has been claimed was the trophy Pratt actually took, particularly when one considers the kudos of acquiring an eagle.[99]

The situation is complicated by a statement of service in the *Royal Calendar* of 1818 by Major Crookshank of the 8th, but commanding the 12th Caçadores in the battle. He asserted categorically that the Portuguese had taken the eagle of the 22[ieme] de la ligne, which Crookshank then presented to Pakenham as commander of the third division, to which the 12th Caçadores were attached. It certainly seems that for several days after the battle Pakenham had an eagle carried behind him wherever he went. Furthermore, Douglas in his memoir (which seems to date from the mid-1840s, the same time as the dispute arose) recollected: 'A little before sunset a Portuguese soldier of our Division picked up an eagle and brought it safe to the lines, to the astonishment of all as you would imagine that a sparrow could not escape between two fires. The eagle was the subject of an account in a book of anecdotes a few years ago, when it was stated to have been captured by an officer of the British. The statement was false. It was taken as I have mentioned. It lay on the ground along with a number of the Regiment to which it belonged, having fallen by our fire, and was free to be picked up by anyone, but it was first discovered among the dead by the Portuguese soldier. But what became of it afterwards I cannot say, as I had other business to attend to.'[100] This would seem to settle the matter, except that the eagle referred to by Crookshank was not found by a Portuguese soldier serving in the fifth division, as Douglas claimed, and Pratt's eagle has never had its number separated from the eagle itself. However, Pearce's eagle, which he took with the help of men from his regiment, was seized just as the actual eagle was dismantled from its number and staff.

It was rumoured at the time that several eagles were taken, but were sold to local Spaniards, who in turn sold them back to the French regiments which had lost them.[101] Also, Charles Boutflower, surgeon to the 40th Regiment, recorded in his journal how the battle was a complete victory, the French losing several general officers, five eagles, twenty pieces of artillery and about 15,000 men. This would explain both the proliferation of eagles, and how more eagles seem to have been taken during the battle than actually remained in allied hands. Indeed, Leith Hay has his own story to add to the confusion. 'Having been removed from the field, I cannot detail the future movements of the 5th division on the night of the battle. They, however, consisted solely of pursuit, capturing many of the enemy; and, as a proof that it had penetrated to the very centre of his regiments, Major Birmingham, of the 15th Portuguese, one of the corps in General Spry's brigade, was seen riding forward carrying a French eagle, which he had, during the melee, torn from the grasp of its bearer.'[102]

To establish how John Pratt might have come across an eagle, if he did, it is necessary to consider what happened to Brennier's division, in which the 22ieme de la ligne served. They were initially caught up in the disaster which engulfed first Thomières' and then Maucune's divisions, but their later stand during Clausel's fight-back suggests this was not when they lost their eagle, which was only likely to happen in a state of complete panic (as happened to the 62ieme de la ligne in Thomières' division). However, they were later harried from the field by the fifth division when Clausel's counter-attack failed, and this would seem the most likely moment for Pratt to have come across the eagle. Whatever the truth of the matter, one thing is certain. The eagle of the 22ieme de la ligne is now at Fulwood barracks as part of a display of the former Queen's Lancashire Regiment, of which the 30th was the senior pre-Haldane regiment. It had been kept at Chelsea Hospital until 1947, but in that year it was ceremoniously handed over to the then East Lancashire Regiment, in acknowledgement that it properly belonged to the 30th.

Chapter 10
An Unacknowledged Victory

The defeat of Marmont at Salamanca, and the hasty retreat of King Joseph, who had been advancing with the Army of the Centre, opened up various strategic possibilities for Wellington. Clausel, still in command of the nominal Army of Portugal, decided to withdraw northwards across the Duero. The Army of the Centre, having halted its own retreat, could have joined him at Aranda which might have threatened the allies but Clausel kept to his planned line of retreat against Joseph's wishes. As a result the two forces went their separate ways, Clausel continuing north to Burgos while Joseph returned to Madrid, the seat and symbol of his limited power. Thus separated, neither army represented a serious threat. From Wellington's point of view, even temporary occupation of the capital of Spain would send a powerful message to those who still believed in French invincibility. Salamanca was a victory which 'had shaken the whole fabric of French domination to its very base, nor did the power of Napoleon in the Peninsula ever recover from the shock. The siege of Cadiz raised, the army of the Duke of Dalmatia [Soult] on the march to the north, the Andalusias liberated, the army of Cataluna and Valencia paralyzed, the guerrilla force tripled – all resulted from the successful termination of that battle.'[103] The occupation of Madrid would merely confirm how unstable was the French position.

The August monthly return for the 30th noted the arrival of a detachment from England of twenty-six rank and file, fifteen of them recruits, seven volunteers from the militia, and four men already in the regiment, although it is not clear if these were transfers from the first battalion or recovered invalids. They came under the command of Ensign Henry Beere. By a cruel irony of fate, the colossal Irishman from Tipperary arrived to the news that his brother, Lieutenant Hercules Beere of the 61st, had been killed at Salamanca. Lieutenant Freear also joined in August from duty at Belem while Lieutenant Eagar was sent to the rear for recovery of health. The battalion acquired another new ensign in Francis Tincombe who had been serving since February as a gentlemen volunteer and now filled a vacancy in the regiment. When a battalion was on active service an impecunious young man could gain a commission in this way.

On 11 August King Joseph and his military chief, Marshal Jourdan, decided to abandon Madrid, recognising that the allied army would easily overcome their own smaller force. Only the Retiro forts were defended and, although adequately provisioned and held by 2,000 men, they were too weak for sustained resistance. Wellington was received in the capital as a hero, and his army, as deliverers. The fifth division remained in bivouac in the park which surrounded the Retiro until the defenders surrendered on 14 August, whereupon the forts yielded a wealth of powder, muskets and ammunition, as well as two eagles. Their support duties complete, the division then retired to higher ground near the Escorial where the high summer heat was less intense. Heat was, in fact, the principal enemy. Two thirds of the battalion were reported sick in the muster of 23 August, although many of them were long-term sick, absent in hospital. Lieutenant Freear and Ensign Beere were sent up country on sick leave, and Ensign Carter, who had joined the battalion in March 1811, died of sunstroke. On the other hand, Captains Chambers and Hitchen, wounded at Badajoz, were able to rejoin after a four-month absence.

There were other problems such as an acute shortage of money. Combined with the extreme heat, this seems to have dispelled the earlier euphoria. '... the want of money was an evil now become intolerable. The army was many months in arrears; those officers who went to the rear sick suffered the most cruel privations, and those who remained in Madrid, tempted by the pleasures of the capital, obtained some dollars at an exorbitant premium from a money-broker, and it was grievously suspected that his means resulted from the nefarious proceedings of an under commissary; but the soldiers, equally tempted, having no such resource, plundered the stores of the Retiro [and anywhere else they could find, presumably]. In fine, discipline became relaxed throughout the army, and the troops kept in the field were gloomy, envying those who remained in Madrid.'[104]

Possession of Burgos, to the north, would prevent a French southwards movement by the reinforced Armies of Portugal and the North. Consequently, the allied third and light divisions were left in Madrid, strengthened by General Hill's second division, which had been brought up from Estremadura, while Cole's fourth division marched north as far as New Castille. Wellington then took the first, fifth and seventh divisions, with Pack and Bradford's Portuguese brigades, towards Burgos, slowly driving back Clausel. At Cuellar the allies joined up with Clinton's sixth division before continuing their advance on Burgos, which was invested on 19 September.

Of the divisions involved in this enterprise, only the fifth had experience of a successful assault. Although the sixth division had finally taken the Salamanca forts, this had been brought about by fortuitous firing rather than by assault.

It must have dismayed the fifth division, therefore, to become a covering force under Sir Edward Paget while the siege was entrusted to the untried first division and the seventh, which had failed to take San Christobal during the previous summer's attempt on Badajoz. Hale recorded the experiences of the fifth division during the next few weeks: 'the remaining part of our army advanced three leagues further, and formed line about one league from the enemy, for they had taken up their position about four leagues beyond Burgos. So there we encamped in a regular way, but without tents; and about one hour before break of day, we stood to our arms till it was quite broad day light, and as soon as our general officers were fully satisfied that the enemy were making no movement, we were dismissed, and parties immediately sent out for wood and water for the purpose of cooking, while our butchers were killing and dressing our meat.

'There we remained, as comfortable as the weather would permit, till towards the end of October; but no engagement took place while we remained there, which was about six weeks.'[105]

Douglas also found something to enjoy. 'We reached Burgos, and marched to the front, to cover the siege of the Castle. Our rations were very good and pretty regular. I think the Spanish, particularly round Burgos and Biscay, make the best bread in the world. I am much of the opinion they put a quantity of honey in it, and that article is plentiful here.' On the other hand, he was frequently obliged to gather brambles in order to provide himself with some light. 'My poor old tattered trousers and coat were no way improved by these excursions and in many cases it would have taken no mean judge to determine the original colour; perhaps a piece of stocking covered a few holes on one sleeve while a piece of biscuit bag covered the other. No matter what the colour was, if we were lucky enough to find a piece it found a place very soon on either coat or trousers.'[106]

Eventually there was some French activity. On 20 October the fifth division came close to action when an enemy force of 10,000 men, who were advancing to the relief of Burgos, tried to drive in the allied outposts at Olmos. Paget was ordered to move the first and fifth divisions to the right, which persuaded the French to retire to Monasterio after the exchange of some desultory fire.

Meanwhile, the siege of Burgos was coming to an unsatisfactory conclusion. As was the usual practice, officers not directly involved in the siege were invited to volunteer as assistant engineers. Since no GSM bars were awarded for Burgos, there is no way of determining how many did so from the 30th. The only one who can be positively identified is Lieutenant Parke Percy Neville. His 1829 statement of service records that he was severely wounded 'Through the left shoulder when employed as Asst. Engr. With the 24th Regt. In the storm of the 1st line of the Castle of Burgos, on the evening of the 4th of Oct. 1812.' He was rewarded with one year's pay. The following year, however, when back in Britain, he received the freedom of the City of Dublin for Badajoz and Burgos. He may also have suffered a slight wound four days earlier if he is the N. who had part of his ear shot off. The events of 4 October are more certain, however. The guns of No. 1 battery had opened up a breach of sixty feet, and a mine charged with a thousand pounds of powder had also been laid. The task of carrying the breach was entrusted to the 2/24th, the regiment to which Neville was attached as engineer. 'It was ordered that the mine should be sprung at 5 p.m., so that the assault might take place during daylight, and the working parties have the benefit of the dusk to commence, and the obscurity of the night to crown the breaches and complete the lodgement within the outer line.

'The 24th Regiment, under Captain Hedderwick, was selected to storm, and for that purpose were formed in the parallel at fifty yards from the mine to be exploded. An advance party, under Lieut. Holmes, was posted as close to the expected breach as was judged consistent with safety, having orders instantly on the explosion to rush up the ruins. Another party, under Lieutenant Fraser, was similarly posted in the nearest part of the trenches to [the] breach, and the remainder of the battalion was prepared to follow the advance as quickly as possible, and form wherever they could obtain cover.

'A reserve of 500 men was brought into the trenches, and a considerable working party paraded in the suburbs of St. Pedro, with gabions, etc, to follow the storming party up the breach, and commence the lodgement ... At the appointed moment the mine was sprung and made an excellent breach ... 100 feet in front, sending up into the air many of the garrison who happened to be posted just above it, but without occasioning the slightest accident amongst the troops of the besiegers closely posted round it.

'The assault was conducted with the greatest regularity and spirit. In an instant the advanced party were on the ruins; and, before the dust created by the explosion had subsided, were in contact with the defenders on the summit of the breach. The party to assault the breach were equally regular and equally successful; and, after a struggle of a few minutes, the garrison were driven into their new covered way, and behind their palisades.

'This gallant achievement, which overcame the greatest obstacle to the success of the siege, was effected with the loss of only 37 men killed, and 7 officers and 189 men wounded.'[107] Among the wounded officers were Jones, whose account this is, and Neville.

Neville, only eighteen, was lucky to survive. 'In the struggle which followed [the explosion of the mine] Neville was conspicuous, being seen engaged with two French soldiers, before he fell. He narrowly escaped being completely covered with earth, but managed to grasp the foot of Lieutenant Pitts of the engineers, and make himself known. A sergeant of the 79th Highlanders carried him to his quarters. Neville pressed his watch upon him, but the Highlander refused it, and when Neville tried to trace him later, he found that he had been killed in the succeeding assault.'[108]

Burgos ended in failure. Five separate assaults failed, proving that courage and the bayonet could not compensate for the lack of siege guns, trained engineers and specialist troops. Volunteers from the ranks, enthusiastic but inadequately equipped, could not make up for this deficiency. By 21 October, with the Army of Portugal threatening aggression, Wellington admitted defeat and withdrew under the guns of the castle, having first given orders for the destruction of the paraphernalia of the siege. But for the exuberance of the guerrillas who were attached to the army, this covert departure might have been achieved without casualties. The sound of their horses galloping over the bridge which crossed the Arlanzan alerted the castle gunners, who immediately opened fire. Casualties were light, however, although the 30th, coming from a different direction, returned one man killed, and another as missing/prisoner.

The fifth division, accompanied by some Galician infantry, Spanish cavalry, and the heavy dragoons, retired from the north of Burgos towards Tardajos on the Urbel river. Near Tardajos they came into contact with the other allied column. During this second day of the withdrawal, the 30th suffered another two men missing/prisoners. Once the two columns had made contact, the men were given several hours to rest and recover and then the march continued, the northern column leading the southern column, with the fifth division at the head of the former.

The route followed by the fifth division took them to Hornillas, where they bivouacked. On 23 October a gruelling march of twenty-six miles brought them towards Torquemada, by which time a further two men from the 30th had been posted missing, a leeching away which was to continue throughout the retreat. While the infantry retreated unchallenged, however, the cavalry rearguard had to hold off the harrying French at considerable cost. That night was spent in and around Torquemada. The fifth division were at Cordovilla, where there was a bridge across the Pisuerga. Thus the men of the 30th missed the temptations discovered at Torquemada itself, where enormous storage vats of wine presented an irresistible attraction. According to Napier, 'drunkenness and insubordination, the usual concomitants of an English retreat, were exhibited at Torquemada, where the well-stored wine-vaults became the prey of the soldiery: it is said, that twelve thousand men were to be seen at one time in a state of helpless inebriety.' The 30th returned no men missing at Cordovilla, suggesting that similar temptations were not encountered there.[109]

The French were now in determined pursuit. On 24 October the two allied columns crossed the Carrion at Palencia and Wellington took up a defensive position on the right bank, extending from Villamuriel on the left to Duenas, on the Pisuerga, on the right. The bridge at Palencia was defended by a Galician division, supported by the third battalion of the Royals. The rest of the fifth division were at Villamuriel, while the first, sixth and seventh divisions extended to Duenas.

Hale's account of the events of this day starts at about 4.00 a.m. 'We stood to our arms in the usual way, and continued our retreat till nearly sun-set in the evening, when we arrived the other side of Palencia, towards Valladolid; there our division formed our camp very convenient to the river Pisuera [sic], at about four miles distance from Palencia, where was a bridge, near Villamuriel. Our regiment [the 9th] was ordered to defend this bridge, and soon after dark at night, a party of engineers was set to work, boring the bridge, in order to blow it up.'[110] Several men of the 30th were similarly employed at the bridge near Baños, upstream on the Pisuerga.

These delaying tactics allowed the sick and the supply trains safe passage. Meanwhile, the French were expected to head for the bridge at Palencia, making the fifth division the allied rearguard. Their task was to hold Villamuriel, which, as Hale noted, was four miles downstream, on the right bank of the river Carrion. Due to staff misdirection, the division was initially sent two leagues beyond this point. They then had to retrace their steps, and only reached their bivouac after dark, to find no rations waiting for them. The French were in close pursuit which Napier claimed led to the loss of the divisional baggage and a large number of men. Douglas, however, maintained, 'As to our baggage, it was left with the Division, while we made the excursion [at the bridge in Palencia]. Consequently it was not within their grasp, and even had they got every ounce that belonged to the Battalion, it would have fallen far short of abundance. And as to prisoners I was nearly the last man over the bridge, and I am quite confident we did not lose a single man as prisoner with the exception of those who fell badly wounded, and whom it was impossible to get away.'[111] Nevertheless, one man of the 30th was returned missing/prisoner, possibly a straggler who was taken by the French.

The action at Villamuriel is often presented as little more than a footnote to the retreat from Burgos, yet the 30th placed it among their battle honours. In Napier's unreliable account General Oswald (who had just arrived from England to take command of the fifth division) is castigated for failing to

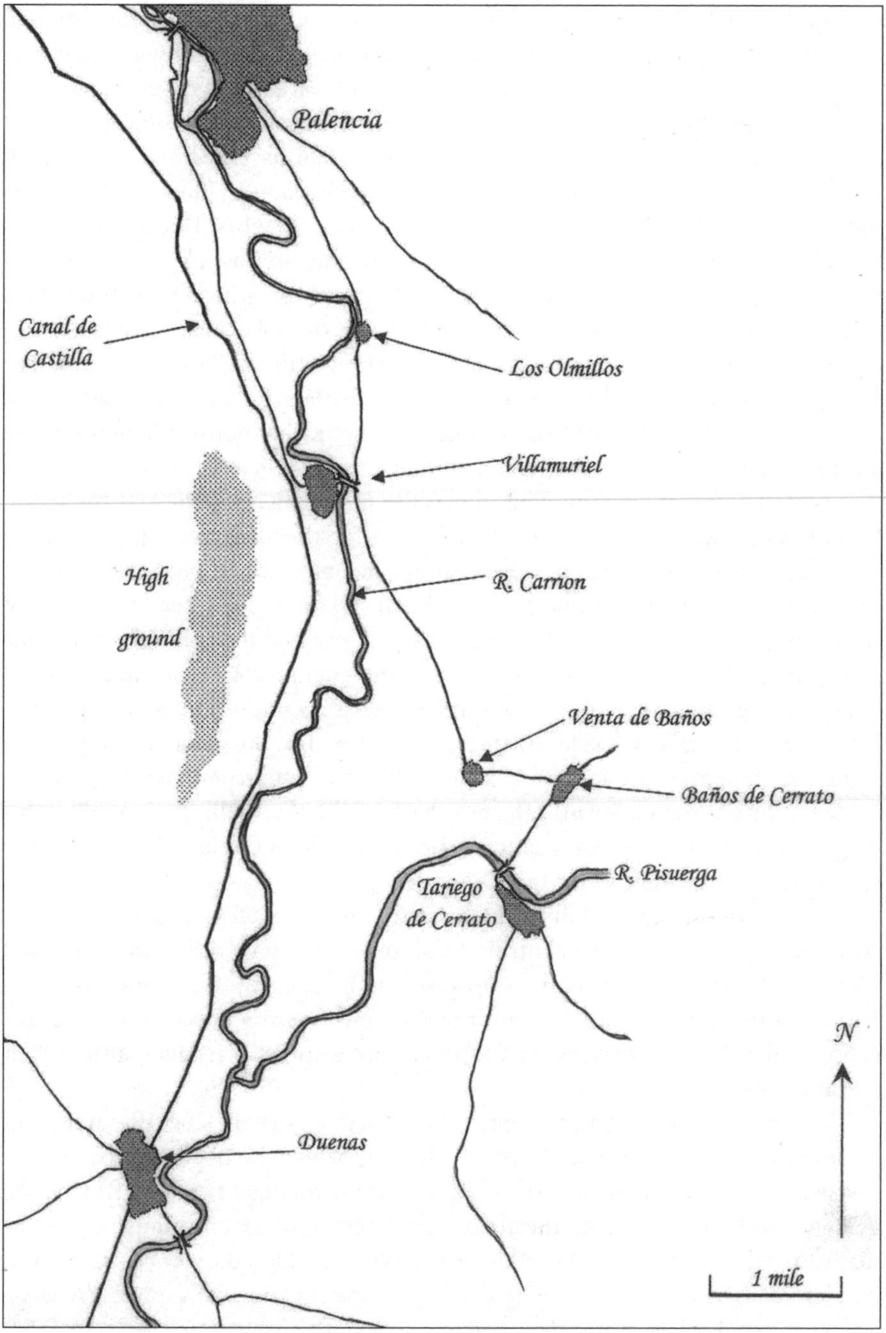

Villamuriel and the surrounding area

exploit the dry bed of the Canal de Castilla, which ran parallel with the Carrion, and also for not occupying Villamuriel itself in sufficient strength. Yet the events which followed the French attack do not support these criticisms.

A more judicious view acknowledges that Wellington's problems started at Palencia. The attempt to hold the bridge failed as General Foy stormed into the town. 'The order had been sent to our Division to blow up the bridge on the evening of the 24th, instead of halting on the heights. But unfortunately the Dragoon who carried the order lost his way in the dark and did not reach the Division until 8 o'clock in the morning, by which time the bridge ought to have been destroyed. This accident was the sole cause of the disasters of the day. As soon as the order arrived, the Artificers and Miners of the Division were ordered down, covered by our battalion and two squadrons of dragoons. But having, I dare say, 4 miles to march, the morning was pretty far advanced ere we arrived there, and to work they went on the bridge ... By this time the enemy were moving down the hills which overlooked the town, keeping up a desultory fire, which was taken for the stragglers shooting pigs; when all in a hurry our leather merchants [shoemakers had been sent into the town to procure leather] came running down the lines and spread the alarm of the enemy being in the town. Scarcely had they reached the column when some close firing took place on the bridge, and the enemy got possession of it.'[112] There is a certain disingenuousness in Douglas's account. The Royals seem to have been particularly casual in their conduct of the business, although they were not helped by the failure of a fuse when the engineers tried to blow the bridge. Nor did the Galicians offer much of a fight. As Wellington wrote in his dispatch, they were 'not in a state of discipline which could gain them either the confidence of their allies or of themselves.'

This failure in Palencia left the fifth division in a perilously exposed position. Not only was Foy firmly in control of the town, only four miles upstream, but General Maucune was advancing to take the bridges at Villamuriel and San Isidro. In this dangerous situation, the division fought a successful rearguard action which enabled the rest of the allied forces to get off safely, although at considerable loss to themselves.

The principal evidence for what happened comes in the dispatches of Wellington himself, and of General Oswald, who was handicapped by the division neither knowing nor trusting him. Unfortunately, there is little private evidence to flesh out these official accounts, and some assumptions have to be made, all of which contradict Napier's version.[113] Douglas echoes several of Napier's criticisms (possibly influenced by the publication of Napier's *History*), although the Royals, after they had extricated themselves from Palencia by clambering up the higher ground, played only a belated part in the action.

neral Thomas Graham, engraved for *The Military Chronicle*, 1811.

A view of Sabugal, drawn by Lieutenant Colonel Leith Hay.

A view of Guarda, drawn by Lieutenant Colonel Leith Hay.

The escalade of San Vincente, Badajoz, by the 2/30th.

Major George Grey,
30th Regiment.

A view of Salamanca, drawn by
Lieutenant Colonel Leith Hay.

The French Eagle captured at Salamanca.

The bridge at Villamuriel showing the high ground to the west.

Quatre Bras, drawn by Craan.

La Haie Sainte, drawn by Craan.

battlefield at Waterloo, from the south,
La Haie Sainte, drawn by Craan.

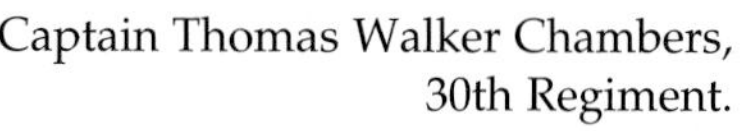

Captain Thomas Walker Chambers,
30th Regiment.

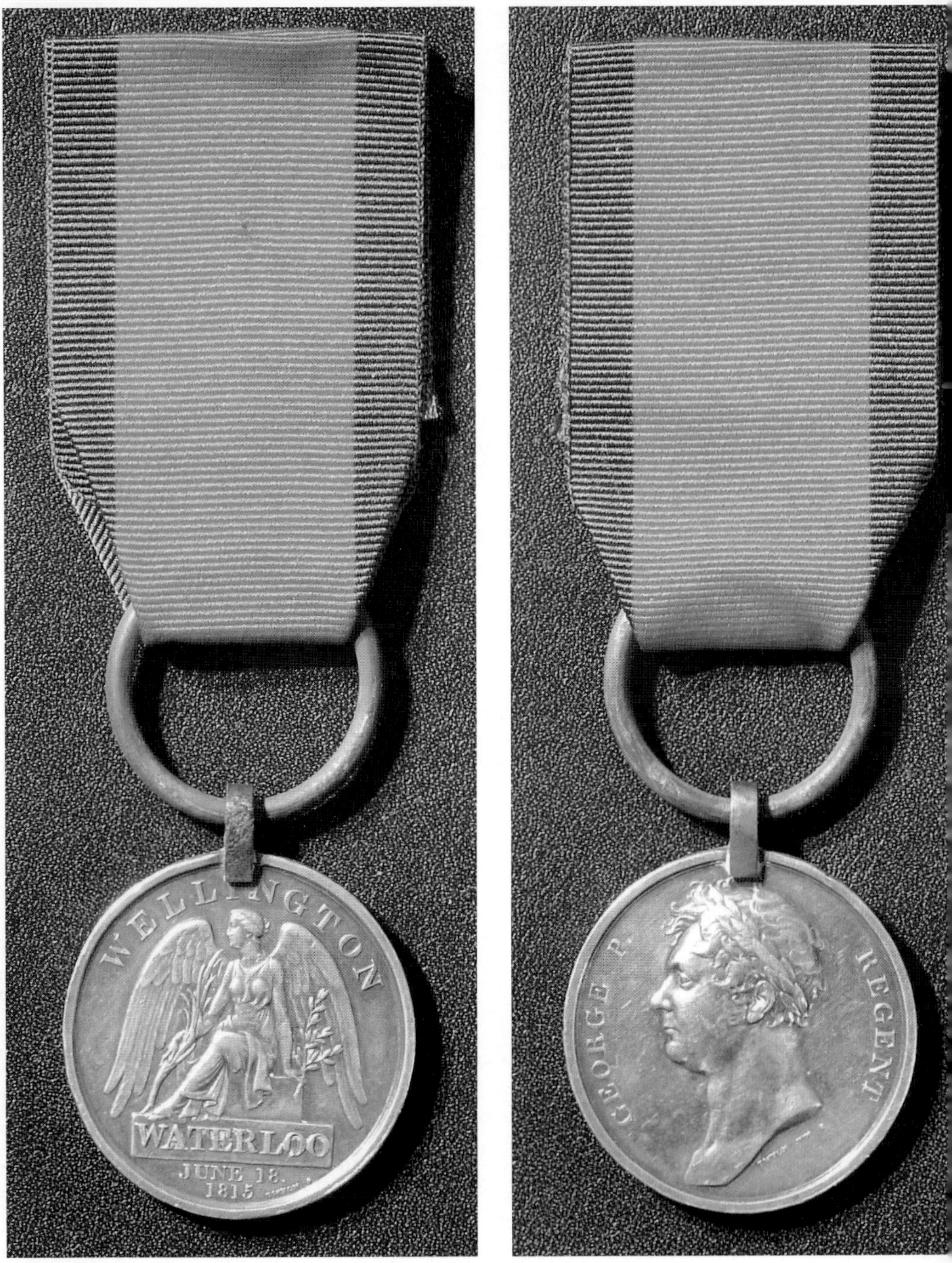

The Scotton Waterloo medal.

Villamuriel, a small village at the time, lies halfway on a straight line between Palencia and Duenas, with the river Carrion on one side and the Canal de Castilla running parallel on the other. Beyond the canal the ground rises gently at first, and then more steeply, to a considerable height. Across the river, though, the land is undulating. There were fords across the river although these were not obvious, so that the only bridge became the French objective.

General Oswald in his dispatch identified the two British brigades in the normal way as the first and second, the latter still commanded by General Pringle while General Barnes commanded the first brigade. By eight o'clock Pringle had positioned the division in a way which Oswald described as 'admirably disposed'. Some of the troops were in the village while others occupied the dry bed of the canal. The rest were in columns of attack with a reserve, ready to take the fight to the enemy if the mines which had been placed the night before should fail, thus enabling the French to cross the bridge. The disposition of the artillery is less clear, since Oswald does not mention it, although Lawson's battery was definitely sited on the rising ground. Similarly unclear is the exact position of the 30th, although they may have been in the dry canal.

Hale is specific about the position of his battalion, in the first brigade. 'We remained there [near the bridge] very quiet till about nine o'clock on the following morning, the 25th October 1812, when we discovered a division of the enemy [Maucune's forces] advancing at a very short distance from us, in consequence of which, about two hundred of our regiment were placed very convenient to the bridge, and the remaining part of the regiment was extended along the river.'[114]

The French attacked with artillery to soften up their opponents, disabling two of Lawson's guns and causing the repositioning of the others higher up the hill. The French guns also inflicted some casualties on the troops in the canal bed. One victim of this bombardment was a British major in the Portuguese service who was decapitated while reading a newspaper.

The enemy then launched an attack on the bridge itself. Hale, who was close to the bridge, wrote: 'The enemy seeing so small a party to defend the bridge, they made a grand push for that place, but fortunately, before they could make their object, the bridge blew up, which put a stop to their pursuit: so then they extended themselves along the river, in about the same direction that we were, by which a sharp skirmishing immediately took place, and continued about four hours.'[115]

While this initial action was happening in Villamuriel, Wellington learnt of Foy's arrival in Palencia, the flight of the Galicians, and the failure to destroy the bridge. 'I had directed the 3d battalion of the Royals to march to Palencia, to protect the destruction of the bridges over the Carrion at that place, but it appears that the enemy assembled in such force at that point, that Lieut.-Colonel Campbell thought it necessary to retire upon Villamuriel, and the enemy passed the Carrion at Palencia.' Although the flooded state of the Carrion made further rapid progress by Foy impossible, the situation had implications for the allied army as a whole. Wellington, therefore, directed Oswald 'to throw back our left, and the Spanish troops upon the heights, and to maintain the Carrion with the right of the division.' As intended, this move successfully halted a French advance before they could assail the heights above Villamuriel and allowed the Spanish who had been ousted from Palencia time to reorganise. These orders were resented by the division, however, being ascribed to Oswald rather than Wellington, and it was muttered among the disgruntled troops that if General Leith had been there they could have beaten the French easily enough.

With the bridge at Villamuriel destroyed, there followed some desultory skirmishing between French voltigeurs and the brigades of the fifth division still in the village. Further upstream General Gaultier was seeking a crossing. Frustrated at San Isidro, where the bridge had been successfully blown up, he advanced further east until he came to Baños where a similar attempt to destroy the bridge had failed. Only the parapets collapsed, so that the French were able to cross and seize the working party, including some men of the 30th. They advanced no further, however, and the day's action remained concentrated upon Villamuriel, where Maucune was searching for the fords in order to throw his troops across the river. Napier gives a dramatic account of how this was achieved. 'The play of the mine, which was achieved, checked the advance of the French for an instant, but suddenly a horseman darting out at full speed from the column, rode down under a flight of bullets, to the bridge, calling out that he was a deserter; he reached the edge of the chasm made by the explosion, and then violently checking his foaming horse, held up his hands, exclaiming that he was a lost man, and with hurried accents asked if there was no ford near. The good-natured soldiers pointed to one a little way off and the gallant fellow having looked earnestly for a few moments as if to fix the exact point, wheeled his horse round, kissed his hand in derision, and bending over his saddle-bow dashed back to his own comrades, amidst showers of shot, and shouts of laughter from both sides. The next moment Maucune's column covered by a concentrated fire of guns passed the river at the ford thus discovered, made some prisoners in the village, and lined the dry bank of the canal.'[116]

Unfortunately, there is no corroborating evidence for this story. Significantly, Hale is silent, although he was certainly in a position to witness such a moment in the action. He does describe how 'One company of our regiment was very convenient to a grist-mill that was on this river, and while they were busy skirmishing with the infantry that was on the opposite side of the river, a troop of French cavalry rushed out from behind the mill, quite unawares to us, and swept away the whole company as prisoners of war before we could give them any assistance.'[117] This suggests that the French had found the fords without attracting the notice of the allies.

The cavalry were followed by eight companies of voltigeurs, who managed to establish themselves on the allied side of the river, where they were held by the light troops of the fifth division. With the Spanish still holding the heights, the division was now formed on their right, which meant that Villamuriel lay in front of them, slightly to the left. In the village itself, after the withdrawal of the British brigades, the Portuguese found themselves under heavy fire, and were forced to retire and take cover as best they could. This enabled the French cavalry to effect a temporary repair of the bridge, untroubled by allied fire. The ladders used for this repair may have allowed the infantry to pass over only a man at a time, but the discovery of a second ford meant that there were soon enough of them across the river to hold the village and the canal. They came no further, choosing instead to set up another skirmish with the allied forces. Despite an additional ten guns which were directed on the new French positions, the action had reached stalemate.

The wider situation, though, was less favourable. The French were in firm control of Palencia and its bridges, and also possessed another crossing point at Baños. Wellington recognised that retreat was the only option, but this could not be executed while the French were on the right bank of the Carrion at Villamuriel. If they advanced beyond the village, they could be charged by the whole fifth division, but Maucune seemed content to hold the ground that he had gained. Consequently, an allied counter-movement was required. Wellington sent orders that the two British brigades should launch an attack, supported by the Spanish.

This presumably is the moment which Napier recorded as: 'Lord Wellington who came up this instant immediately turned some guns upon the enemy and desired that the village and canal might be retaken; Oswald thought that they could not be held, yet Wellington, whose retreat was endangered by the presence of the enemy on that side of the river was peremptory, he ordered one brigade under general Barnes to attack the main body, while another brigade under general Pringle, cleared the canal, and he strengthened the left with the Spanish troops and Brunswickers. A very sharp fire of artillery and musquetry ensued, and the allies suffered some loss, especially by cannon-shot which from the other side plumped into the reserves.'[118]

At best, this could only have been reported to Napier and there is no way of identifying his informant, although a wish to praise Wellington may have coloured the narrative. There is also implicit criticism of Oswald in Douglas's account. 'On Wellington's coming to the hill which commanded a full view of the scene of attack and defence, he ordered our Brigade to drive the enemy from their snug berth down the hill. The Royals and the 38th went, which was none the easiest jobs as it was very steep and broken. The fire of the enemy slackened on seeing us move down, until we came on a level with their guns, and then the play began. Our first fire and advancing with the bayonet cleared the canal and here, if Wellington's orders had been obeyed, our loss would have been trifling as we were to halt and keep possession of it and then it would have been impossible for those dispossessed of their lodgings to have escaped, as they became exposed to two fires. But, instead of occupying this post, we were ordered to follow the fugitives to the river's brink, exposed to a front and flanking fire of round and grape shot with occasional shells.'[119]

The 9th had been withdrawn half a mile before the French crossed the river in force but 'We had not been sitting more than half an hour, when we beheld the enemy fording the river, and the Spaniards [who had relieved the 9th] retreating in an unsoldierlike manner; in consequence of which our brigade was again ordered to stand to our arms and give them a charge, which we immediately did with great vigour, and in a few minutes we captured about four hundred prisoners; there were also a great number killed and wounded in endeavouring to make their escape back across the river: therefore they did not make any further attack that day.'[120]

It is possibly significant that Hale was writing before the publication of Napier's work, and Douglas, afterwards.

But what about the second brigade? Hale's account summarises what happened from the perspective of Barnes's brigade, but the counter-attack ordered by Oswald involved the whole division, and the Spaniards. As the first brigade was launched against the left flank of the enemy, the second was initially required to march in support, extending to the left to help the Spaniards, who were under frontal attack. They were soon in confusion and on the verge of retreat when General Alava, Wellington's Spanish liaison officer, despite being wounded, put himself at their head and steadied them.

Oswald himself led Barnes's brigade against the French left flank, while the steadiness of Pringle's brigade, in support, enabled the Spanish to rally on them after they had suffered heavily from French artillery fire. The first brigade cut off the French retreat, allowing the Spanish to pursue the enemy into the river where many of them were killed. At the same time, the second brigade used the bayonet to clear the canal. A second-hand encomium of their action was included many years later in the obituary notice of Colonel Hamilton. The friend who wrote it cited Hamilton's own words: 'The 30th and 44th did rather a dashing thing when they advanced in line against seventeen pieces of cannon, cleared the adjoining village and took more prisoners than their own force was composed of.' Although artillery and infantry continued to fire into the night, the French had effectively been pushed back to where they started. The fighting had been fierce to achieve this degree of success; the British troops used more than their allotted sixty rounds of ammunition in a struggle which lasted from daybreak until well after darkness fell. The position had been held, however, and the rest of the allied army was able to retire during the night, crossing the Pisuerga at Cabezon, while the fifth division covered them at Villamuriel. In the early hours of the morning the fifth division followed them, unmolested.

If the British and Portuguese showed their usual backs-to-the-wall determination, and the Spanish demonstrated that they could be rallied by steady troops, the French exhibited less than their usual élan. Obviously, the lesson of Salamanca had not been forgotten but it also seems that the British had not been the only troops to raid the wine cellars at Torquemada. What they had left, the French had finished off and French drunkenness on this occasion surpassed British. But whatever the reason for the muted French attack, there can be no denying that the fifth division had fought a valiant and determined action and achieved a notable defensive victory.

Chapter 11

Out of the War

Although Villamuriel was a successful action, the cost was considerable. In the 30th alone a sergeant (Francis Keith) and two privates were killed, while seven officers were wounded: Captain Hitchen, Lieutenants Andrews, Rumley and Brissac, and Ensigns Beere, Madden and Tincombe. A volunteer, Mr John Hughes, was posted missing, along with seven other men, although these may have been taken at Baños, and nine wounded men were taken prisoner after the French crossed the river. A further twenty-five men were wounded, meaning that more than a fifth of the 250 men involved were casualties. As already noted, there is some uncertainty about where the 30th were actually positioned. The 8th Caçadores were certainly in the dry canal and they lost ten officers wounded. In the other two battalions in Pringle's brigade, the 4th and the 44th, two and four officers respectively were wounded against seven in the 30th, which would suggest that the 30th were on the left in the dry canal where the troops came under particularly heavy fire. If officer casualties are related to overall casualty figures, then losses would be heaviest for units in this position. It would also be the 30th's rightful position, as second in seniority.[121]

Fortunately for the seriously depleted battalion a detachment of ninety NCOs and other ranks was on the march from Lisbon. In command was Captain Richardson, who had obtained his captaincy in June 1812 during a period of twelve months' leave from India for recovery of health which had already extended into its second year. Nor were the second battalion to see much of him. He spent most of his time on leave once the retreat was over although he did not finally leave the regiment until 1814. He was accompanied by three subalterns: Lieutenant Theophilus O'Halloran from the 54th, and Ensigns Samuel Robert Poyntz and Thomas Kelly. Poyntz was the second son of the first battalion's former quartermaster. Samuel Robert's elder brother, Arthur, served briefly with the 30th as an ensign before transferring to the 17th, while his younger brother, James, was still a student at the Royal Military College but would soon rejoin the regiment. Samuel Robert, like O'Halloran, remained with the second battalion until disbandment in 1817, when he went on half-pay.

Reinforcements were a mixed blessing because they had no immunity against the local diseases and the rigours of campaigning in an alien climate. Many of the new men, and one of the officers quickly fell sick. Ensign Kelly succumbed to the extreme circumstances of the retreat soon after he joined and, as the monthly return for December records, 'died of fatigue in a hospital wagon' on 2 December, near Celorico where there was a base hospital.

The retreat continued towards Salamanca. On 29 October, at the confluence of the Pisuerga and the Duero, the allies crossed to the left bank of the Duero at Puente de Duero and Tudela. These bridges were subsequently destroyed, as were the bridges at Cabezon, Valladolid, Tordesillas and Quintanilla. Headquarters were established at Rueda, and this position was maintained until 5 November. Four days later the allied army reached San Christobal, above Salamanca, where they were reunited with General Hill's forces. There had been considerable straggling since Villamuriel. The 30th, though, posted only two men missing for this period, a figure which supports General Oswald's claim that the fifth division remained well-disciplined.

If Wellington had moved faster to join forces with Hill, he might have attacked either the Army of Portugal or the united force of King Joseph and Marshal Soult. There were strategic considerations which deterred him but also, as he wrote to Lord Bathurst at the War Office, 'The two corps of this army, particularly that which has been in the north, are in want of rest. They have been continually in the field, and almost continually marching, since the month of January last; their clothes and equipment are very much worn, and a period in cantonments would be very useful to them.' On the French side Soult certainly advocated a battle, particularly after the two French forces combined, but the poor condition of his army actually delayed their advance. A probing attack on Alba de Tormes was made on 10 and 11 November, but the French commanders recognised that Wellington's position on San Christobal (which four divisions, including the fifth, were holding) was too strong for a frontal attack. Soult then successfully advocated turning the allied right, even though it required a complete realignment of the French forces.

Initially, Wellington was unclear about the purpose of these manoeuvres but by 13 November he recognised that the French had decided upon a flanking movement. His response was dependent upon how the French conducted their re-alignment. If they advanced in detached columns, then another Salamanca was possible whereas a concentrated attack would necessitate a retreat upon Ciudad Rodrigo. Wellington brought his own troops forward to the Arapiles position and a battle remained a possibility until the morning of 15 November, when it became apparent that Soult was not to be outmanoeuvred. At this point Wellington decided upon retreat and as he did so the light rain ominously intensified to a downpour.

Hale describes the misery of the retreat: 'the weather and the roads were then very bad, and in consequence of so much rain, the rivers began to run; very strong, and every brook and ditch was overflowing with water; so that I might venture to say, that we had several brooks or rivers to ford more or less every day. In consequence of that, and for want of food and regular rest, our army began to straggle and get very much fatigued, so that many were left behind, who, we might easily suppose, fell into the hands of the enemy.'[122] Douglas includes some more colourful detail: 'The weather was now become very wet, and the country between Salamanca and Ciudad Rodrigo, being generally flat, we had most miserable spots to encamp on. If inclined to sleep we were obliged to repose like so many turkeys, on the branches of trees, to keep us out of the water and mud. On our first march from Salamanca we received a draft of 250 men. Poor wretches! I pitied them. Being unaccustomed to such work, they stood in mid-leg shivering with cold, not knowing what to do.'[123] The men who joined the 30th after Villamuriel were undoubtedly in a similar state.

The route lay through forest. The rain was incessant, hence the flooded streams and the mud, and there were no rations, thanks to the incompetence of the quartermaster-general's department, which sent the stores in the wrong direction. The French kept up a continual harassment, snapping up stragglers and baggage, until the order was finally given for the baggage to be sent ahead to Ciudad Rodrigo. On the third day the allies traversed a waterlogged plain, boggy enough to suck the shoes off the soldiers' feet. Still without rations, many collapsed exhausted. Fortunately, the French were in similar straits and left the pursuit to small bands of cavalry. The losses of the 30th during these three days, according to the casualty returns for November and December, were one death, five men taken prisoner and three posted missing. Another five men fell out but were later saved from falling into French hands by allied cavalry. If we accept Napier's figure for the losses during the retreat from Burgos[124], the forty-five dead and missing suffered by the 30th (including Villamuriel) suggests a disciplined unit. Furthermore, details of regimental courts martial (there were no general courts martial) in the inspection return for January 1813, which covered the last six months of 1812, involved only nineteen men, six of whom were tried *en masse* for losing or destroying their blankets. The others were variously drunk on guard (including 'repeatedly surly for guard'), accused of theft, unsoldierlike conduct and disrespect to an officer, all predictable offences of the time.

Towards the evening of 18 November the weather improved. Dry bivouacs were secured, and fuel and rations distributed. Previously it had been impossible to find anything that would burn, while the sweet acorns that abounded in the oak forests brought little comfort to empty stomachs. A day later the allied forces were safely lodged in villages around Ciudad Rodrigo.

Discipline certainly did break down during the retreat, and all units lost stragglers, but the officers of the 30th were probably among those who bitterly resented Wellington's subsequent circular, *Memorandum to Officers Commanding Divisions and Brigades*. As its title suggests, it was intended only for the higher echelons of command, but some copies reached the colonels of regiments and, through them, the contents became general knowledge and caused widespread resentment. 'The discipline of every army after a long and active campaign becomes in some degree relaxed – but I am concerned here to observe that the army under my command has fallen off in this respect to a greater degree than any army which I have ever served or of which I have ever read. Yet this army has met with no disaster. It has suffered no privations which but trifling attention on the part of the officers could not have prevented, nor has it suffered any hardships except those resulting from the necessity of being exposed to the inclemencies of the weather when they were most severe.

'It must, however, be obvious to every officer that the moment the troops commenced their retreat from the neighbourhood of Burgos on one hand and from Madrid on the other, the officers lost all command over their men. Irregularities and outrages of all descriptions were committed with impunity and losses have been sustained which ought never to have occurred ...

'Generals and field officers must get the captains and subalterns of their regiments to understand and perform the duties required of them, as the only mode by which the discipline and efficiency of the army can be restored and maintained during the next campaign.'

Wellington seems not to have appreciated the failure of the commissariat; there is no supporting evidence for his claim that three days' supply of bread was issued at Salamanca. Indeed, all the personal accounts comment upon the lack of rations. If meat became available, it could not be cooked. According to Lieutenant Grattan, with the tough Connaught Rangers in the third division, 'The rations arrived alive (I mean the meat), as usual after midnight, but no kettles reached us for over an hour after the poor famished beasts had been knocked on the head. Each man obtained his portion of the quivering flesh, but before a fire could be re-lighted, the order for march arrived, and the men received their meat dripping with water, but little, if anything, warmer than when it was delivered over to them by the butcher. The soldiers drenched with wet, greatly fatigued, nearly naked, and more than half asleep, were obliged either to throw away the meat, or put it with their biscuit into their haversacks, which from constant use, without any means of cleaning them, more resembled a beggarman's wallet, than any part of the appointment of a soldier. In a short time, the wet meat completely destroyed the bread, which became perfect paste, and the blood which oozed from the undressed beef, little better than carrion, gave so bad a taste to the bread, that many could not eat it; those who did were in general attacked with violent pains in the bowels, and the want of salt brought on dysentery.'[125]

Furthermore, an army without pay since the beginning of the year had every reason to feel disgruntled. This, at least, was put right when arrears were settled to 24 August. Money in the men's pockets, new uniforms to replace the rags and tatters of the year's campaigning, and a free issue of boots went some way towards raising morale.

Nevertheless, the *Memorandum* continued to rankle. 'Those [junior] officers asked each other, how or in what manner they were to blame for the privations the army endured on the retreat? The answer uniformly was – in no way whatever. The junior officers had nothing to do with it at all. Their business was to keep their men together, and, if possible, to keep up with their men on the march, and this was the most difficult duty they had to perform; for many, very many, of these officers were young lads, badly clothed, with scarcely a shoe or boot to their feet – some, attacked with dysentery, others with ague, and more with a burning fever raging through their system, had scarcely strength left to hobble on in company with their more hardy comrades, the soldiers. Nothing but a high sense of honour could have borne them on; and there were many who would have remained behind, and run all risks as to the manner in which they would be treated as prisoners, were it not for this feeling.'[126] Ensign Kelly, dead from exhaustion, proves the justice of Grattan's sentiments.

The allied forces were now dispersed in cantonments for the winter. The fifth division returned to the area around Lamego, and the 30th spent the next five months in Vila Nova del Rey, a village high above the Douro. They probably shared Hale's impressions.

'This part of Portugal is a rough, mountainous, hill country, and mostly covered with shrubs, bushes, and ragged rocks; and in some places a great quantity of very large stones lying on the surface of the ground; in my opinion, some are as large as wind-ricks or small wheat-ricks that are made in our country. There are some vineyards it is true, and here and there an olive orchard and a few chestnut trees; there are also some hares and rabbits to be seen. The streets in the towns and villages are very narrow, and the roads about the same, and in general so very bad, that we frequently found great difficulty in getting our guns along. It was also dangerous marching in the night, for in some places we might tumble over loose stones that lay in the road, almost as big as our knapsacks; and in other places, tumble headlong into great holes.'[127]

Divisional headquarters were at Lamego, a fine town with an impressive elevation of pilgrimage steps as its principal landmark. The various regiments of the division were quartered in the villages and hamlets which surrounded the town. Vila Nova del Rey appears only on the *carte militaire*, and even today has little distinction. It would be interesting to know whether the men of the 30th shared Hale's opinion that the Portuguese lived 'in a very dirty beastly manner . . . Most of the houses that belong to the lower classes of people are very mean, mostly only a ground floor, and perhaps no other light than what comes in at the door, or at least at a hole made in the upper part of it, but certainly, they have some light that comes in through the roof. In many of these poor habitations the fire is placed in the middle of the house, their seats are some rough-made stools or blocks of wood. Some of the natives, perhaps half-naked, and as yellow with smoke and dirt as a parcel of tawnies, some covered in vermin, in this manner will huddle round a bit of fire, to all appearance as comfortable as that live in a palace.'[128]

Mean habitation, perhaps, but there was regular provision of good supplies. After a campaign when food could fail to materialise three days out of four, the certainty of being fed every day was even more welcome than the payment of arrears. The retreat took its toll, however, as the monthly and casualty returns of the second 30th bear out. The November returns record twelve rank and file as sick present, while thirteen sergeants, five drummers and 326 rank and file were sick absent. By December the situation was a little better. A sergeant and nineteen rank and file were sick present, while ten sergeants, four drummers and 298 rank and file were still sick absent. In addition, nineteen men died in December, including Sergeant Patrick McIlhatton, whose wife back in Ballymena eventually received his credits, presumably with the news of his death. In January there were a further twelve deaths, including another sergeant, Alexander Murdagh, whose wife was with the battalion. It would be interesting to know whether she followed custom and remarried within the battalion but the surviving records do not record such intimate details.

Soon after the 30th reached Vila Nova del Rey orders arrived from Wellington which brought about a drastic reorganisation. On 6 December, by general orders issued from Frenada, Wellington's headquarters, the battalion was ordered to transfer all effective men into four companies. These four effective companies were to form a provisional battalion with four companies of the 2/44th, under the overall command of Lieutenant Colonel Hamilton, and the remainder were to be sent home.

Although this reorganisation probably came as a surprise, it fitted into the policy of organising the army into service (first) and home (second) battalions. Various military misadventures such as the retreat to Corunna and the

Walcheren campaign, as well as the need to protect British interests in India, Canada, the West Indies and elsewhere, had led to the temporary suspension of this policy. For regiments such as the 30th, however, with one battalion in India and the other in the Peninsula and both suffering steady depletion, the situation was problematic. For example, in mid-January 1813, before the re-organisation of the second battalion, the relative strength of the two battalions was fifty-two/thirty-eight sergeants, forty-eight/twenty-six corporals, twenty-one/fourteen drummers, 878/468 privates. These figures demonstrate two uncomfortable facts: the needs of the senior battalion took precedence over the fighting second battalion; and, however energetically the recruiting parties pursued their activities, the depot would never have enough men to supply both battalions. Second battalions kept at home could perform their primary function of preparing men for service in the senior battalion.

By 1812, the Duke of York, Commander-in-Chief, had troops which he could exchange with Wellington's weakest second battalions. Wellington did not submit readily to losing acclimatised troops that had proved their worth on campaign. The provisional battalions he now set up (there were three others), formed upon the best men of the depleted units, were his attempt to preserve the strongest of his proved troops, while reluctantly letting the rest return to England. In February 1813 Wellington wrote to Colonel Torrens, Military Secretary to the Commander-in-Chief: 'I am of opinion from long experience that it is better for the service here to have one soldier or officer, whether of cavalry or infantry, who has served in two campaigns, than it is to have two, or even three who have not. Not only the new soldiers can perform no service, but by filling the hospitals they are a burden to us. For this reason I am unwilling to part with the men whom I have formed into the provisional battalions; and I never will part with them as long as it is left to my discretion.'

The Duke of York, however, was not prepared to tolerate the provisional battalions. 'Experience has shown that a skeleton battalion composed of officers, non-commissioned officers, and a certain foundation of old and experienced soldiers can be reformed for any service in a short time: but if a corps reduced in numbers be broken up by the division of its establishment, such an interruption is occasioned in its interior economy and *esprit de corps*, that its speedy recompletion and reorganization for foreign service is effectually prevented.' Wellington prevaricated by agreeing to send the weakest provisional battalion home. This unit was the fourth, comprising the 30th and 44th but it was April before their departure was sanctioned and in the meantime both battalions undertook the reorganisation required by Wellington. On Christmas Day 1812 the second 30th mustered in their entirety for the last time in Portugal. Seven weeks later the weaker men, six sergeants, three drummers, and sixty-six other ranks, embarked from Lisbon under the command of Captain Bamford. They were accompanied by eleven subalterns and enjoyed a relatively easy journey back to England on the transport *Sovrig*, landing at Portsmouth on 24 February.

The strength of the four companies left in Portugal was thirty-one sergeants, ten drummers, and 438 rank and file. Of these, twenty sergeants, nine drummers, and 189 rank and file were present, fit, at headquarters. The remainder were sick absent, or on command. Also retained were three staff sergeants, Sergeant Major Woods, Armourer Sergeant Artis and Drum Major Vipond, all of whom had served with the battalion since its formation. The officers who remained in Portugal, in addition to Lieutenant Colonel Hamilton, were Captains Hitchen (on command), Chambers and Richardson, Lieutenants White, Mayne, Heaviside (on command), Garvey, Eagar, Freear, Rumley, Harrison and Campbell, and Ensigns Pratt and Lockwood. The quartermaster, Kingsley, had returned to England for recovery of health, but the other staff officers were retained for duty with the new provisional battalion. They were the adjutant, Garland, the paymaster, Wray, and the assistant surgeons, Evans and Clarke. Still in the Peninsula, but doing duty elsewhere, were Captain Malet, on attachment to the Spanish, Captain Craig, serving as Deputy Assistant Adjutant General, Captain Stewart, with the second division, Captain McNabb, commandant at Figueras, with Lieutenant Daniell as his acting quartermaster, Lieutenant Charles, aide-de-camp to Sir Robert Wilson, Lieutenant Hughes, attached to the Portuguese army, and Ensign Travers, attached to the 71st Regiment. He never served with the 30th, since he died whilst still with the 71st.

There is little information on how the two battalions functioned in their new combined role, since they continued to produce separate monthly returns. The 30th, with their staff in Portugal, returned to their headquarters at Vila Nova del Rey. The 44th, however, located their headquarters in England with their senior officers and staff. There are no returns for their four companies in the Peninsula, although the names of those who remained in Portugal can be identified from the muster rolls. The two battalions were long-standing fellow campaigners, however, and seem to have functioned efficiently as a joint unit. Given Hamilton's experience in training units for active service and the thanks he subsequently received, it can also be assumed that the provisional battalion was worked hard to make it ready for the anticipated campaign.

An order dated 10 May and issued from Frenada disappointed these hopes, instructing the battalion to march to Lisbon and embark at the first opportunity. Wellington conveyed his thanks to the commanding officers, and the men for their services, and further thanks were received from General Robinson, who had taken command of the fifth division in March. He particularly remarked upon the state of readiness to which Hamilton had brought the battalion. The four companies then marched to Lisbon and embarked on 18 June. Hamilton, with the staff and the majority of officers and men, travelled on board the transport *Atlas*, while a smaller detachment accompanied Captain Richardson, Lieutenant Freear, and Assistant Surgeon Clarke in the *Mary*. Some officers travelled independently. One of them, Lieutenant Richard Mayne, may have been delayed by a personal matter. His soldier servant, William Sloane, who had served with the battalion since volunteering from the Antrim Militia in 1808, deserted on 16 June, taking with him 130 dollars, the property of Mayne. Although it can only be suspicion, there may have been a woman involved. Many men entered into relationships with Spanish and Portuguese women who could not be brought home. It is possible, therefore, that with 130 dollars in his pocket, Sloane decided upon a life of his choice in Portugal.

All the officers on detached duty were left behind with the departure of the four companies. In addition, Captain John Hitchen and Lieutenant James Eagar were both appointed to the 12th Royal Garrison Battalion, stationed at Lisbon. Hitchen had done sterling work with the 30th, having served with the second battalion since its formation. He had been wounded at Badajoz, thus missing Salamanca, and wounded again at Villamuriel. His background was unusual; before embarking on a military career he had been a wine merchant. The long-serving RSM, David Glass, who had been with the second battalion since its formation, also left at this point, having been commissioned as an ensign into the 4th Royal Veteran Battalion. About sixty men remained in the Peninsula, on command or sick, under the command of Lieutenant Daniell.

The four companies landed at Cowes, Isle of Wight, on 29 August, after a protracted homeward voyage, and three weeks later they were reunited with the rest of the battalion in Jersey, where the six companies were already established in Grouville Barracks. These companies had initially marched to the depot in Hull. They were joined a month later by Major Norris William Bailey, who took command. He had been appointed to the 30th in July 1811, but did not join until April 1813. The six companies and the depot then moved to Berwick, where their stay was brief. On 26 June they left Holy Island for Jersey, arriving at St Aubin on 16 July. A footnote to these movements is to be found in the monthly return for July. Two men had been left sick in Hilsea upon arrival from Portugal and, upon recovery, 'marched to Berwick shortly after the regiment left that quarter. They are now on their way to join the regiment'. A very long detour from Portsmouth, and it must be hoped they completed the second leg of their journey by sea rather than having to march back to Portsmouth.

On Jersey, Bailey remained at headquarters with fifteen officers, five sergeants and fifty-two other ranks. A detachment of two officers, seven sergeants and 122 other ranks was in camp on Saumarez Hills, while smaller detachments of an officer, a sergeant and fourteen other ranks were at Bonnuit and Bouley Bay. In addition, three privates manned the signal stations at Bouley Bay and Virchut. After the four companies joined, there was a greater concentration at headquarters, but detachments remained at Bouley Bay and Bonnuit, as well as manning the signal stations, while another detachment of a sergeant and fourteen other ranks were posted to Rozelle under the command of a lieutenant. All these postings were on the side of Jersey vulnerable to French attack.

When the four companies arrived home, many men were given furlough and some of these were subsequently pensioned off, or dismissed because they had completed their seven years' service. The monthly return for August instances Private Thomas Horner, discharged at Chelsea on account of his blindness, the result of the explosion at Puntales battery in Cadiz when Private William Page was killed. In November Privates Patrick Garner and Daniel McCann were also discharged at Chelsea 'being unfit for service from wounds received in action in the Peninsula.' Others were dismissed as 'worn out', the contemporary description of a soldier past his military best. On the other hand, the recruiting parties had brought in a steady stream of new men, while there were also several arrivals from the militia. The half battalion which arrived in Jersey in July consisted of twenty-nine sergeants and 335 other ranks, which contrasts with the six sergeants and sixty-nine other ranks that sailed from Portugal in February. Some of these additional men came from the depot but most were new to the regiment. In November, the strength of the battalion was thirty-seven sergeants and 580 other ranks.

There were also changes among the officers, although the most significant of these did not directly affect the second battalion. Colonel Lockhart, who was promoted to major general in June, had been with the first battalion since 1803. Lockhart's promotion meant that Major Christopher Maxwell, in India, secured the vacant lieutenant-colonelcy and Brevet Major Charles Vigoureux of the 38th was promoted major in the 30th and was attached to the second battalion. Before joining them, though, he distinguished himself during the Vitoria campaign. He had also been involved in an action at Ladoera in August 1810 between the 13th Light Dragoons and a troop of Portuguese Dragoons on one side and a patrol of French Dragoons, over sixty strong, on the other. 'Major Vigoureux, who was employed on the reconnoitring service, gave Captain White [in command] information of the presence of the enemy, and concerted with him the plan of attack. He requested Captain White to mount him, which he did, on one of the largest horses of the troop, and being a very tall and powerful man, his appearance was most formidable. He charged with Captain White at the head of the Thirteenth, and rode with uplifted sabre straight at the French commanding officer who was leading: on their meeting, that officer, instead of defending himself, dropped his sword to the salute, and turning it, presented the hilt to Major Vigoureux.'[129]

Promoted out of the regiment were Captain Bamford (6th West India Regiment) and Brevet Major Spawforth (96th Foot). A third loss was Captain Malet, who had been attached to the Spanish army since 1810. He was killed at the passage of the Bidassoa (Bridge of Vera) on 31 August, only the second officer from the battalion to be killed in action.[130] A fourth departure was the adjutant, Garland, who was promoted into the 73rd Foot for meritorious conduct. His place was taken by Lieutenant Matthias Andrews.

Another development which affected the battalion was the appointment of colour sergeants. This rank had been instituted by the Prince Regent on 6 July as a reward for outstanding service by non-commissioned officers. Its implementation in the second battalion was delayed until Hamilton's return from the Peninsula; and all of the original colour sergeants had distinguished themselves in Spain and Portugal. Their reward for meritorious conduct, as well as the new rank, was 2/4d a day, against the ordinary sergeant's pay of 1/10d.

Hamilton's ability to create an efficient unit in a short space of time is evident in the inspection report of General Hatton in November 1813. He reported of the non-commissioned officers: 'The greater part are very young. They perform their duties with promptitude and energy and attend to the best of their abilities the discipline of the Regiment ... The privates with the exception of about 100 much too young for any service, are a good body of men with the appearance of health and cleanliness, and of a [illeg] standard ... they are for the time well drilled, attentive, and well behaved ... Their interior oeconomy is well-regulated, and the interior arrangements of companies duly attended to the conduct of the men in quarters, on duty and soldierlike ... One hundred and ten have joined since the last inspection. Every attention appears to have been paid in perfecting them in their duty. From the general appearance they are an acquisition to the Corps, with the exception of ten, who from slight make, and indifferent health, do not promise to improve.' There was similar approval for the performance of field exercises and movements which 'were performed with precision, and the formations made with correctness, and a proper degree of celerity.'

General Don, in overall command, added the following in his letter to the Adjutant General: 'In addition to the remarks contained in the Major General's reports I take the liberty of making the following observations . . . 2nd Battalion 30th Regiment This Battalion is commanded by Lieut Colonel Hamilton, who pays particular attention to it. 372 men of the Battalion now present are fit for duty in the field, besides which number there are 75 rank & file recruiting, and 58 rank & file on furlough considered fit for duty in the field.' This implicit recommendation would soon bring the battalion back into active service.

Chapter 12

Flanders

While Wellington was harassing the French in the Peninsula, defeating them at Vitoria, and then driving them over the Pyrenees, Napoleon's fortunes elsewhere were also on the turn. 1812 had witnessed the Russian adventure and the disastrous retreat from Moscow. Although at the beginning of 1813 Napoleon staged a remarkable military come-back, his defeat at Leipzig in October led to a conflagration of revolt. The Dutch, under French control since 1795, rose up in November. To help them in their bid for freedom, a force under Sir Thomas Graham was sent to Holland.

Graham had an army of 6,000 men, later augmented to 9,000. It comprised mainly second battalions, or groups of four companies from some first battalions, which led the Duke of York to apologise for sending him such a weak force. Furthermore, apart from three Guards battalions who had fought under Graham at Barossa and 2/81st, veterans of the Corunna retreat, only the 2/30th and their long-time comrades, the 2/44th, had spent a protracted period in the Peninsula. Overall it was not a force to inspire confidence, which may explain why it achieved so little.

The campaign started at the beginning of 1814, before the 30th arrived in Holland. Graham landed at South Beveland and, putting his army into entrenched cantonments between Antwerp and Bergen-op-Zoom, made contact with a Prussian force under von Bülow which was threatening Antwerp, where most of the French forces were concentrated under the command of Lazare Carnot, Minister of War from the heady days of the revolutionary Republic. On 10 January Graham advanced to join the Prussians. Three days later there was a combined Anglo-Prussian attack on Merxem. The French were driven back to Antwerp, although with considerable loss on both sides. On 25 January von Bülow took Bois le Duc before investing Antwerp, although he focused on the French fleet rather than the fortifications of the city. There was another joint attack on the French outposts on 1 February which met with mixed fortunes. Then, a few days later, von Bülow was summoned to join the main Prussian army as it concentrated against Napoleon himself, and the British were left to continue the campaign alone. By this point, though, the French held only the strongholds of Antwerp, Ypres, Conde, Maubeuge and

Bergen-op-Zoom. The last of these became Graham's immediate objective. The place had excellent defences, sixteen bastions, three gates and twenty-six sally-points. Furthermore, there were water-filled dykes and ditches to make any advance difficult, but Graham was determined, particularly as he was running out of time, having been informed that his force would soon be withdrawn for service in North America.

The 30th, meanwhile, prepared to join Graham from Jersey. Despite the imminence of active service, however, they were still weakened by a draft for India which sailed on 1 January 1814. A day later the rest of the battalion embarked in the transports *Union*, *Saragossa* and *Earl of Cathcart*. The first two ships were destined for the Low Countries, Hamilton and the headquarters wing sailing in the *Union*, Vigoureux and the left wing in the *Saragossa*. Aboard the *Earl of Cathcart* was the depot detachment. All three ships reached Portsmouth on 19 January. The depot marched for Winchester under the command of Lieutenant Nicholson, who was accompanied by Ensigns Tincombe and Drake, the quartermaster, Kingsley, eleven sergeants, and 151 other ranks. Of these, sixteen were lads and boys, and twenty were invalids for discharge. Nominally on the strength of the depot were another 204 men variously on furlough, in the Peninsula, recruiting or prisoners of war.

The transports carrying the 30th and the 81st to join Graham's force sailed from Spithead on 22 January, accompanied by HMS *Rinaldo*. For the headquarters wing it proved a perilous voyage. The winds were contrary and all the ships in the convoy except the *Union* had anchored under the Downs by 28 January. The master of the *Union*, apparently drunk, sailed on to Dover where, despite being anchored, the ship was caught in a ferocious gale which lasted two days. The anchors were expected to give and men of the local garrison regiment stood by to attempt a rescue. In local churches prayers were offered for the safety of those on board. The wind finally changed direction to blow offshore on the evening of 29 January, and the following morning a pilot was able to board the ship. Under his direction the *Union* was brought into Ramsgate harbour, but was so unseaworthy that the men on board were transferred to the *Sophia*. They then rejoined the convoy and reached Helvoet Sluys on 10 February.

The *Saragossa*, meanwhile, had become detached from the convoy at the very beginning of the voyage and did not reach Helvoet Sluys until 14 February, after the men had spent forty-two days on board, harbour-bound. Reunited at Willemstad, the two wings of the battalion marched to Loenhout, arriving on 2 March to join Graham's force.

While the main part of the battalion was struggling against gales to reach Flanders, an even worse fate awaited the party of men who sailed for England from Portugal at the same time. The *Queen*, a government hired transport, tonnage unknown, commanded by Captain Joseph Carr, left Lisbon just after Christmas 1813. She sailed in convoy with eight other transports, all protected by the 36-gun frigate, *Melpomene*. On board the *Queen*, according to newspaper reports of the time, were 325 men, sixty-three women, sixty-eight children and a crew of twenty-one. Among the men were ten French prisoners of war, while the rest were, for the most part, invalids returning from the Peninsula. The whole detachment was commanded by Lieutenant Robert Daniell, who had with him thirty-two men of the 30th who had been left in Portugal on detached duties, as well as his wife and five children.

The *Queen* reached Falmouth on 7 January after a rough homeward voyage, although a relatively fast one. Arriving to strong easterly winds and very unsettled weather, the ship anchored in Carrick Roads, which were exposed to easterly gales, while the anchorage itself was open to southerly winds. In this potentially dangerous position, about three hundred fathoms off Trefusis Point, the *Queen* remained at single port anchor with only thirty-five fathoms of cable, considerably less than local knowledge deemed advisable. In this situation the ship was caught up in the gales, described in the press as hurricanes, which swept across southern England.

On Thursday 13 January, in the early hours of the morning, violent south-easterly winds whipped up tremendous seas, while the whole area was blanketed in a snowstorm. The anchor began to drag but the lookout failed to notice and by the time Captain Carr was told of the danger it was too late to save the ship. The starboard anchor was *catted* with no cable attached, and while the necessary cable was being brought up the port anchor cable broke. This seems to have happened at about six o'clock, leaving the vessel adrift with the wind blowing her onto Trefusis Point.

By this time nearly all the men were on deck but the women and children were still below. There followed 'A scene of indescribable confusion and horror . . . the sea breaking in an awful manner over the ship, whilst the endeavours of those who were below to get on deck, and the alarming shrieks of the women and children, whom neither force nor entreaty could render quiet, augmented the distress.'[131] Huge seas swept over the ship and poured through the hatchways. Attempts to fire a gun to alert potential rescuers failed because the guns had been swamped. As the ship listed, Carr ordered the masts to be cut away but as they were cut the foremost mast fell aft, crushing or knocking overboard a great number of people. Also, as the masts fell, the ship lurched violently, the guns broke loose, the bulwarks smashed, and the hull collapsed, drowning or crushing to death the unfortunate passengers still trapped below. The ship now began to break up and within twenty minutes was little more than a half-submerged hulk.

Some of the troops had already managed to clamber ashore and these first survivors ran to the village of Flushing, where they raised the alarm. By the time help was at hand, however, there were bodies everywhere. 'The return of day presented a shocking spectacle ... dead bodies of men, women and children, many of them mangled, several of them naked and others scarcely half-dressed, strewed on the shore.'[132]

The final tally of survivors was eighty-nine soldiers, including all but five of the 30th, nine women, a child, and four prisoners of war, as well as all but two of the crew. Most of the crew were able to swim ashore, while some passengers escaped in boats, and others, by clinging to casks and pieces of wreckage. Yet more were saved by a Mr Fox of Falmouth, and Mr John Plomer, a farmer from Trefusis. The former came with his servants and clerks to help in the rescue and opened his house in Trefusis to the survivors, while the latter, with his labourers, risked his life to save survivors from the rocks. Many of the local villagers provided blankets and beds, which helped to preserve those who had reached the shore, although some still died of shock and hypothermia.

In contrast to these humanitarian efforts there were also reports of looting. Several soldiers were later tried by court martial for robbing the dead, while some wretches were intent upon plunder, and carried off several boxes and packages of considerable value. The newspapers reported the case of a sergeant seen breaking open trunks and chests until stopped by Mr Plomer, who threatened to arrest him. None of the miscreants seem to have belonged to the 30th, however.

In the sad aftermath of the disaster, 250 bodies were finally recovered. Buried in a common grave in Penrhyn churchyard were the five men, ten women and nine children who had been washed ashore at that point on the coast. A far greater number were found at Flushing, 136 being buried in a mass grave at Mylor, where a memorial tablet was erected by the villagers: 'To the memory of the warriors, women and children who, returning from the coast of Spain, unhappily perished in the wreck of the *Queen*, transport, on Trefusis Point, January 14th 1814. This stone is erected as a testimony of regret by the inhabitants of this parish.'

As for Lieutenant Daniell, in command, he managed to scramble ashore 'though much bruised' but he lost his wife and children. He erected his own memorial to his family. 'In memory of Catherine, wife of Lieut. Robert Daniell, 30th Regiment; also their children, viz Margaret, Eleanor, William, Robert & Edward Alexander, who unhappily perished in the wreck of the *Queen*,

Transport, on the awful morning of the 14th Jan 1814. Leaving an unfortunate husband & father to lament their loss to the end of his existence.'

Lieutenant Colonel Hamilton later wrote to the War Office on Daniell's behalf, and received a reply, signed by Lord Palmerston, Secretary of State for War, and dated 8th February, 1816. 'I have the honour to acknowledge receipt of your letter of the 27th November last and to acquaint you that the Prince Regent has been graciously pleased to approve the grant to Lieutenant Robert Daniels [sic] of the Regiment under your command of a Royal Bounty of £10 per annum from the 15th February 1814 in consideration of the loss of all his property and family by shipwreck the preceding day on the passage from Lisbon to England. I am to add that the Lieutenant should apply to the Right Honourable the Pay Master General for the payment of the said Allowance which may now be to due to him.' Daniell later remarried, but it is unlikely that even the royal bounty compensated him for the loss of his family.

Of the five men from the 30th who drowned, the most puzzling casualty is Private George Rawdon, a labourer from Lincoln who had enlisted in 1807 while still a boy along with his cousin James (who died in Portugal in 1811). According to all the regimental records, George was lost in the wreck of the *Queen*, yet in 1848, when the GSM was belatedly awarded to survivors of the Peninsular War, George Rawdon applied for and received a GSM with a bar for Badajoz. Did his family make the application *in memoriam* (which was against the rules), or, having safely reached the shore after the shipwreck, did he decide that he had had enough of soldiering and simply disappear?

To return to the second battalion in Flanders, once again there was an imbalance of junior officers to senior. The three field officers were Hamilton, in command, and two majors, Vigoureux and Bailey, the latter arriving by mail packet on 27 March, after what was probably a speedier and more comfortable crossing of the North Sea. According to the return of 25 February, there was only one captain present, Chambers, who commanded the light company, along with fifteen lieutenants and five ensigns. Captain Machell was in Holland, but once again was on detached staff duties, although he returned to the battalion in April. The confusion which existed between the two battalions by this time can be demonstrated by noting that Chambers and Machell should both have been with the first battalion in India, where seven captains properly belonging to the second battalion were doing duty. Of the remaining four who should have been with the junior battalion, McNabb was on leave, James Fullerton was superintendent officer of recruiting in Derby, Henry Craig was still deputy Assistant Adjutant General in Portugal, and Stewart was with the depot, recovering from wounds he had received at the siege of Pamplona.

A particular problem was the absence of a quartermaster. Kingsley had been ordered to replace the recently appointed Nicholas Wilson, who was with the first battalion in India but properly belonged to the second battalion. Wilson himself had replaced Arthur Poyntz but he had subsequently died in India. Kingsley, however, sailed out before this news arrived. To complicate matters further, the second battalion was expecting not Wilson but Quartermaster Sergeant John Williamson as Kingsley's replacement. Williamson did eventually join the battalion from the Peninsula but the confusion was symptomatic of communication difficulties when the two battalions were so far apart.

The February return indicates the strength of the battalion as twenty-nine officers, forty-six sergeants, ten drummers, a drum major, and 745 rank and file. Of these last, 208 were on command or still on furlough, reducing the number in the ranks present at headquarters to little over 500, half the 'paper' strength of a battalion.

At this point Edward Nevil Macready (son and brother of actors) joined the second battalion as a volunteer. He subsequently kept a journal of his experiences, so that the Flanders campaign and the later events which culminated in the Battle of Waterloo can be amplified by his lively account. His initial impression of Holland was not encouraging. 'It froze and snowed very hard in our faces and as the road ran along the dyke of the river, the wind was cruelly piercing.'[133] Macready had hoped to join the 69th where one of the majors was a connection of his mother but General Graham sent him to the 30th with the words: 'No, I would rather you joined the Thirtieth; I know Colonel Hamilton well [from Malta, Egypt and Cadiz] and I am certain he will take care of you.' Macready then 'hired a guide, and after a walk of six miles through the snow, with trembling steps I entered the house or rather hovel of my future commander. He was a veteran officer who had served under Abercrombie and Nelson in his younger days, and had shared in the late campaigns in Portugal and Spain. He welcomed me most kindly, asked me to dinner, assigned me a quarter in a windowless room, already occupied by a dozen officers, and on the 28th February 1814 I was placed on the strength of the light company'[134], as was customary for volunteers.

The next morning the 30th marched to a village near Brasschaat where their task was to build a battery which could sweep the road between Breda and Antwerp. The position was reached at 6.00 a.m., and immediately half the battalion was engaged in breaking up the frozen soil with pickaxes and spades. This was to be the men's employment for the next three weeks, twenty-four hours on duty, twenty-four hours off, in appalling conditions. 'The snow was at this time deep on the ground, and continued so till late in April. This with the thick fogs, frequent sleet-showers, and chilling breezes, rendered our working-day very harassing. The villages we occupied had been abandoned by their inhabitants, and destroyed by the Prussians. Not an article of furniture nor a pane of glass was to be found in them – they were mere sheds – and when we awoke in the morning we were petrified with cold, and frequently covered with snow.' Macready ascribed his survival to 'the accomplishments of smoking and gin-drinking', which he quickly mastered.

Nor was night duty any more pleasant. 'The cold was intense. Our shed was open on two sides, and the enemy not near enough to make the duty interesting. [Lieutenant John] Rumley and I walked round and round the sentries, examining every loiterer we could catch, and even sent off some who were particularly unintelligible as spies to head-quarters. We talked of everything, did everything that could divert us, but could not kill the time. We often awoke shivering with cold, and expecting it to be morning called to the sentry for the hour and he has answered "Past ten." Our first sleep being over, our boiled eggs and potatoes all eaten, and our patience exhausted, there we would sit over our expiring fire and damn the climate till day-break.'[135]

These harsh conditions may have been a shock to a newcomer like Macready, but no doubt the Peninsular veterans, of whom there were many in the light company (distinguished by their darkened complexions and tendency to swear in Portuguese), listened to the complaints of their inexperienced comrades with amused contempt.

While the 30th were toiling at the battery, the long-awaited assault on Bergen-op-Zoom ended in disaster. The first news which reached the battalion was encouraging. The place had been stormed. Since the next stage in the plan was an attack on Fort Lillo the following night, involving the 30th, there was keen anticipation of action. The order actually arrived to march to Kalmthout, preparatory to the attack, but was almost immediately countermanded. Far from being a success, Bergen had ended in disaster. Graham's plan was feasible, but chaotically implemented. 'Over three thousand men were thrown into the fortress with little effort; and yet these, though they fought with uncommon courage and tenacity, were vanquished by a heterogeneous garrison of twenty-seven hundred. This remarkable result was due chiefly to three causes: first, to Colonel Henry's squandering of his troops in a real attack, which according to Graham's plan should only have been a feint; secondly, to Skerrett's blunder in leading his men along the northern instead of the southern ramparts, and thus failing to join his force to that of Carleton and Cooke; thirdly, and chiefly, to the helpless imbecility of Colonel Muller [of the Royals], who, instead of opening communications with Skerrett on one side and with Cooke on the other, so as to throw his reserve in with decisive effect, kept the Royals useless and inactive at the Water-gate for six hours, and then without any sufficient warrant surrendered them as prisoners.'[136]

The disgruntled men of the 30th, even as they realised that they had been marched thirty miles for no good purpose, learnt that 2,000 men had been lost, dead, wounded or prisoners. No wonder the veterans growled, 'Why weren't we sent for?' After all, they had succeeded at Badajoz.

They were now relieved from battery-building, and moved into quarters in Putte while Graham devised an alternative strategy. Batteries had already been erected on the Scheldt to cut Antwerp off from Bergen, and the battalion was required to occupy the gun positions twice a week. In front of them were the riflemen of the 95th, and beyond lay the river, a mile wide because the French had opened the sluices and flooded the countryside. In this setting, the forts and houses were islands connected by roads and dykes.

The first day and night passed quietly enough apart from some skirmishing between the advanced posts from which the riflemen emerged the winners. The following morning the 74-gun *L'Anversoise* was spotted with her stern chasers pointed at the battery. This did not initially distract anyone from his breakfast but suddenly the enemy fired a broadside which demolished the house where Macready was enjoying an egg. He was merely showered with bricks and dust, but the unfortunate woman who supplied the eggs was cut in two by round shot. At once the whole battalion retreated to the shelter of the dykes, where mud and ice slushed around them as the ship's guns kept up their attack. The British guns returned the fire, but it took a battery of Congreve rockets which arrived at eleven o'clock to persuade the *L'Anversoise* to cut her cables and retire.

The 30th lost their drum major, Thomas Vipond, a Manchester cotton spinner who had served with the battalion since augmentation. His widow received not only his arrears of pay but also extra contributions, a not unusual gesture of battalion generosity. According to the casualty returns for 24 March Vipond had both legs carried away by a cannon ball and died of his wounds the same day. A similar fate befell Private Joseph Gabbett and both men were buried that night at Putte with full military honours. Four other men were wounded. Hamilton had the luckiest escape, however. Taking his breakfast near the colours, he narrowly missed serious injury when a round shot passed close to him. Under his legs, which were drawn up, so amazed witnesses claimed.

The battery where the 30th had taken their casualties remained a target for French ships which were trying to force a passage from Antwerp to Bergen. When these efforts were finally abandoned, however, the British force was reduced first to a wing and then to a party of 100 men under a captain and two subalterns. On one such occasion Macready was under the command of Chambers with ten men when they had to drive off an attack on the riflemen who shared the position. Chambers acquitted himself with his usual competence, while inspiring the others to do likewise. This, however, seems to have been the only real action experienced by the battalion and soon afterwards they were withdrawn to Brasschaat, where the officers were packed a dozen to a room, while the men were similarly crammed into barns and stables. No wonder when the village was also occupied by the 2/52nd, 2/73rd, and 2/81st.

Elsewhere the situation was improving. News that Paris had been taken reached Graham on 4 April and as a result an armistice was concluded between Graham and Carnot, followed by the withdrawal of all but a French skeleton force from Flanders. The 30th were then able to move into the suburbs of Antwerp, arriving on 1 May. The next day they moved on to Malines. Four days later they were placed under the command of the Prince of Orange, popularly known as 'Slender Billy'.

For Graham it had been a campaign strong on strategy and weak in execution but he was rewarded for his services over twenty years (starting as a volunteer in Toulon) with the title of Lord Lynedoch and a pension of £2,000 a year. For the men he commanded, tedium, inadequate and overcrowded quarters, and bitter weather (warmed by swigs of Hollands) seem to have been the most notable features of the campaign.

Like Graham, the 30th had a history in the wars which went back to Toulon, where Napoleon first established his military reputation. Now, with the Emperor's abdication, they must have felt that the fighting was over and a long period of peace stretched ahead, taking for them the form of a somewhat unfocused existence in Flanders as they moved randomly from place to place. Not that the officers missed the opportunity to enjoy themselves. After three weeks in Malines, where Macready recorded luxuriating in the comfort of a real bed, the battalion moved to Brussels. Here the officers enjoyed socialising in a city set upon pleasure. Macready certainly regretted the order which took them to Ath, and then on to Tournai, a march which was enlivened by an encounter with the French 33^{ieme} de la ligne. What started as banter in Spanish between the veterans of the two corps quickly threatened to become a fight with swords and bayonets and the officers only parted the contending parties with difficulty. A friendlier contest took place on the same march between the grenadier and light companies, the latter having been detained in Ath to act as a guard of honour for the Grand Duchess of Oldenburg, sister of Czar Alexander I. Macready recalled how 'as we marched left in front, the grenadiers swore they would run over us. The challenge was no sooner given than the lights shouted "double quick", and away we went – a musket on my shoulder and sixty rounds in my cartouche-box. We stopped at Lenza, about 7 miles from Ath, when only three bacon bolters (and these were overgrown light bobs) were visible. I was in high favour with the greasy rogues for keeping up, and received three or four pats on the shoulders which nearly shook out the little wind I had left, accompanied with the assurance I "was of the right stuff".'[137] As a volunteer, Macready marched with the men, although he messed with the officers.

During the month spent in Tournai the officers celebrated the second anniversary of Salamanca in style. They also made the acquaintance of Kielmansegge's Hanoverians, with whom they would stand shoulder to shoulder at Waterloo. At the beginning of August, however, they were on the move again, marching back to Antwerp by way of Avelghem, Oudenarde, Ghent and St Nicholas.

At Locheren, on the way to Ghent, the Peninsular veterans spotted a sergeant of the 44th travelling in a cart in the opposite direction. His journey was quickly interrupted. 'As soon as his button was recognised, a scream of congratulation was heard through the column, and every canteen was unstrapped in an instant. He was dragged from his seat and shoved from rank to rank, every fellow stopping his mouth with his canteen and shouting, "Good luck to the old boys, and how are they?" till the worthy non-commissioned officer was replaced in his seat speechless and motionless. This is certainly an instance of killing kindness, but as an affectionate remembrance of auld lang syne even the most starched disciplinarian must forgive it. For my part I felt a thrill of joy and pride at this rough exhibition of feeling in our fellows.'[138]

In Antwerp the battalion came under the command of Major General Colin Halkett, another Peninsular veteran. Halkett's task was to resolve a dispute with the French over shipping and stores, and no doubt the presence of the 30th and other British battalions strengthened his bargaining position, although it was the Congress of Vienna which finally settled matters.

A cause of contention at this time was the general filth of the city. Such, at least, is Macready's explanation for Halkett's sudden departure. 'General Halkett, who was much beloved, was ordered to give up the command to General Mackenzie, in consequence of his disagreement with the civil authorities. They would not keep the town clean, and I believe he sent fatigue parties, who collected the filth and deposited it at their doors. Whatever was the real cause he was ordered away, and the officers of the garrison resolved to give him a dinner. We sat down 300 red jackets, English and German, neither nation remarkable for temperance. All were soon drunk, and wine having got the better of our manners, we attacked the head of the mayor with champagne corks.'[139] Macready reckoned that seven hundred bottles of champagne were drunk on this occasion.

One of Halkett's last duties before leaving was to inspect the battalion. Hamilton was praised as 'an old and zealous officer whose exertions had been unremitting for the instruct [sic] of his Corps, and is acquainted and steady in the performance of the movements presented by His Majesty's Regulations.' As for the officers, those 'present at the inspection appear in every respect fit for service. Attention has been paid to the instruction of the Subaltern Officers, and they have acquired a good knowledge of His Majesty's Regulations. The Captains and officers in command of companies are acquainted with the internal oeconomy, and competent to the charge of their companies. The officers appear to understand their duty and are zealous in the discharge of it. Unanimity prevails and the commanding officer states that he receives the necessary support of his officers.' The non-commissioned officers were described as 'attentive and intelligent, perform their duty with zeal and support a proper authority.' Furthermore, since there had been few complaints from the local inhabitants, Halkett considered 'the Battalion to be regular and orderly in Quarters.' For a second battalion which had been so seriously weakened in the Peninsula, and then quickly brought up to strength with recruits, the observation that they were 'a fine body of men with a healthy and clean appearance, and they are well-drilled and conducted' was praise of a high order.

The description of Hamilton as an old officer is somewhat surprising. He was definitely old in service but even after twenty-seven years with the 30th he was still only forty, and would remain with the regiment for another fourteen years. There seems little doubt, though, that his exertions on behalf of his regiment had been unremitting. He had succeeded a very effective lieutenant colonel in William Minet, and had, if anything, surpassed his predecessor's high standards.

A particularly enjoyable occasion which also preceded Halkett's departure was a subscription ball organised by the First Military Society of the Garrison of Antwerp, of which Halkett was patron. Two officers of the 30th, Lieutenant Colonel Bailey and Elkington, the surgeon, were among the five directors. The invitation, sent to the commanding officers of regiments, announced: 'It being decided to give a Ball and Supper, on the 31st instant [January], to such of the Ladies and Gentlemen of the Town, friends of the Officers subscribing, as attend the Thursday's Ball at the Sodalite; you are requested to send in the names of those officers of the Corps under your command, who may be desirous of attending, and the number of Tickets required by each, together with the names of the Ladies and Gentlemen purposed to be introduced. It being intended to give a handsome Fete upon this occasion, the price of Tickets cannot be ascertained until the amount of expense shall be known.'

Each officer who brought guests to this 'handsome Fete' had to pay an appropriate proportion of the total expense, which promised to be considerable. Eighteen months later the 30th organised a similar occasion in Limerick which left the officers seriously out of pocket, so this ball and supper may have caused similar consternation when the time came to pay. Certainly, Macready, on his ensign's pay (having been commissioned on 9 September), did not attend.

The strength of the battalion in February 1815 was thirty-eight sergeants and 569 other ranks. Some discharged invalids had returned to England under the command of Captain Chambers but in October 1814 Captain Ryan arrived with a detachment of five sergeants and 210 rank and file. He had with him Captain Sinclair, from India, Lieutenants Nicholson and Daniell, and Ensigns Rogers and Drake. There were also twenty-two women and children. Nicholson was a particular friend of Chambers and, like Chambers, having come to Europe from India for recovery of health promptly joined the second battalion, to which he did not properly belong. Also like Chambers, he had suffered a period of estrangement from the other officers of the first battalion, so it is possible that he imitated his friend in joining the more congenial second battalion. As for Chambers himself, while in England he secured promotion to major and was now on his way to join the battalion in Flanders.

Two other officers were absent, Machell serving as town major in Antwerp and Neville once more with the engineering department. Major Vigoureux had been transferred to the first battalion, but he remained with the second throughout the Waterloo campaign.

Meanwhile the depot, stationed at Chelmsford and commanded by Captain Stewart, comprised fifteen sergeants, and 141 other ranks, although some of these were on command, including twenty-nine still in Portugal, or recruiting. The rest were the men identified by General Hatton in Jersey as too young or too weak for active service, or not recovered from wounds received in the Peninsula. Some of these, however, formed the last detachment to travel to Flanders before the Waterloo campaign.

Among those at the depot were the four officers and eighty men who had survived eight years as prisoners of war after the loss of the *Jenny*. They had been released in a general exchange after Napoleon's abdication. The officers, Captains Roberts and Hawker, Lieutenant Howard, and Ensign Sullivan, all received a step in rank, while the men were given a sovereign apiece. For Major Hawker this homecoming was not without its problems. He was soon being dunned for unpaid bills, probably pre-dating the shipwreck. Roberts purchased a lieutenant-colonelcy in De Rolls Regiment in December 1814, which opened the way for Chambers to purchase the vacant majority, but Howard, Hawker and Sullivan remained with the regiment for some years to come. Among the other returned prisoners of war were thirty-one of the thirty-five men who had been captured in the Peninsula.

Several new officers had come into the battalion during 1814 and subsequently served in Flanders. Captain Arthur Gore, from half-pay, replaced the recently retired Captain Richardson, while Captain Matthew Ryan, also from half-pay, exchanged with Captain Thomas Williamson. Going in the opposite direction were Ensign Madden, who was promoted into the 89th Foot, and Lieutenant White, into the 14th Foot. Further reinforcements arrived in April 1815, when Lieutenant Tincombe, accompanied by Ensigns James and Bullen, arrived with two drummers and twenty-nine rank and file.

Hamilton had definite ideas about the officers he wished to serve with the battalion. In October 1814 Captain McNabb, who was home from Portugal on leave, received a summons to join which he obeyed in December. Majors Bailey and Vigoureux had been ordered to sail to India but Hamilton was able to retain their services. One other officer he particularly requested was Captain Henry Craig but instead of joining he exchanged into the 102nd with James Finucane, who came to Flanders in Craig's place. Not without difficulty; he was in France when Napoleon returned from Elba. After the border with Belgium was closed he had to find a sea route, while being careful to avoid arrest. He finally took ship at Bordeaux.

In the return for 25 May 1815, the last before Quatre Bras and Waterloo, the strength of the battalion present was given as three majors, five captains, twenty-one lieutenants, seven ensigns, thirty-six sergeants, fourteen drummers and 591 rank and file. (Hamilton was omitted because he was on leave.) Compared with other units in Wellington's 'infamous army' they were a seasoned battalion. Of the forty-three officers who later received the Waterloo medal, twenty-six had seen active service in the Peninsula with the 30th, while others had done so with their previous regiments. As for the men, three quarters of the subsequent casualties were owed Peninsular prize money. Most of the men had survived the rigours of Graham's brief Flanders campaign. In other words, 'the men who carried the regiment through the awful day at Waterloo had served in it for at least twelve months, and most of them had served under Hamilton in the Peninsula. The non-commissioned officers, although still young men, were veteran soldiers.'[140] An inspection return of October 1815 (April 1815 is lost) makes the point. None of the men, from private to sergeant, had served less than two years, including the four who were under eighteen. Similarly, none of the sergeants had served less than five years, although half of them were under thirty. Macready remembered his light company: 'They were the prettiest company I ever looked at. "Ashes to ashes; dust to dust" – poor fellows! A few years have left little of this gallant band, but recollection so dear and deep, that time alone renders them more indelible.'[141]

Chapter 13
The Road to Waterloo

In the early 19th century the victories of the army were celebrated but those who achieved them were viewed with suspicion as a folk memory of Cromwell's major generals lingered on. Furthermore, peacetime armies were expensive luxuries. As a result, the government was always quick to reduce the strength of the army at the first opportunity. Napoleon's abdication gave Lord Liverpool's administration the excuse to reduce numbers. By the end of 1814 twenty-four second battalions had been disbanded, the men discharged, the officers placed on half-pay. The 2/30th were initially spared this fate because a military presence was required in Flanders but by the beginning of 1815 their days must have seemed numbered. And then came the news of Napoleon's escape from Elba.

Particularly pleasing for the battalion was the general order which placed them in Halkett's brigade, as part of Alten's third division of the Anglo-Dutch army, under the overall command of the Duke of Wellington. Macready waited eagerly to be ordered forward as preparations for the anticipated campaign were expedited. 'We had inlying and outlying pickets, fatigue parties loading stores for the frontiers, guards at every turn, guns and tumbrels rattling through the streets, and all the fuss and confusion of a commencing campaign.'[142] On the 8th April the long-awaited order arrived. The route took them through Malines and Vilvorde, and they reached Brussels on the 10th, staying for three weeks before moving on to Hal where they joined the rest of the brigade, which consisted of the 33rd, the 2/69th, and the 2/73rd. Although all three of these units had been part of Graham's Flanders force, none of them had served in the Peninsula, which made the veterans of the 30th feel their superiority.

The events of the brief campaign which culminated at Waterloo are sufficiently well known not to require a detailed repetition. The following account, therefore, focuses on the actions of the 30th. Inevitably, some of the moments for which Quatre Bras and Waterloo are best remembered receive only a passing reference but as Wellington himself remarked: when comparing a battle to a ball, some might recall 'all the little events by which the great result is the battle lost or won, but no individual can recollect the order in which, or the exact moment at which, they occurred ...'

On 20 May the battalion, along with the 33rd, moved to Soignies where 'His Royal Highness of Orange continued to annoy us and increase the sick list by his detestable drills, and Lieutenant Colonel Bailey, who commanded the battalions composed of the light companies of our brigade, exposed us to the weather, and himself to our ridicule, on every opportunity. He clubbed a battalion sooner, and laughed thereat more heartily, than any officer I ever saw.'[143] Macready, it seems, had a distaste for drill, and resented those who inflicted it.

In the wider world, meanwhile, matters were becoming critical. The border between France and Belgium was closed on 12 June, creating a virtual embargo on information, and increasing the expectation of action. A general order issued two days later brought about a concentration of all divisions at their respective headquarters, and a general movement to the left. So rapid and unforeseen was the French advance that Bailey, on leave in Brussels, was left behind when the allied army moved in response and only caught up with the battalion on 17 June.

On 15 June Macready and some other officers heard a rumour that the French had crossed the border. General Halkett himself rode up and ordered Macready, as a light infantry officer, to parade the men in ten minutes. The three light company officers, Rumley, Pratt, and Macready himself, had the men in position at the appointed time and were then ordered to do picket duty at Naast, a village about two leagues from Soignies. By evening news of the French advance had been confirmed, although the Prussians to the east were thought to be Napoleon's immediate objective.

The next morning, Macready was sent to make contact with the rest of the battalion, and fetch some necessaries. When he reached Soignies, however, he found the place deserted, all the battalions having left at 2.00 a.m. for Braine-le-Comte. Rumley and Pratt, meanwhile, had learnt that the French had crossed the Sambre and reached Charleroi, from which position they could threaten the retreating Prussians. The light company officers now found themselves in a quandary. If they obeyed orders and remained where they were they would miss the action, yet to disobey orders and leave their post might be considered a gross dereliction of duty. In the end 'the hopes of young ambition' outweighed the risk to their commissions and they decided to follow the rest of the battalion to Braine-le-Comte, only to discover that the whole division had advanced to Nivelles. Continuing the pursuit, they quickly overtook the baggage at the rear of the division. They could hear the sound of cannon fire, from Ligny, where the French and Prussians were fully engaged. With difficulty they forced their way through Nivelles, which was full of non-combatants, including the regimental wives who 'came up, blessed us, and kissed their husbands – many for the last time. These moments agitate the hearts even of soldiers' wives, the most insensible and callous creatures in existence.'[144]

At Nivelles they learnt that the rest of the division was little more than an hour ahead. They were also able to collect their stores, from which they gave every man an allowance of spirits. 'Thus reinforced, our boys started double quick, for the firing increased. It was now past three o'clock. We passed the division of Guards. Rumley had some words with a staff officer about crossing their line of march, and our fellows began to laugh and jeer them. They had some cause, for I never saw such a number of men knocked up in my life. "Shall I carry your honour on my pack?" said one of ours to a Grenadier Guardsman, as he was sitting down. "Haven't you some gruel for the young gentlemen?" shouted another, and continued, "It's a cruel shame to send gentlemen's sons on such business – you see, they don't like it – they've had quite enough at Bergy-my-Zoom." '[145]

This chaffing nearly led to fisticuffs but the light company officers managed to extricate their men and continue the march, still at double quick time, across the fields. Now it was the turn of the light company to experience exhaustion. They had already marched about eighteen miles and as they ran the last six all of them felt the effort. Some even fell out, 'black in the face and senseless. Many of them reeled while replying to our encouragements, "Never fear, sir, I'll keep up." We cut their pack straps, took off their stocks, and left them gasping. At length we had a confused view of the field, with our troops and the enemy firing away, under their sulphurous canopy – clouds of birds were flying and squealing above the smoke. We loosened our ammunition, and pushed on for it. Hedges, streams, and ditches, were passed like thought.'[146]

The light company now found themselves in contact with men from the Nassau Usingen contingent, whom the French had just driven out of the wood of Bossu. They learnt from a staff officer that the rest of the 30th had arrived about fifteen minutes earlier, and were on the opposite side of the wood. To join them they would have to pass through or round the wood, which was firmly in French hands. 'This we were convinced of by numerous round shot coming from it, one of which slashed dirt and mud over the whole company. "Close your files, and hould up your heads, my lads," roared an old campaigner, named Terry O'Neil. One feels a thrill at these moments. We soon reached Quatre Bras, where the Brunswickers and some of Picton's people were in square; and on turning the end of the wood, found ourselves in the hurly-burly of the battle. The roaring of great guns and musquetry, the bursting of shells, and shouts of combatants, raised an infernal and indescribable din – while the galloping of horses, the mingled crowds of wounded and fugitives, the volume of smoke, and flashing of fire, struck out a scene which accorded admirably with the music.'[147] Thus the light company joined the action.

The rest of the battalion had commenced their movements much earlier, while the light company was still at Naast. As the battalion surgeon, J.G. Elkington, recorded in his journal: 'At 2 a.m. we commenced our march on the road to Braine-le-Comte, on the Brussels road, and from then took the road to Nivelles, where we arrived about 1 p.m., and proceeded to a small stream near Hautain le Val, where the men were ordered to cook, but before they had half finished they were ordered forward. There was heavy firing in our front, shortly after the men were put into double quick to keep up with the Artillery that were much wanted. Shortly after 4 p.m. we reached the North of the Wood of Bossu, the men had now been nearly fourteen hours marching.'[148]

Napoleon's strategy aimed to drive apart the Allied and Prussian armies, sending them back on their divergent supply lines. While he dealt with the Prussians at Ligny, about five miles to the east, Ney was to hold Wellington's forces at Quatre Bras. Once the Prussians had been defeated, Napoleon would then deal with the Anglo-Dutch army. Even if a second victory were not achieved, the retreating Prussians would move north-east, taking them away from Wellington, who would retire towards the coast, thus exposing Brussels to an unopposed French advance.

Quatre Bras itself had been held since 15 June by 4,500 Nassau infantry and a battery of six guns under the command of Prince Bernhard of Saxe-Weimar, who had taken the initiative to occupy the crossroads when he heard that the French had crossed the Sambre. They had arrived just after a detachment of Polish lancers had found the ground unoccupied, which may explain why they were able to take unchallenged possession of this crucial crossroads.

Salient points of the battlefield were the wood of Bossu, and the two farms of Gemioncourt and Piermont. All three were initially occupied by allied troops. Pressing forward, the French under Marshal Ney took possession of the wood of Delhutte, the only other feature of the landscape which offered any cover. Ney's position was highly favourable. He had fifty thousand men at his disposal, although only a third of them, with ten cartridges apiece, were near enough to start the action. This should have been sufficient to sweep away the Nassauers and why Ney hesitated so long can only be surmised. He had experienced Wellington's tactics in the Peninsula and may have suspected that the small force he could see was part of a larger, hidden army. Nonetheless, the situation was critical and if the Nassauers had been overwhelmed a very different sequence of events would have developed. Under great pressure they held their position from eleven o'clock when Ney finally attacked until mid-afternoon when the first reinforcements (Picton's fifth division) arrived. Gemioncourt

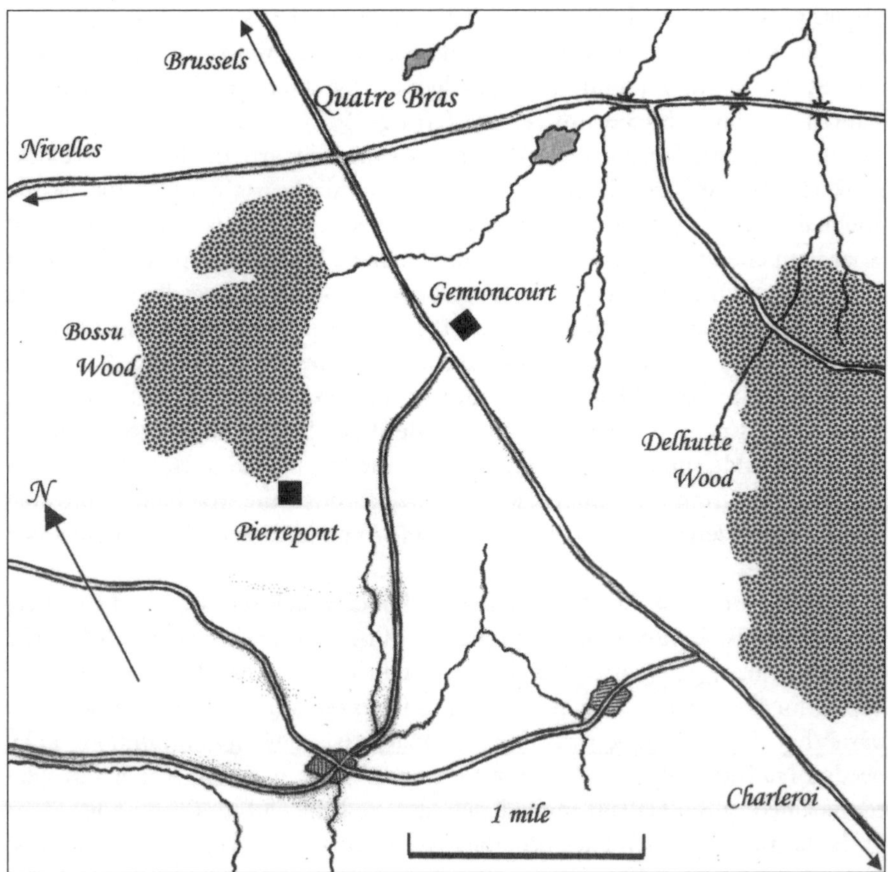

Quatre Bras, topological details

was lost and Bossu Wood was under fierce attack, despite the presence of the Brunswick corps, which had followed hard on the heels of the fifth division. Although stiffened by Picton's two British brigades, the Brunswickers began to give ground after the death of their duke.

Despite Wellington's presence on the battlefield, the situation for the allies might have proved catastrophic had Count d'Erlon's corps not been drawn off towards Ligny and then brought back towards Quatre Bras as Napoleon and Ney sent contradictory orders which marched the corps out of both actions. For two hours Picton's division, the Brunswickers, and the remnants of the Nassauers, now close to collapse, fought a desperate defensive action. All the units involved suffered heavy losses as they were forced into square by cavalry charges and came under heavy artillery fire. Macready observed the effects.

'As we passed a spot where the 44th, our old chums, had suffered considerably, the poor wounded fellows raised themselves up and welcomed us with faint shouts, "Push on, old Thirtieth – pay 'em off for the poor 44th. You're much wanted, my boys. Success to ye, my darlings." '[149]

The first two brigades of Alten's division had arrived by five o'clock. Halkett's British brigade took up a position to the right of Picton, while Kielmansegge's Hanoverians moved to the left. Halkett's own account of what happened next is contained in the letter he wrote to Captain Siborne in 1837 and, even allowing for the lapse of time, seems to broadly suggest the situation which confronted him. 'I was the only General Officer in the Division in a field betwixt Quatre Bras and Nivelles. Unexpectedly, I received an order to move on towards Quatre Bras, and on clearing the wood that ran down towards the Enemy's left I received an order from Sir Thomas Picton to bring the left shoulder up of the leading brigade, the 5th British of the 3rd Division ... My order from Sir Thomas was to move through the wood and if possible to fall on the left of the French Army, and further to act as I thought most advantageous.'[150]

Halkett's first task was to clear Bossu Wood, which required him to wheel the marching columns into line, so that the 30th were on the extreme left of the position, closest to Quatre Bras. Before the brigade reached the wood another appeal for help arrived. An aide-de-camp from General Pack arrived with the news that Pack's brigade was running dangerously low on ammunition. They needed Halkett's support if they were to hold their position, which was vital to the allied cause. Halkett immediately directed the 69th to form under cover of the farmhouse which Pack occupied (Piermont) and to act on Pack's orders. Halkett then returned his attention to the situation in Bossu Wood where the Brunswickers were in retreat. He made contact with their commanding officer, Olfermann, and was able to steady them and bring them up under cover of a ditch which ran nearly parallel with the French line. He then remained in support of the Brunswickers, awaiting further orders.

After the 69th had been detached, the three remaining battalions, with cover provided by a flank battalion under Major Vigoureux, deployed and advanced. (Normally this flank battalion would have been made up of the light companies, as at Salamanca, but as the light company of the 30th had still to reach the battlefield their place was taken by number nine company, under Lieutenant Heaviside.) Calculations of manpower and distance, as well as the testimony of the battalion's officers, lead to the conclusion that the 33rd and 73rd actually entered the wood, while the 30th, to the left of them and about two hundred yards further back, advanced in echelon across open ground. In the wood the Brunswickers were still falling back (as Halkett noted), their retreat accelerated by the final collapse of the Nassauers. Thus Halkett satisfied himself with steadying the Brunswickers, instead of giving support to Picton's division. He also sent a warning to Pack, based on his own reconnaissance, that a French cavalry attack was imminent, and suggested that the 42nd and 44th, under Pack's command, as well as the detached 69th, should form square. These three units lay to the east of the Charleroi road. The 30th, apparently still in column, were two hundred yards in the rear, to the west of the road. To the right of them, emerging from the wood, were the 33rd and 73rd.

What happened next is somewhat problematic. There seems little doubt that all four of Halkett's British battalions were ordered to form square, either by Halkett himself or by Picton, and that the order was then countermanded by the Prince of Orange, either because he resented a challenge to his authority, or because he was unaware of the imminent cavalry attack and reasoned that both Picton's division and the Brunswickers needed the support of line fire. Hamilton, with a degree of independence which was typical of him, proceeded to form square while the 69th remained in line, ready to be rolled up by Kellerman's approaching cuirassiers and Piré's lancers. Meanwhile, the 73rd retired towards the wood and the 33rd formed square as the horsemen swept towards them.

In a letter to Siborne, Captain Brooke Pigot explained that Major Henry Lindsay made two companies of the 69th halt and 'face to right about, in open Column, and commence firing upon the Cuirassiers. But for this we should have got into square, as it was those Companies [that] were really cut down. Poor man, to the day of his death he regretted having done so, but at the time he did it for the best.'[151] The 69th suffered the inevitable catastrophe as they belatedly struggled to form square. Unable to resist such a tempting target, the cuirassiers charged them down, causing the battalion about 150 casualties and the loss of the king's colour.

Meanwhile, the 33rd, suffering artillery fire as well as the threat of cavalry, and no doubt appalled by the fate of the 69th, retreated expeditiously and in no good order to the shelter of the wood. As for the 73rd, although apologists would question it, Sergeant Morris's account suggests an undisciplined retreat. 'The ground, for a considerable distance, being covered with rye, and of an extraordinary height ... prevented us from seeing much of the enemy; but, though we could not see them, they were observing us. We continued to advance, the glittering of the tops of our bayonets guided towards us a large body of the enemy's cuirassiers, who, coming so unexpectedly upon us, threw us in the utmost confusion. Having no time to form a square, we were compelled to retire, or rather to run, to the wood through which we had advanced'.[152]

The 30th now demonstrated the advantage of experience and thorough training. Thanks to their Peninsular veterans and Hamilton's ability to bring unseasoned men up to scratch, they remained in square and beat off the French attack. 'The steadiness of the 2/30th is demonstrated by their behaviour 16/6/15 at Quatre Bras when the spectacle of the 2/69th being ridden down and cut up by the French cavalry so unnerved the 33rd and 2/73rd that they broke and ran for the cover of the Bois de Bossu, whereas the Thirtieth quite calmly formed square and dealt with the situation most effectively and without fuss. Surely this reflected the fact that, alone in Halkett's Brigade, they had served in Spain.'[153] The exposed flank battalion rallied to their square and together they were able to repulse the French with two volleys. Furthermore, there is reported evidence from Colonel Morrice of the 69th that the steady fire of the 30th saved his battalion from even heavier losses. Morrice told Captain Rudyard R.A. that he believed the Guards were responsible but there were no Guards in action at this point, although their approach was expected. The 30th were the only unit that could have provided this supporting fire but Morrice's death at Waterloo meant his initial impression remained uncorrected.

A letter to Siborne from Lieutenant Colonel Harty, a captain in the 33rd in 1815, describes events from the perspective of the flank battalion, which 'consisted of the Light Companies of the Brigade under the command of Lieutenant-Colonel Vigoureux of the 30th Regiment, and we were under him, acting in the vicinity of, and in connection with, his own Regiment commanded by Lieutenant-Colonel Hamilton, so much so that we (the Battalion) formed square with that Corps when charged by French Lancers, on which occasion the firm conduct of the Square called forth the unqualified approbation of the late Sir Thomas Picton, who was an eye-witness, and galloped up; and, calling for the commanding officer, told Colonel Hamilton that he would report their gallant conduct to the Duke.'[154] In another version, 'Picton, who had watched the repulse of the cavalry with delight from his own side of the Charleroi road, galloped over as soon as he could and called out, "Who commands here?" and upon Colonel Hamilton answering, "It is the 30th," Picton said with one of his customary oaths, "That is not my question." Finally he said he would make the highest report to the Duke of the commanding officer <u>and</u> the regiment. Owing to his death at Waterloo this report was not made.'[155]

Halkett's brigade now manoeuvred to the right in response to a renewed French attack. Fortunately, the 30th were forewarned by Hamilton, who had ridden forward to assess the danger, but at the cost of being wounded by a French sharpshooter hidden near Gemioncourt. Elkington recorded how he met Hamilton, wounded in the leg. Hamilton remained in the saddle while the surgeon dressed the wound. Hamilton was unwilling to leave the field but the wound was serious enough to need further medical attention. Something of his character is brought out by his remarks to the light company, whom he now passed as he rode off for further treatment. Recollecting a severe wound he had received in his right leg at Toulon twenty years before, he told them, 'They have tickled me again, and now one leg cannot laugh at the other.' Further inspection of the wound, however, revealed its seriousness, and he was lucky not to lose his leg. Twice a tourniquet was applied, preparatory for amputation, and twice the surgeon was called elsewhere.

Elkington had been a close observer of the action thus far. 'The Regiment passed Quatre Bras and proceeded some way down the Namur road and entered the cornfields. It was certainly five o'clock now. Soon after there was an order to receive Cavalry, and I fell back and stood on the Namur road with my Hospital Sergeant, and Bat Horse, having my instruments and medicines. I had the Regiment in view, knowing it more particularly by the Adjutant, Andrews, having a white horse.'[156]

Upon receiving Hamilton's warning the battalion again formed square and were now joined by the light company at the run just as two sides of the square were attacked by cuirassiers and lancers. Once more the attackers were driven off by a defensive volley so tremendous that their assailants were thrown into total confusion. They fled beyond Gemioncourt, pursued by the light bobs who dashed out in pursuit until they were brought to a halt by their French equivalent, a line of tirailleurs. Picton was quick to congratulate the battalion again, calling them noble fellows, but when this comment provoked loud cheers he immediately damned them for making a noise like devils. There seem to have been congratulations on all sides at this point, but it was probably a cheer directed at him personally which provoked the old hero's blasphemy.

As more allied reinforcements arrived, Halkett was able to extend his light troops as far as Gemioncourt, while the Guards finally drove the French out of Bossu Wood. With the light fading, the French withdrew in good order and the 30th were finally able to advance. 'We now descended a slope towards our right in the direction of a deep ravine, across which the Royal Scots and ourselves drove a heavy body of infantry after a severe fire. A retrograde movement was perceptible along their whole line, and it was performed in beautiful style; their skirmishers and columns kept their alignment and distance as if on parade ... Major Chambers of ours was pushing on with the two companies towards a house in our front, and I joined with as many of the light infantry as I could collect. We rushed into the courtyard, but were repulsed; he reformed us in the orchards, directed the men how to attack, and it was carried in an instant, by battering open the doors and ramming muskets into the windows. We found 140 wounded and some excellent beer in the house.'[157]

At ten o'clock the battalion finally piled arms and settled down to sleep, protected by the ravine to the front of them. According to Macready, the presence of dead and dying all around was ignored.

The battalion suffered four officers wounded, a sergeant and four men killed, two sergeants and twenty-seven men wounded, and five men missing. Of these last, two returned the next morning. These relatively light casualties reflect the steadiness displayed against cavalry attack. Also they received no direct artillery fire. Two of the wounded officers, Lieutenants Harrison and Roe 2 (there being two John Roes in the battalion) were able to stay with the battalion. Hamilton's wound disabled him for the rest of the campaign. The most seriously wounded casualty, however, was Lieutenant Lockwood of the grenadier company. He joined the light company in pursuit of the French cavalry and 'dropped with a shot in his head as he was speaking to [Macready]. He was a noble fellow, and as he was led by the regiment, his last words were an exhortation to his company to do their duty.'[158] Elkington continues the story. 'I also received Lieutenant Lockwood with a wound of a musket ball in the front sinus. I sent him to the farm at Quatre Bras, whilst I saw the Artillery on my right open fire on the advance of the Cavalry, up the Charleroi road. Shortly after the repulse of the Cavalry I was ordered up to the front to some of the wounded of the Regiment. I attempted to pass down the high road but my horse would not pass the numerous dead men and horses of the French that lay in the road, and I entered the fields on my left and dressed some men at a farm-house. I then returned to Quatre Bras and extracted the ball (as I thought) from Lieutenant Lockwood's frontal bone, but three weeks after a portion was found in the sinus and the trephine was used to extract it.'[159]

Writing to his brother in mid-July Lieutenant Tincombe was not hopeful of Lockwood's recovery. 'Our loss this day was Lt-Col Hamilton and Lt Lockwood wounded, the latter very dangerously, very little hopes of his recovery being entertained. He was shot in the forehead and part of the ball was found under the bone.' Nevertheless, Lockwood recovered and survived for another forty-four years, to the age of sixty-seven, serving as Captain of Invalids at Kilmainham Hospital. As a result of his wound, he had a silver plate in his skull, engraved with the words 'bomb proof'. This he kept covered with a black silk band. As a further, ironic note, remembering how Lockwood saved the young nun at Badajoz, there is a story that at the point where he had been given up for dead a nun noticed that he was still alive and urged the surgeons to continue treating him.

Quatre Bras has been overshadowed by Waterloo, yet for the 30th it was an opportunity to demonstrate that steadiness and determination which they had learnt in the Peninsula, steadiness and gallantry which won them the commendations of the Prince of Orange, and Generals Alten, Halkett and Kielmansegge. In a wider context, 'Nothing could exceed the coolness and intrepidity of the troops engaged at Quatre-Bras, where a small body of men, assembled in haste, and exposed for a considerable time, without either artillery or cavalry, displayed the most surprising bravery, in resisting the impetuous attacks of a superior army.'[160] The battle may have been desperate and improvisational, with no choice of position and little room for manoeuvre but the position was held and Napoleon's grand strategy suffered its first check. The Prussians, although defeated at Ligny, were not retreating along their supply lines and an Anglo-Dutch force still barred the road to Brussels.

Chapter 14
Into the Storm

After the turmoil of the action at Quatre Bras, only the light company was disturbed during the night, by rumour of a French attack which came to nothing. Otherwise the battalion bivouacked undisturbed until daybreak when the order came to stand to arms. According to Elkington, the wounded were now sent to the rear, while the brigade remained in front of Piermont until about two o'clock, expecting the French to renew their attack after the indecisive closure of the previous day's action. Indeed, it is still open to conjecture why Napoleon let the morning pass without some aggressive action against the battered but undefeated Anglo-Dutch army. Once Wellington learnt that the Prussians were retreating in good order on Wavre, however, he withdrew his own forces towards Brussels.

James Shaw Kennedy, Deputy Assistant Quartermaster General attached to the third division, recorded many years later his view of the situation. 'The division was severely engaged on the 16th, and was in a position of great delicacy to be withdrawn from on the 17th, as it occupied Piermont and part of the great road towards Brye, and consequently became exposed to the advance of the army under Bonaparte from the field of Ligny. I was ordered to reconnoitre the country from the position of the division, near Piermont, to the Dyle, and to fix upon its line of retreat, and upon the point at which it should pass the Dyle, so as to leave the passage at Genappe free for the other portions of the army. The division retired upon the line as fixed upon in this reconnaissance. Marching by Bezy, it passed the Dyle by the bridge of Wais-le-Hutte, and, by a cross march, joined the great road leading from Genappe to Waterloo. This operation was a very delicate one, – that of withdrawing six thousand men from before so great a force, in open day, under Napoleon, with which force they were in open contact, and having during their retreat to cross a considerable river. The operation was, however, perfectly successful.'[161]

The retreat of the division began without the French noticing, and thereafter the three brigades which made up the division (Halkett's British, Ompteda's King's German Legion, and Kielmansegge's Hanoverian) preserved an echelon formation which enabled them each in turn to form up on favourable ground while the other two brigades retired past them. Thus they were in a constant state of readiness should the French attack. Once they reached the Genappe-Waterloo road, however, they were able to march in regular order.

'Every one now said that the heights of Genappe would be the scene of action, and this report acquired credit from our halting near a village for a considerable time; but this delay was merely occasioned by the passage of troops on the high road, as we were destined to be the rear division of the army. As we re-commenced our march, at about three or four o'clock, a most furious storm occurred. The rain came down in torrents, and in a moment we were drenched to the skin. The thunder rolled over our heads, and the lightning glistened among the bayonets. The enemy's artillery, pushing on closer every minute, mingled its roar with this hubbub of the elements.'[162] Macready's description of the ferocity of the storm is substantiated by Elkington. 'During the retreat we encountered a most severe thunderstorm with heavy rain, and perhaps I may say that a more severe night was never experienced by the British Army, who were lying out in cornfields up to their knees in mud, Colonel Vigoreaux [sic] and myself lay together, having my hospital panniers to windward our only shelter.'[163] Elkington also recorded the arrival of Major Bailey from Brussels. He had been searching for both the battalion and his baggage without success until he met up with Elkington. Still in mufti, he exchanged his civilian coat for Elkington's red one.

The retreat was not without its problems. 'As we descended a steep declivity our men rolled head over heels from top to bottom, and the road in the low ground was knee-deep for a quarter of a mile. About half-past five we came on the Charleroi chaussee as the covering division. Our Jägers and the Brunswicks were busy on the flanks, the cannonade was brisk, and report said that the enemy had captured two of our guns. At this time the 7th Hussars charged some Red Lancers near Genappe, and were sadly beaten. The Life Guards then came up and fully revenged them. I saw a regiment of Heavy Dragoons deploy to support the Household if necessary; they had on their red cloaks, and looked like giants.'[164] And all the while the rain continued to pour down.

Finally, the 30th moved beyond Genappe and took the ground which had previously been held by the Guards, who had been moved to the right to occupy Hougoumont and its enclosures. This position, reached about 8.00 p.m., was an uncomfortable one, exposed to the rain, with corn and mud as the only bedding. Here they spent the miserable night described by Elkington, initially harassed by some light French artillery, although these were later silenced by the counter-fire of Cleeve's nine-pounders.

Nor had the day been without its casualties. According to Macready, the battalion's total loss was one killed, three wounded and eight missing. The casualty lists tell a slightly different story, however. Three men are returned as killed on the 17th: Francis Glinn, a weaver from Longford, John O'Brien, a labourer from Tipperary, and George Smith, a nailer from Dudley. Two of these, of course, could be men who were originally posted missing.

As the wet night progressed, hunger became a torment. The Guards in their haste had left behind biscuits and firewood and Rumley, Pratt and Macready were able to share 'a fowl, which we roasted, or rather warmed on a ram-rod, and a third of this animal, with an onion at Genappe, some beer at the captured farmhouse, and a couple of biscuits, was all that exhilarated my inward man on June 16th, 17th and 18th. We lay down on the mud around our fires, and the rain continued pouring on us all night. In the morning we were almost petrified with cold, many could not stand, and some were quite stupefied. Poor Pratt, who had fainted the day before at Genappe, set off (at our earnest entreaty, and promise to call him when things looked serious) towards Mount St Jean, and shortly after we found him at our fire unconscious of where he had been or what he was about. I had occasion to pull open the buttons of my cloths 9 o'clock on the night of the 17th and was not able to rebutton them until dawn this morning. It was a miserable night – however, motion brought us about in some degree, and we began to gape and stroll about the field, and the rain having ceased, our soldiers were busily employed in firing off and cleaning their pieces in readiness for action.'[165]

Elkington also observed the invigorating effect of movement. 'Early in the morning [the weather] began to clear, the men and the officers were actually benumbed, being so saturated with the wet. After a little running about, wringing their blankets, and the issue of some spirits, the circulation returned, and by 10 o'clock the muskets were all in good order.'[166]

Macready summed up the feelings of the Anglo-Dutch forces as they awaited the onset of battle. 'About half past ten o'clock the enemy began moving his forces, and displayed strong columns of infantry and cavalry opposite every part of our position ... Thus, at near eleven o'clock, stood the contending armies. Our battle might amount to more than 60,000 men, and their's most probably exceeded 80,000. We (I mean the multitude) were not aware that Blücher could afford us any assistance, as we heard that he was completely beaten and hotly pursued; but no British soldier could dread the result when Wellington commanded. Our poor fellows looked wretchedly, but the joke and laugh was bandied between them, heartily and thoughtlessly as in their happiest hours.

'About eleven o'clock some rations and spirits came up; the latter was immediately served out to the men, but I dared not drink on my empty stomach. I had just stuck a ramrod thro' a noble slice of bull beef, and was fixing it on the fire, when an aide de camp galloped up, and roared out, "Stand to your arms". We were in line in an instant.

'Considerable movements were perceptible among the enemy's columns, and from the number of mounted officers riding to and from one group of horsemen, I should think Napoleon was there, issuing his decrees. Our artillery arrived full gallop, and the guns were disposed on the most favourable ground in front of their respective divisions. The regiments formed column and marched a little to the rear, under cover of the brow of the hill; our company and the 73rd Grenadiers were ordered as coverers to Cleve's and Lloyd's brigades of guns. The men were in great measure covered by the crest of the hill, but the whole French army, with the exception of the reserve, was exposed to our artillery.

'There was a pause for some minutes, and I imagined there were few of the many thousands assembled that did not experience a sort of chill, a rising sensation in their breasts. It was indeed a spirit-stirring sight – the chivalry of two mighty nations in grand and deadly rivalry.'[167]

Waterloo has been summed up as 'a ferocious battle, an experience both harrowing and thrilling for the men who survived it: the total defeat of an empire, inflicted in a single Sunday afternoon on a field of battle only two miles long and two-thirds of a mile across.'[168] Although this is inevitably a simplification, Waterloo is indeed a remarkably small battlefield to accommodate the estimated 135,000 men who fought there. The three focal points of the allied position were Hougoumont, La Haie Sainte, and Papelotte. If the French were to be victorious, they needed to take at least one of these, either to turn the allies or to break through the centre. As always when Wellington took up a defensive position, his forces were placed as far as possible on a reverse slope. Apart from the troops holding Hougoumont and La Haie Sainte, only Saxe-Weimar's Nassauers, well forward and nearest to Papelotte, Bijlandt's Dutch-Belgian brigade, and the battalion of the 95th Rifles who held the knoll and the sandpit near La Haie Sainte were in exposed positions. Bijlandt's brigade, however, would seem to have been pulled back either just before or just after the commencement of the battle.

To the east of Wellington's army were the Prussians at Wavre. Wellington already had a promise of support from Blücher but although Wavre was only ten miles away the roads were unpaved and difficult to traverse in wet weather, particularly for artillery. For that reason, and some poor staff work which led to units crossing each other's paths, the Prussians could not be expected until late in the day. The best that Wellington could hope for was to hold his position until the Prussians arrived to tip the numerical balance. Napoleon, however,

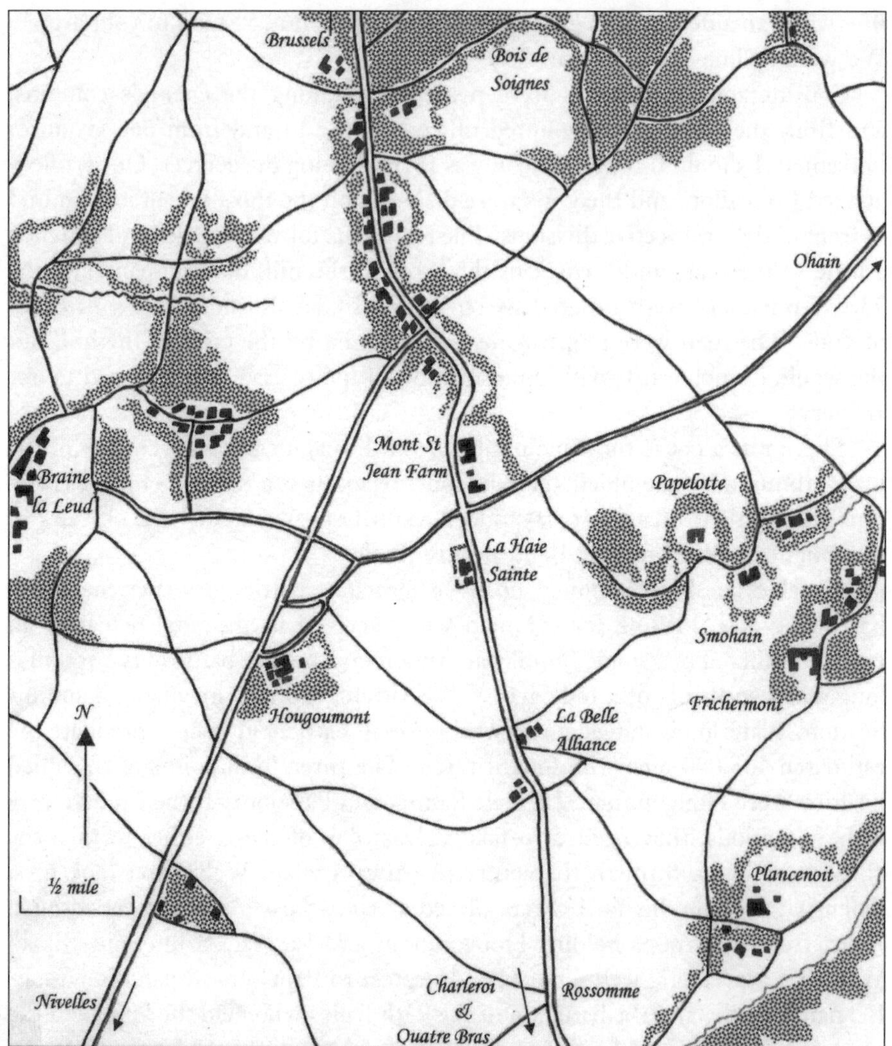

The Battlefield of Waterloo, shown with surrounding area

confidently anticipated sweeping his opponents from the field while Marshal Grouchy dealt with the Prussians and then marching in triumph to Brussels.

For Alten's third division, the crucial feature of Wellington's chosen ground was La Haie Sainte. The farmhouse itself, and the attached orchard, was held by the 2nd light battalion of the King's German Legion, with the 1st light battalion in support. To the right were the 5th and 8th line battalions of the Legion, under Colonel Ompteda, while further right still were Kielmansegge's

Hanoverians. On the extreme right was Halkett's British brigade. The 30th and 73rd, united as a single corps, lay in front and to the left of the similarly combined 33rd and 69th. Behind them, a little to the left, was a reserve of Nassau troops.

The amalgamation of the four battalions into two larger units which in the Peninsula would have suggested depleted numbers probably had a different cause at Waterloo. Although exact figures for the morning of the battle are difficult to establish, neither the 30th nor the 73rd had taken heavy casualties during the preceding two days. That the exact positioning of the brigade caused some concern is brought out by Shaw Kennedy's notes. He describes how the Prince of Orange and General Alten discussed this issue for some time. When

Shaw Kennedy's Sketch Map of the Position of the Third Division at Waterloo

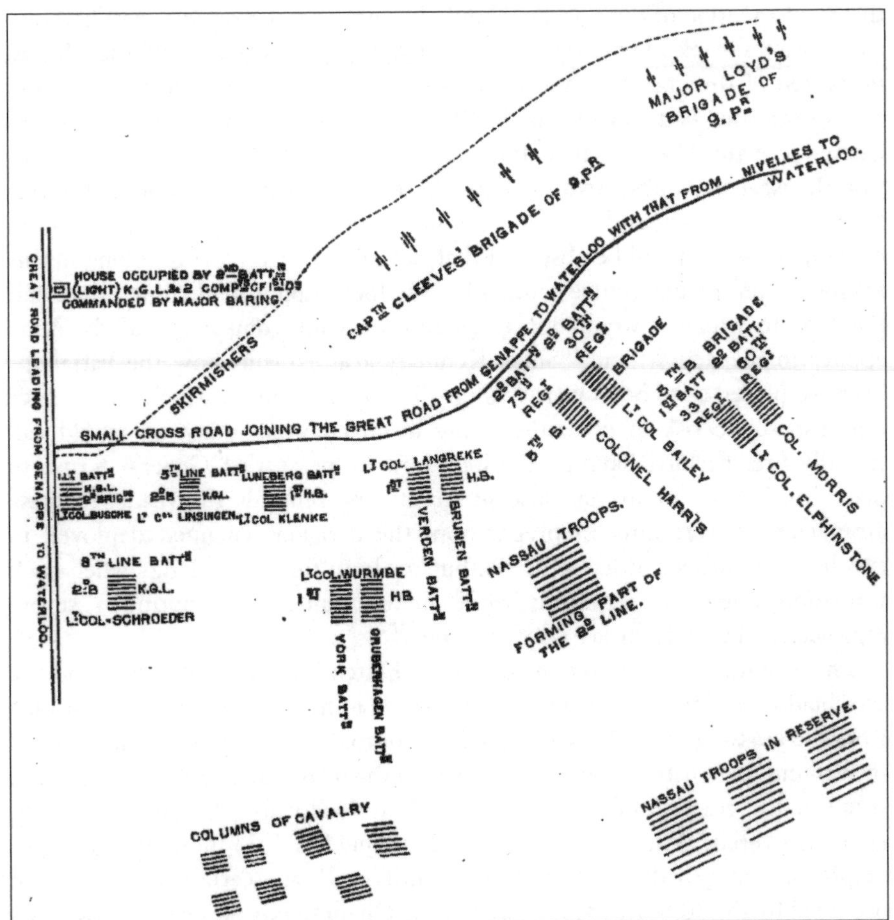

Wellington was consulted, he merely instructed them to form in the usual way. The problem remained, however, that 'in the usual way' they would be exposed to both artillery and cavalry.

'I asked General Alten if he would allow me to form the division; to this he at once and unqualifiedly assented; upon which I instantly left him, and proceeded with the formation ... The principles and considerations which guided me in making the formation were as follows:- The French cavalry had, on the 16th, proved itself very formidable at Quatre Bras in its attacks upon the third division. That cavalry, in immensely augmented numbers, was now forming opposite to the division, and the ground between them and us presented no natural obstacle whatever. It was at the same time evident, from the way in which the French guns were taking up their ground, that the division would be exposed to a severe artillery fire. It was, therefore, of the highest importance that the formation of the division should be such that its passing from line into a formation for resisting cavalry should be as rapid as possible; and that the re-formation of the line should also be made rapidly. To carry these views into effect the strong battalions formed each an oblong on the two centre companies [these were the Hanoverian battalions] and, when the battalions were weak [the British companies], two were joined, the right-hand battalion of the two forming left in front, and the left-hand battalion right in front, each in column of companies ... It will be observed that, when a battalion forms oblong in this manner upon the two centre companies, the formation is made in *less* than half the time in which it would form square on a flank company, and the same applies to the deployment.' Shaw Kennedy also explains how the battalions 'were so placed as to be as nearly as possible in exchequer', which would have diminished the risk of casualties being taken by what today we would call friendly fire. Finally, having described how he persuaded General Kruse to place his Nassau troops in close proximity, he reminds the reader: 'These arrangements were only in preparation; the division remained deployed in two lines, its proper order of battle, but ready to form in oblongs when such formation might be required; while merely under the continued severe cannonade, the division lay down in line.'[169]

The ground in the middle of the Anglo-Dutch line was undulating and the area held by the third division rose fifty yards in five hundred yards westward from the crossing of the Wavre and Charleroi roads. Contemporary sketches of the ground demonstrate the degree to which the lie of the land has changed as a result of the erection of the Lion Mound, as Macready's friend, John Pratt, later discovered. When he revisited the battlefield in 1833 he found the topography so changed that he could not identify with any certainty the position occupied by the 30th. In 1815, however, the Ohain to Nivelles road was sunken on the left of the third division's position but was at ground level within four hundred yards. The cover from artillery fire was generally good just south of the road, and where the 30th and 73rd were placed the ground rose to a crest just in front of them. If they were required to hold this rise at any point, however, they would find themselves exposed to enemy artillery fire, particularly if the French managed to bring their guns closer to La Haie Sainte.

Allied artillery covered the position of the two battalions. To the right and a hundred yards to the front was Lloyd's battalion. Major Rudyard, a captain in 1815, wrote to Siborne twenty years later that 'Early on the morning of the 18th our position was taken up on the very crest of the slope in front of our Division; the Regiments were the 69th and 33rd in our rear; the grain, I can't say whether wheat or barley, it was above our head, but soon trodden down. From this position we never moved one instant until the Battle closed.'[170] Rudyard's comments, like Morris's in relation to Quatre Bras, remind us that corn crops grew very much higher in the early nineteenth century than they do today.

To the left of Lloyd's battery and also well forward were Cleeve's guns of the King's German Legion. In such a confined battle area, artillery was a powerful and deadly weapon; so crucial, in fact, that the French attack was delayed until Napoleon was certain his guns could manoeuvre on drying ground.

As for the strength of the 30th on the morning of the battle, a certain amount of speculation is required but a figure of just under 500 (which allows for some losses to sickness and exhaustion) is probably about right. This compares almost exactly with the strength of the battalion in the May monthly return and seems to take no note of the casualties of the 16th and 17th but, on the other hand, the officers who had joined from detached duties since that date would have brought their soldier servants with them. In the other half of Shaw Kennedy's oblong, the 73rd seem to have had about 450 rank and file.

With Hamilton incapacitated by his wound, the battalion was under the command of Major Bailey. Chambers commanded the left flank while Vigoureux commanded a skirmishing line of the light companies of the brigade, reinforced in the case of the 30th (and possibly the other battalions) by the grenadiers. These lay some way to the front of the guns, linking up with the Guards, and extending from La Haie Sainte to Hougoumont. As for the command of companies, the subsequently produced Waterloo Roll causes some confusion by naming the notional commanders, many of whom were in India, and also leaving several officers unattached. It would seem, though, that all but one of the companies had a captain in command, the exception being number eight company, commanded by Lieutenant Nicholson.

The men were undoubtedly feeling the effects of hunger. The light company had suffered worse than the rest of the battalion because they had missed out on the full rations distributed on 16 June. Even so, the meat from those full rations, which the men had started to cook during a brief halt on their march to Quatre Bras, had to be abandoned, and biscuit alone was consumed. The next evening there was the limited amount of biscuit which the Guards had left behind, and on the morning of the battle it was biscuit again, with spirits to alleviate the effects of a cold, wet night. Nor did the situation subsequently improve. Nothing was supplied the next day and only on 20 June did regular rations reach the division. Significantly, two days after the battle the Deputy Assistant Commissary General of the third division was dismissed for failing to do his duty. He had lingered in Brussels while the division marched and countermarched to Quatre Bras and Waterloo.

Shaw Kennedy timed the first cannon-shot at 11.30 a.m., while Elkington wrote in his journal: 'We could now distinctly see the movements of the different French Corps. At noon the action commenced. The Artillery in Front of our Brigade opening fire on the enemy advancing on Hougoumont. (I took out my watch as this took place.)'[171] Elkington was responding to the sound of the allied guns, which themselves started firing as the divisions of Prince Jérôme, Foy and Bachelu (of Reille's second corps) advanced on Hougoumont. Shaw Kennedy, on the other hand, was undoubtedly responding to the first French bombardment which, it is said, decapitated a man of the 69th. This provoked his quartermaster to remark: 'It is time for all peaceable non-combatants to be off.' It also persuaded Alten to draw his lines further back from the crest of the ridge.

While the battalions of Halkett's brigade retired, the flank companies under Vigoureux received specific orders from Halkett himself, as included in John Pratt's communication with Siborne: 'To cover and protect our Batteries. To establish ourselves at all times as much in advance as might be compatible with prudence. To preserve considerable intervals between our extended files for greater security from the fire of the Enemy's Batteries. To show obstinate resistance against Infantry of the same description, but to attempt no formation or offer useless opposition to charges of Cavalry, but to retire in time upon the Squares in our rear, moving in a direct line without any reference to Regiments or Nations. When the charge was repulsed, to resume our ground.'[172]

The struggle for Hougoumont continued unabated for two hours (according to Shaw Kennedy) before 'The second act of the great drama commenced at half-past one o'clock P.M. No one can doubt, who knows the field of battle, and who is even tolerably informed of the circumstances, that Napoleon's plan of attack was that of breaking Wellington's centre at La Haie Sainte, overthrowing the left of the Allied line, and thus going far to ensure the defeat of the Anglo-Allied army; to separate it entirely from that of Blücher; and to gain the command of the great road to Brussels.'[173]

As Shaw Kennedy further points out, Napoleon had wasted two hours in a fruitless attempt to take Hougoumont and thus turn the allied line, a manoeuvre which continued as a sideshow to the main action for the rest of the battle, drawing in men who could have been used more profitably elsewhere. Now Napoleon focused on the fifth division, lying to the left of the Brussels road. The attack began with a bombardment by a battery of seventy-four guns which was suffered both by Picton's division to the left of the road and Alten's division, to the right. Then came the great infantry attack by d'Erlon's corps. Although the destruction of the fifth division was its principal objective, an attack was also launched against La Haie Sainte which drove the defenders from the orchard and the garden, while a detachment of cuirassiers moved to the left of the advance where the skirmishers of the third division lay exposed to their onslaught.

Macready's account of his experiences in the skirmishing line up to this point in the battle gives a lively impression of what happened from this forward perspective. He starts with the attack on Hougoumont. 'At length the enemy's left appeared in motion towards Hougoumont, and old Cleve [sic] slapped away at them. When the first shot was fired I threw off a wet blanket I had wrapt round me, gave myself a shake and, like Joe Miller's soldier, considered all as clear gain that I might bring out of the battle. Cleve's guns, which told most gloriously on the columns as they approached the orchard, were unanswered for some minutes, but we soon saw the enemy's artillery trotting down the hill, and at once they opened from 200 paces. The cannonade extended along the whole line. The skirmishers were soon ordered to extend and to descend the slope to protect the guns.' The defence of Hougoumont was fierce and determined. 'From its doors and windows our gallant Guardsmen poured an unceasing shower of bullets, and the enemy fell dead in heaps. After two hours of most determined exertion they retired from this spot, leaving it covered with bodies of their countrymen. The conduct of the Guards was most glorious. On the retreat of the enemy, the firing still continued at this point; but it was no longer considered as an attack, merely occupation for both parties.'[174]

Macready was able to witness the action from the elevated position occupied by Halkett's brigade, and distance lent a certain detachment to his view. Nevertheless, the situation was uncomfortable for the third division. 'During the contest for the chateau our columns were lying at length under the hill to shelter themselves as much as possible from the showers of shot and shell which were tearing up every part of the field ... The artillery on both sides, covered by their respective light troops, who kept up a brisk fire, were dealing destruction around them; and the only bodies in motion were the groups of staff officers, who attracted the fire of the enemy and the curses of their friends wherever they appeared. Our company and the 73rd Grenadiers, after a pretty long skirmish, had pushed the French Tirailleurs close under their guns, and our shot began to whistle among the artillerymen, when we perceived a body of cavalry coming down on us at the gallop. We were too far extended to attempt any formation, and the ground was quite open, so Colonel Vigoureux gave the word to us to make off, and away we went at score. Pratt, with some men, reached a Hanoverian square; Rumley, one of the Nassau's; and I, with about a dozen men, made our own. The rest of our men were dispersed into La Haye Sainte and various squares, and some few of them were cut down. Our rapid retreat was peculiarly dangerous, as we had to run through high corn towards our own guns, which opened with grape on the enemy's cavalry. Kielmansegge's Jägers, who were on our left, trusting to their numbers and the nature of their ground, stood, and were annihilated.'[175]

Macready's subsequent sentiments, confided to his journal, may now appear vainglorious but they undoubtedly capture the feelings of a young and inexperienced subaltern as imminent tragedy descended into farce. The French cavalry, having dealt with the Jägers, galloped up the slope, sabred the greater part of Lloyd's artillerymen, and charged a Hanoverian square. They were repulsed, and, before they could effect their retreat, were destroyed by a squadron of Life Guards, who advanced through the third division. 'These ruffians laughed at us as we scudded from their uplifted sabres, but, as their own proverb says, "il rit bien qui rit le dernier." I could not help grinning at some of "les bon sabreurs", though certainly they made noble-looking corpses. Their charge was a gallant piece of service – of course, as they were destroyed, it will be called a rash one; but had they been satisfied with the destruction of a regiment of Jägers and a brigade of artillery, they might have returned to their comrades covered with success and glory.'[176]

The light company of the 30th now formed up in the shelter of Cleeve's guns. Here they remained until the tirailleurs advanced once more, whereupon they descended the slope and returned to the business of skirmishing.

Meanwhile, d'Erlon's attack on the fifth division had achieved some success. Bijlandt's brigade, after an initial stand, was overwhelmed; a gap was opened up between Kempt and Pack's brigades; Papelotte fell to the French; and Picton, rallying his men, was killed by a shot to the head. The line held, just, and was then rescued by the cavalry of Sir William Ponsonby's Union brigade, the Royals, the Scots Greys and the Inniskillings, who charged down the French infantry and swept on towards the guns. That they went too far and were decimated by the counter-attack of French lancers and cuirassiers is one of the tragedies of the battle. The fifth division had been rescued, however, and Saxe-Weimar's Nassauers were able to re-take Papelotte.

Indeed, at this stage of the action Wellington's army could congratulate itself on holding a sequence of French attacks which had tried and failed to take any of the salient points or breach the most vulnerable part of the allied line. For the third division, however, the battle had hardly started; the worst was yet to come.

Chapter 15
To the Last Man . . .

John Kincaid of the Rifle Brigade, reflecting on the later stages of the Battle of Waterloo, remembered thinking, 'I had never yet heard of a battle in which everybody was killed, but this seemed likely to be an exception, as all were going by turns.'[177] As the French changed their tactics, the 30th were about to encounter this possibility.

So far the centre of the allied line had suffered only limited attention from the French. The cannonade had affected them and the skirmishers had found themselves under attack from cavalry, but the reverse slope position and the intervention of the Household Brigade had prevented any serious losses. Indeed, French losses seriously outnumbered allied losses; the infantry of d'Erlon's corps had suffered severely; their batteries had been weakened; and three hours had been wasted to no good purpose. Napoleon needed to adopt different tactics if he were to break through to Brussels, particularly as he had now received the first indications that the Prussians were advancing on his right.

'The interval between this [d'Erlon's] attack and the next was very considerable, and no one in the Anglo-Allied line could imagine what the next move would be;- that is, how the third act of the drama would begin; and when it did open, it was certainly in a manner quite unexpected. General Alten and his staff, being near to where the Belgian Lion now stands, had a commanding view of the enemy's position and movements, and watched with anxiety during this lull of the action what the next move of the French would be. The attacks on La Haie Sainte and Hougoumont were continued, but not with much violence, and the cannonade was moderate. But at about four o'clock the cannonade became violent in the extreme, probably as much so as has been witnessed in any open field of battle. This was evidently the prelude to some serious attack. To our surprise we soon saw that it was the prelude to an attack of cavalry upon a grand scale. Such an attack we had fully anticipated . . . would take place at some period of the day; but we had no idea that it would be made upon our line standing in its regular order of battle, and that line as yet unshaken by any previous attack by infantry. The moment that it was observed that the movement of the great masses of the French heavy cavalry were directed towards his division, General Alten passed the order to form oblongs, into which formation the division rapidly passed; the Guards formed squares on the right of the 3rd division; the two divisions thus filling up the space between the Charleroi and Nivelles roads; the artillery stood in front of the infantry on the front slope of the position, so that its fire might be effectual against the attacking force.'[178]

Forty squadrons of Milhaud's heavy cavalry now launched themselves obliquely from across the Brussels-Charleroi road and up to the ridge. 'This was effected in beautiful order, and the formation and advance of that magnificent and highly disciplined cavalry had, as a spectacle, a very grand effect. These splendid horsemen were enthusiastic in the cause of Napoleon – full of confidence in him and in themselves – thirsting to revenge the reverses which had been suffered by the French armies – led by most experienced and able cavalry commanders – and they submitted to a heavy discipline. Their advance to the attack was splendid and interesting in the extreme. Our surprise at being so soon attacked by this great and magnificent force of cavalry was accompanied with the opinion that the attack was premature, and that we were perfectly prepared and secure against its effects, so far as any military operation can be calculated upon.'[179]

Whether the man in the ranks shared the confidence of the staff is doubtful, although the 30th had already demonstrated at Quatre Bras that an infantry square could stand against cavalry. As to why the French embarked upon such questionable tactics, a possible explanation has Napoleon concentrating on the Prussian threat from the east and sending an ambiguous order to Marshal Ney, who himself may have misinterpreted several units retiring at Wellington's command, combined with the wounded being conveyed from the field, as a general retreat by the centre of the allied line. Even when this proved palpably false, he could not abandon the tactic, continuing to send (and lead) wave after wave of cavalry against the steadfast squares.

The twelve-pounders on the heights near La Belle Alliance and the lighter guns already deployed in a forward position commenced a barrage, the forward guns protected by the usual swarms of tirailleurs. 'The line of Tirailleurs opposed to us was not stronger than our own, but on a sudden they were reinforced by numerous bodies, and several guns began playing on us with canister. Our poor fellows dropped very fast, and Colonel Vigoureux, Rumley and Pratt, were carried off badly wounded in about two minutes. I was now commander of our company. We stood under this hurricane of small shot until Halkett sent to order us in, and I brought away about a third of the light bobs, the rest were killed or wounded, and I really wonder how one of them escaped. As our bugler was killed, I shouted and made signals to move by the left, in order to avoid the fire of our guns, and to put as good a face upon the business as possible.'[180]

Pratt's own account suggests that he was wounded later in the battle, and Macready seems to have confused two separate moments when the light company were dangerously exposed. Pratt himself recollected how 'Between 2 & 3 P.M. our attention was directed towards the orchard of La Haye Sainte, whence we saw debouching from the high road a heavy column of infantry directing its march towards the flank of Hougoumont, and winding along the foot of the British position. This was a very critical movement, and entirely absorbed our individual attention. We had only a few scattered light troops to oppose this formidable force. The Prince of Orange had been gone for some time, and there was no staff or mounted officers present to send for aid. I have a distinct recollection, in my nervous anxiety, to arrest the progress of this important movement, urging Captain Cleeve (whose attention indeed we had directed to it, as he had been occupied with his brigade) to point his guns towards the advancing Column & endeavour to drive it back. He appeared however at once to have taken his resolution and permitted the column to continue its advance unmolested until it reached the point of the valley immediately in its front and upon which he had concentrated the whole fire of his battery. We now quietly but anxiously watched their progress & the column had cleared more than two thirds of the distance between La Haye Sainte & Hougoumont, when, having well entered his line of fire, three rounds from each gun were thrown in with astonishing rapidity, wonderful accuracy, & awful effect. As soon as the firing had ceased by sound of trumpet, and the smoke had dispersed, we had the inexpressible satisfaction of beholding the whole column in complete deroute, flying back in confusion towards La Haye Sainte for shelter, the ground in our front upon which the fire had been directed affording the best proof of its deadly accuracy, from the number of bodies which were lying there.' Pratt could not be sure how many times this manoeuvre was repeated. He also mentions that 'In the interval we experienced more than one charge of cavalry.'[181]

At this point Macready calmly surveyed the battlefield. 'When I reached Lloyd's abandoned guns, I stood near them for about a minute to contemplate the scene: it was grand beyond description. Hougoumont and its wood sent up a broad flame through the dark masses of smoke that overhung the field – beneath this cloud the French were indistinctly visible – here a mass of long red feathers could be seen, there, gleams as from a sheet of steel showed that the Cuirassiers were moving; 400 cannon were belching forth fire and death on every side; the roaring and shouting were indistinguishably commixed – together they gave me an idea of a labouring volcano. Bodies of infantry and cavalry were pouring down on us, and it was time to leave contemplation, so I moved towards our columns, which were standing up in square.'[182]

The flank companies were now withdrawn by Halkett in response to the imminent cavalry attack. The cuirassiers were in the lead, with lancers in support, and chasseurs as a reserve. The right of this body was directed against the squares of Verden and Bremen and the square comprising the 30th and the 73rd. According to Alten, 'The cannonade by this time on the part of the enemy was most destructive of our infantry squares, yet none showed even a disposition to give way but filled up the space over the bodies of their brave comrades as they fell. The enemy's cavalry now appeared in crowds upon the position, charged the square of the 30th and 73rd, the one of the Grubenhagen and Osnabruck and that of the Bremen and Verden field battalions five or six times, but were as often repulsed by the coolness of our troops who reserved their fire until they approached within twenty paces.'[183]

Captain Arthur Gore remembered that 'From this moment the most desperate and successive charges were made upon the squares of the Allies, formed in echelon, some in advance, others a little to the rear, upon a declivity, gradually descending from the crest of the position, where, notwithstanding they were repeatedly attacked on every side and harassed without intermission, they remained immovable, presenting with unshaken firmness, an impenetrable bulwark to the violent shocks of the daring and intrepid cuirassiers; whose broken squadrons, although frequently charged by the allied cavalry, re-formed with unexampled quickness, and returned to the assault.'[184]

Lieutenant Picton wrote in 1816 of the 30th and the 73rd, 'To no square did the artillery, and particularly the cuirassiers pay more frequent and tremendous visits, and never were they shaken for a minute. Their almost intimacy with these death-bringing visitants increased so much, as the day advanced, that they began to recognize their faces; their boldness much provoked the soldiers; they galloped up to the bayonet points, where, of course, their horses made a full stop, to the great danger of pitching their riders into the square. They then rode round and round the fearless bulwark of bayonets, and, in all the confidence of their panoply, often coolly walked their horses, to have more time to search for some chasm in the ranks, where they might ride in. – The balls absolutely rung [sic] upon their mail, and nothing incommoded the rider, except bringing down his horse, which at last became the general order; in the event he generally surrendered himself, and was received within the square till he could be sent prisoner to the rear.'[185]

Macready offers a personal perspective. 'In a few minutes after, the enemy's cavalry galloped up and crowned the crest of our position. Our guns were abandoned, and they formed between the two brigades, about a hundred paces in our front. Their first charge was magnificent. As soon as they quickened their trot into a gallop the Cuirassiers bent their heads, so that the peaks of their helmets looked like visors, and they seemed cased in armour from the plume to the saddle – not a shot was fired till they were within thirty yards, when the word was given, and our boys peppered away at them. The effect was magical. Through the smoke we could see helmets falling – cavaliers starting from their seats with convulsive springs as they received our balls, horses plunging and rearing in the agonies of fright and pain, and crowds of the soldiery dismounted – part of the squadron in retreat, but the more daring remainder hacking their horses to force them on our bayonets. Our fire soon disposed of these gentlemen. The main body re-formed in our front, and rapidly and gallantly repeated their attacks. In fact from this time (about four o'clock) till near six, we had a constant repetition of these brave but unavailing charges. There was no difficulty in repulsing them, but our ammunition decreased alarmingly – at length an artillery wagon galloped up, emptied two or three casks of cartridges into the square, and we were all comfortable.

'The best cavalry is contemptible to a steady and well-supplied infantry regiment – even our men saw this, and began to pity the useless perseverance of their assailants, and, as they advanced, would growl, "Here come those damned fools again!"'[186]

As the struggle ebbed and flowed, allied cavalry took advantage of each French withdrawal to drive them further down the hill, while the gunners, who sheltered in the squares during the attacks, returned to their guns and commenced a bombardment on the retreating horsemen. Undeterred by the inevitable failure of these cavalry attacks, Ney tried again – and again. Kellerman's cavalry of the reserve and the heavy cavalry of the Guard joined the attacks. As many as eleven separate attacks were made until eventually all impetus was lost. The horsemen rode round the squares in desultory fashion, firing into them with their carbines before being swept away by an allied counter-attack. One colonel of cuirassiers tried a desperate *ruse de guerre*. Riding up to the front of the square, he lowered his sword to General Halkett. Despite being urged by several officers to accept the surrender, Halkett immediately gave the order to fire. He knew the trick of old. The volley sent the colonel and his cuirassiers into retreat, accompanied by the derisive laughter of their opponents.

Tincombe, attached to a centre company, which gave him a different perspective from Macready, later wrote to his brother, 'We lay down for some considerable length of time, but at length the French Cavalry came on and we were moved forward to support our guns, which they had charged and taken five out of the six of our Brigade belonging to the Division, but fortunately when they saw us they left the guns and charged. We could not fire before the Artillery were clear of us, many of whom came into our square for protection. At length the moment came. We gave them a terrible fire which no troops could withstand. They ran, formed again and charged – off again – charged several times but could not come near us.'

At this juncture Lieutenant Robert Hughes performed one of those gestures which remind us that even in the midst of war men may still retain humanitarian instincts. When 'the adjutant of the 6th Cuirassiers had his horse shot and fell in front of the side of the square formed by the 30th. Lieutenant Hughes saved him from the bayonets raised to kill him, and taking him by the hand drew him into the square and for further safety made the young Frenchman take his arm. They stood thus until the Imperial Guard formed up for the attack on the heights near La Belle Alliance nearly two hours later, where the adjutant implored Hughes to send him to the rear that he might not be killed by his friends. Hughes pointed out to him that his life would not be worth a minute's purchase if he left the square, but in a moment of confusion they were separated and in all likelihood the young Frenchman was killed in attempting to escape.'[187] Hughes was a casualty during the battle; he seems to have received his wound at this 'moment of confusion' while attempting to rally some panicking foreign troops.

Although the squares had successfully withstood the French cavalry, the French now made a determined attack upon La Haie Sainte where lack of ammunition forced the few surviving defenders to withdraw. This success gave the French a forward position from which to launch a renewed attack on the allied line. The Prince of Orange intervened to counter-attack with the fifth battalion of the King's German Legion but the result was a catastrophic defeat which included the death of its commander, Ompteda.

This was the point when John Pratt was wounded. 'Towards the close of the day I found myself for the last time near the bottom of our slope with the few Light Troops that were remaining. The firing on the left had slackened or ceased, and the enemy's position in our immediate front was being covered with Infantry. Their Artillery also had taken up a position much in advance and was firing, chiefly grape, amongst the scattered Light Troops, which were gradually retiring before the overwhelming force opposed to them. La Haye Sainte being in possession of the Enemy, our left was necessarily much thrown back, so as to place us in *echelon* with the crest of the position. It was at this period that I was wounded, and, of course, I ceased to be an eye-witness of what took place afterwards.'[188]

Tincombe wrote: 'At length they brought Artillery within range of us and poured grape, canister, and everything they could think of into our square and nearly cut us to pieces. The Belgian Cavalry ordered to support us ran away. The other square [33rd and 69th] was in our rear rather to the right. They were ordered up but I am sorry to say did not behave as well as we could have wished. Lord Wellington was frequently with us and was very anxious for our position which was the centre. Two of his ADCs were killed within our square. Every one of the mounted officers belonging to the 73rd and 30th were killed or wounded.' The casualties included the former adjutant of the 30th, John Garland, now with the 73rd, who lost a leg.

Gore described the fate of Wellington's ADCs. 'The place where Sir Alexander Gordon was wounded is considerably to the right of the monument, and in front of the hedge which marks the centre of the plateau. This gallant officer was removed from the field by Sergeant-Major Woods, of the 2nd battalion 30th foot, to the village of Mont St Jean; where, after suffering the amputation of a leg, he terminated his mortal life, in the flower of his youth, universally regretted by his friends and brother officers.

'Near the same spot fell, mortally wounded, Lieutenant-Colonel Canning, also Aide-de-Camp to his Grace the Duke of Wellington ... When this gallant officer fell, I was near him; I held his hand in mine, while that distinguished young nobleman, the Earl of March, received his last farewell.'[189]

Shaw Kennedy recognised the seriousness of the situation. 'We have already seen that La Haye Sainte was in the hands of the enemy; also the knoll on the opposite side of the road; also the garden and ground on the Anglo-Allied side of it; – that Ompteda's brigade was nearly annihilated, and Kielmansegge's so thinned, that those two brigades could not hold their position. That part of the field of battle, therefore, which was between Halkett's left and Kempt's right, was unprotected; and being the very centre of the Duke's line of battle, was consequently that point, above all others, which the enemy wished to gain. The danger was imminent; and at no other period of the action was the result so precarious as at this moment.'[190]

In Siborne's opinion, the two British squares of the 1st Guards and of the 30th and the 73rd, from their advanced position, were most exposed to both French cavalry and French artillery fire. They suffered the immediate onslaught of the cavalry attacks and the unremitting attention of the French gunners. Yet both squares stood their ground throughout the battle.

Macready also recorded his painful memories. 'At about six o'clock I perceived some artillery trotting up our hill, which I knew by their caps to belong to the Imperial Guard. I had hardly mentioned this to a brother officer when two guns unlimbered within seventy paces of us, and, by their first discharge of grape, blew seven men into the centre of the square. They immediately reloaded and kept up a constant and destructive fire. It was noble to see our fellows fill up the gaps after every discharge – I was much distressed at this moment. I ordered up three of my light bobs – they had hardly taken their station when two of them fell horribly lacerated. One of them looked up in my face and uttered a sort of reproachful groan, and I involuntarily exclaimed, "By God, I couldn't help it!" We would willingly have charged those guns, but, had we deployed, the cavalry that flanked them would have made an example of us.'[191]

To Macready's relief, 'our dear old rags' were taken to safety; he recognised that in their weakened condition the two battalions would not be able to defend four stand of colours.

Many of the battalion's casualties fell to artillery fire during this phase of the battle. Heavy casualties were also taken by the nearby German squares, while some Nassauers (who may have been Tincombe's Belgians), brought up by the Prince of Orange, immediately retreated when the Prince was wounded. 'Of such gravity did Wellington consider this great gap in the very centre of his line of battle, that he not only ordered the Brunswick troops there, but put himself at their head; and it was even then with the greatest difficulty that the ground could be held; but Count Kielmansegge soon led back his gallant Germans to the spot; the Brunswickers held their ground supported by part of the Nassau force; and ultimately Vivian's brigade of cavalry supported these troops; and the artillery officers responded to the utmost of their available means in strengthening this most vulnerable and dangerous part of the position.'[192]

By this time, about 7.30 p.m., the Prussians were fiercely engaged at Plancenoit. Napoleon had to deal with the Anglo-Dutch forces before the Prussians overwhelmed the units he had sent against them. To this end he ordered the twelve battalions of the Imperial Guard to attack the allied line.

'It was near seven o'clock, and our front had sustained three attacks from French troops, when the Imperial Guard [the Middle Guard] was seen ascending our position in as correct order as a review. As they rose step by step before us, and crossed the ridge, their red epaulettes and cross belts, put on over their blue greatcoats, gave them a gigantic appearance, which was increased by their high hairy caps and long red feathers, which waved with the nod of their heads as they kept time to a drum in the centre of their column. "Now for a clawing," I muttered; and I confess, when I saw the imposing advance of these men, and thought of the character they had gained, I looked for nothing but a bayonet in my body, and I half breathed a confident sort of wish that it might not touch my vitals.

'While they were moving up the slope, Halkett, as well as the noise permitted us to hear him, addressed us, and said, "My boys, you have done everything I could have wished, and more than I could expect, but much remains to be done

– at this moment we have nothing for it but a charge." Our brave fellows replied by three cheers. The enemy halted, carried arms, about forty paces from us, and fired a volley. We returned it, and giving our "Huzza!" brought down the bayonets. Our surprise was inexpressible when, pushing through the clearing smoke, we saw the backs of the Imperial Grenadiers – we halted and stared at each other as if mistrusting our eyesight. Some nine-pounders from the rear of our right poured in the grape amongst them, and the slaughter was dreadful – in no part of the field did I see carcasses so heaped upon each other. I never could account for their flight, nor did I ever hear an admissible reason assigned for it. It was a most providential panic. We could not pursue on account of their cavalry, and their artillery was still shockingly destructive.'[193]

Shaw Kennedy, from his perspective, described what happened in the following terms. 'These two columns of attack of the French Imperial Guard did not attack simultaneously, the attack by the right column having considerably preceded that made by the left column. The head of the right column directed its march upon that part of the British position occupied by Maitland's brigade of Guards, who were lying down, rather under the slope of the ground, for protection from the cannonade; so that this French column, in its advance, suffered from a very severe fire of artillery, and was at a very short distance assailed by Maitland's brigade, which then rose, and, being in a four-deep formation, was seen for the first time by the French Guard. Maitland's brigade now opened a heavy and most destructive fire upon the French Guard while in column, and the fire from the right of Colin Halkett's brigade must also have told upon that column, which soon got into utter confusion and could not deploy. Maitland's and part of Halkett's brigade advanced upon it when in this state of confusion, and drove it back in a state of rout. Maitland's brigade was thrown into some confusion by this advance, but both it and Halkett's right soon resumed their proper position in the line in good order.'[194] Although the routed French Guards were eventually able to form, they were later driven into final retreat by the advance of the 52nd.

This was not the end of the battle for the 30th, however. Although the Middle Guard had been repulsed, the situation suddenly became chaotic. Alten had been wounded some time before and replaced by Kielmansegge, who now received incapacitating wounds. Halkett took his place, so he may have given the order to retire as the division was suffering greatly from French artillery. Who gave the order to form square is not known but the results were calamitous for the 30th. Two officers were killed, two received wounds from which they later died, and forty men were killed or wounded.

Macready's account is graphic. 'There was a hedge in our rear, to which we were ordered to move, as some cover from the fire. As we descended the declivity, the enemy thought we were flying, and, according to their invariable custom, turned a trebly furious cannonade upon us. Shot, shell, and grape came like a hurricane through the square, and the hurly burly of these moments can never be erased from my memory. A shriek from forty or fifty men burst forth amid the thunder and hissing of the shot. I was knocked off my legs, by the fall of a brother officer, and just as I recovered my feet, an intimate friend, in the delirium of agony occasioned by five wounds, seized me by the collar, screaming, "Is it deep, Mac, is it deep!" Another officer was seen to halt, as if paralyzed, and stare upon a burning fuze, till it fired the powder and shattered him to pieces. At this instant the two regiments on our right rushed amongst us in frightful confusion, and our men passed the hedge at an accelerated pace. The exertions of the officers were rendered of no avail by the irresistible pressure, and, as crying with rage and shame, they seized individuals to halt them, they were themselves hurried on by the current. Such a jumble of curses, screams, sobs and laughter as arose amongst our mob. At this moment, someone huzzaed, we all joined, and the men halted. Major Chambers ordered me to dash out with our light bobs and grenadiers, while the regiment marched up to the hedge and reformed – the whole brigade was within an ace of ruin. Our men were as steady as rocks till the others came amongst them, when the disorder was extreme. The officers did wonders, but the shout alone saved us. I never could discover who raised it.'[195]

Years later, Macready made it clear that the men whose panic caused the chaos were British, and must, therefore, have been the 33rd and the 69th. He also commented that 'Nothing could be more gratifying than the conduct of our people at this disastrous period. While men and Officers were jammed together and carried along by the pressure from without, many of the latter, some cursing, others literally crying with rage and shame, were seizing the soldiers and calling on them to halt, while these admirable fellows, good-humouredly laughing at their excitement, were struggling to get out of the *melee*, or exclaiming, "By God, I'll stop, Sir, but I'm off my legs." '[196]

Although the squares regained some sort of order and came into line with the Brunswickers, the danger was not yet over. The Imperial Guard might have been repulsed and the supporting columns (particularly Donzelot's) brought up short but they still possessed firepower. According to Macready, as everyone stood around in a state of listlessness, there was a sudden outbreak of musketry which disabled Halkett as he was trying to restore order and also killed Chambers, who had taken command after both Bailey and Vigoureux were wounded.

Captain Robert Howard now assumed command of the 30th, while overall command of the British brigade was taken by Major Kelly of the 73rd, a staff officer from the Quartermaster General's Department. His first task, according to his own account, was to order the intermingled battalions to resume their former order and then to form an extended front. He instructed the men to lie down to protect themselves, at the same time checking and preparing their weapons for a renewed attack. (Macready later claimed that Chambers gave these orders, and Kelly only took over after Chambers's death.)

The attack came quickly enough, composed of the 28^ieme^ and 105^ieme^ regiments. 'Their advance was, as usual with the French, very noisy, and evidently reluctant, the officers being in advance some yards cheering their men on. They, however, kept up a confused and running fire, which we did not reply to till they reached nearly a level with us (that is they topped the ridge), when a well-directed volley put them in a confusion from which they did not appear to recover, but after a short interval of musketry on both sides they turned about to a man and fled.'[197] The 30th retained a drum belonging to the 105^ieme^.

Soon afterwards the order for a general advance was received. The British brigade of the third division, however, halted on the ridge which had been their main defensive position throughout the day.

Macready recorded the melancholy details of the officer casualties. The first to die was Henry Beere, an Irishman from Tipperary. He was killed during the cavalry charges. 'As I entered the rear face of our square I had to step over a body, and, looking down, recognised Harry Beere, an officer of our Grenadiers, who about an hour before shook hands with me, laughing, as I left the columns – I was on the usual terms of military intimacy with poor Harry – i.e. if either of us had died a natural death, the other would have pitied him as a good fellow, and smiled at his neighbour as he congratulated him on the step – but seeing his Herculean frame and animated countenance thus suddenly still and motionless before me (I know not whence the feeling could originate, for I had just seen my dearest friends drop almost with indifference), the tears started in my eyes as I sighed out, "Poor Harry!"'

Two ensigns, John James and James Bullen, died from round shot. 'Poor young Bullen was much regretted; he had left his home contrary to the wishes of a fond mother, and had only been with us three weeks: – his legs were both terrible shattered. Just before the amputation of one of them, he was smiling and saying he must now return to his mamma, and he thought £150 per annum (his half-pay and two pensions) would make her more comfortable – he bore the operation nobly, but as soon as it ended, exclaimed, "Gentlemen, you have done for me!" and breathed his last.'[198]

The circumstances of Chambers's death are less certain. According to one account, which his brother-in-law received from soldiers of the battalion invalided to Yarmouth, he was shot through the heart as he galloped his horse into the safety of the square. Another version has him standing with a group of officers, just before the final French attack, joining in the general congratulation that they had survived the day, when a stray shot to the heart killed him instantly. Yet a third version, that of Arthur Gore, is perhaps the most ironic: 'there is none more worth "of the voice of praise," than my friend and companion in arms, Major T. W. Chambers ... he was an active, zealous, and intelligent officer, and a great loss to his regiment, both as a soldier, and a gentleman ... About half past six in the afternoon, at the moment he was declaring, "that he had hitherto escaped unhurt, and that he was too small to be hit," he received a ball through the heart, from a tirailleur of the guards, and instantly expired.'[199]

Gore was not alone in regretting his death. 'When Chambers fell, his friend Nicholson threw himself on the body and sobbed aloud, "My friend – my friend!"'[200] No wonder that he was grief-stricken; in India they had stood alone against the animosity of the rest of the first battalion. Macready also described, in relation to Chambers, how two officers who had been at odds for some time were reconciled when one of them, general assumed to be Chambers, saw the other (Macready himself) behaving gallantly. Macready was inclined to be intolerant, while Chambers set high standards for himself and everyone else, and some ill-spoken words by the former had alienated him from the latter.

Two officers were killed at the same point that James and Bullen received their ultimately fatal wounds. Captain McNabb, the Canadian officer, was killed by grapeshot. The fate of Lieutenant Edmund Prendergast was, if anything, worse. It was he who stared at the burning fuse until the shell exploded, obeying the convention that an officer should not flinch away from a burning fuse.

Various casualty lists were produced for the battalion. The June muster list has six officers and fifty-one other ranks killed. This was later amended by Hamilton to thirty-six other ranks, and this figure is probably correct. After a battle men could be 'missing', and thus presumed dead, for some time. The number of wounded is more problematic. Elkington recorded fifteen officers and 208 other ranks wounded, while Macready estimated 228 other ranks wounded. Both the medal roll and the pay list for June give fifteen officers and 202 other ranks wounded. Elkington may only have counted the men he sent to the general hospital, while Macready included another twenty who had their wounds dressed at the regimental hospital. Furthermore, by the time the pay list was drawn up, some of Elkington's casualties had rejoined.

Not all the wounded survived, although the number that did is surprising, considering that both antiseptics and soporifics were as yet undiscovered. We cannot be certain that all the men who subsequently died in Brussels died of wounds, but if they did the figures are still impressive. Assuming the figure of 202 recorded in the pay list is accurate, only eighteen men are definitely returned as died of wounds, with another eight who died in Brussels and may have been casualties. This says much for the skill of the surgeons within the limitations of the time.

As for the wounded officers, Macready made the following list in his journal: 'the wounded were, Lieutenant Colonels Hamilton [at Quatre Bras], Bailey and Vigoureux, Captain Gore, Lieutenants Mayne, Andrews, Elliott, Rumley, Daniell, Harrison, Hughes, Roe 2nd, Lockwood [Quatre Bras], Pratt, Warren, and Moneypenny and those that escaped unhurt were Capt Howard (shot thro' the cap), Bt-Maj Ryan, and Captains Sinclair and Finucane; Lieut Nicholson, Heaviside, Gowan (shot thro' the cap), Freear, Tincombe, O'Halloran, Latouche, Drake, Rogers (cap shot off) and Ensign Macready.'[201] Not present with the battalion were Captain Machell and Lieutenant Baillie, who were both in Antwerp on staff duty, Lieutenant Roe 1, on baggage duty, and Lieutenant Neville, once again serving as an assistant engineer.

Macready subsequently suggested that not every officer behaved well. While in London in 1817 he chanced to meet Lieutenant Latouche, a young man possessed of both distinguished connections (his Huguenot forebear founded the Bank of Ireland) and wealth. Latouche offered his congratulations to Macready, who had just returned to the regiment from half-pay, but Macready believed these good wishes to be false. His reflections on Latouche's character led him to conclude: 'my first cause of dislike was the dismal abuse in which he indulged on our profession for which however he soon discovered his unfitness. When sober he was an uninformed, silly fellow and when drunk as outrageous in his insolence as he was pusillanimous in its support. At Waterloo he put the finishing stroke to a character truly despicable.'[202] Macready was intolerant of anything he perceived as cowardice or dereliction of duty, and his strictures against Latouche may stem from this. Latouche's half-pay return of 1829 suggests some justice in the comments, since he himself explained that he went on half-pay soon after Waterloo because he had caught a cold during the battle.

The last word on the feelings which many must have experienced after the cataclysmic events of the 18th June can be given to Macready. The next morning 'about ten o'clock, we left this glorious spot encumbered with thousands of the dead and dying. Our acquaintance with the enemy had been but short, and we had some reason to complain of a few atrocities on their part; but while valour and heroic devotion to a cause are commendable, their praise as soldiers cannot be refused them. Our own countrymen excited a softer feeling – they were our friends and fellow soldiers, but they died the death that every soldier looks for, and they fell by gallant foemen. "Peace to the souls of the heroes, their deeds were great in battle!"'[203]

Chapter 16

Army of Occupation

There were unprecedented rewards for the survivors of the battle of Waterloo. In addition to the thanks of a grateful nation, expressed in addresses to both Houses of Parliament and by the Prince Regent, all combatants were to receive a medal irrespective of their rank, an innovation suggested by Wellington. Surviving field officers were made Companions of the Order of the Bath. For the 30th, this meant Hamilton and Bailey, since Vigoureux had already received the honour for his service at Vitoria. Later in the year, the commanding officers of the 33rd, 69th and 73rd Regiments received the Dutch King Wilhelm's order, fourth class. Only Hamilton was omitted, according to Macready because he refused to ask for it, although his intemperate criticism of the Prince of Orange at Quatre Bras (when ordered to get into line) may have been the real reason.

There were also pecuniary rewards. Prize money was computed in relation to the number of captured guns and for the 30th varied from £433.3.4d for the field officers to £2.11.4d for the drummers and rank and file. The subalterns were credited with two years' extra service, which meant an extra shilling a day after five years' service instead of seven. The NCOs and men, henceforth known as 'Waterloo Men', received the same reward, with implications for pay and pension. For example, when Colour Sergeant Joseph Scotton was discharged at Chelsea in September 1816 'in consequence of gun shot wound of right leg received at Waterloo', he had served a total of seventeen years and 298 days, of which eight years and thirty-six days were with the 30th. His pension, however, was based on a notional service of nineteen years and 298 days because of his presence at Waterloo.

For officers the main concern was promotion, because vacancies caused by death in battle did not require purchase. Chambers's majority, which he had purchased only a few months before the battle, went to Samuel Bircham, a man who had seen no action since Egypt, and, paradoxically in view of his friendship with Chambers, Nicholson got Bircham's company. McNabb's company went to Lieutenant Lewin in India, while Ensigns Windus (India) and Donnelly were promoted, vice Beere and Prendergast. Nicholson's lieutenancy went to Macready and Lewin's to James Poyntz. Macready 'was delighted to hear, about the beginning of August, of my promotion to a lieutenancy. This was particularly gratifying to me, as it was not my turn by regular advancement, being put over the head of Mr Stewart a senior officer. On our march to Paris I received a note from Rumley, assuring me that I should be promoted; and though I was puzzled to discover the cause of this unexpected good fortune, I expected to be posted to another corps. However, I was gazetted to a lieutenancy in the 30th, 20th July, 1815, and no earthly notice taken of the gentleman above me. I have to thank Colonel Hamilton, and Andrews, our adjutant, for this service. They drew up a strong recommendation of me, mentioning that I had had the honour to command the eighth company of our regiment through a great part of the 18th of June, and personally led them on in different periods of the day. This effected my promotion in the corps, under circumstances to which I do not know a parallel.'[204]

18 June was not the end of the campaign, however, and many anticipated that the French would make another stand, probably just north of Paris. Initially, the Prussians took up the pursuit. In the days which followed some of the allied battalions also had to deal with pockets of French resistance but for the 30th their direct contact with the enemy was over. They were commanded until 30 June by Captain Howard (who received brevet rank as major on 18 June) and formed part of a column headed by Belgian cavalry, followed by the first and third divisions, with Belgian infantry bringing up the rear. Paris was their objective as they marched through Nivelles, Bavai, Caulaincourt and Senlis.

Several incidents enlivened this advance. Elkington was much struck by the depredations of the Prussians. On one occasion he was greeted as a saviour: 'halted at Seneffe, where I was gladly received by a farmer, whom the enormous numbers of Prussians, Belgians, and English stragglers had greatly alarmed by repeated firing and demanding rations. He was about to quit his house when I arrived and promised protection for the night. This I was able to do having collected a good many of the 30th Regiment and kept them with me.' As for damage, he wrote on 30 June: 'On this day's march we fell in with the route the Prussians had advanced by, we found the villages completely plundered, there was nothing to be got but vegetables and pigeons, that still remained about the houses.' The next day, 'To Annay, a small village only four leagues from Paris. There was some nice villas here, and the one I occupied had been beautifully furnished, but the Prussians had broken everything, the most beautiful pier glasses were destroyed.'[205]

Macready focused on the physical discomforts of the advance. On 21 June, the day the 30th crossed into France, there was some expectation of action. '[We] loosened our ammunition on hearing a heavy but irregular fire in front of us. A commissary met us, riding like John Gilpin, and swearing he did not turn back until his pistol ammunition was expended. In half-an-hour we reached the field of action, and found the Hanoverians hard at work cleaning their pieces! We halted near Bavai, a neat town abandoned by its inhabitants. We next lit our fires and remained in the wood of *Crevecoeur*. This rest was most welcome to me, as my boots, which had been on my feet since the morning of the 15th, had become hardened by the mud and turned on one side, so as to cut me dreadfully, and during the last march I was obliged to support myself by Heaviside's stirrup leather, walking on the sides of the soles. I had them cut off my legs here, and procured a good pair of shoes from the light bobs. These fellows furnished me with everything. When they could not find wine for my dinner, I have known them to go and buy it from the sutlers at five franks [sic] a bottle, and bring it to me, declaring that they made (i.e. stolen) it, lest my delicacy should prevent my accepting it. A field officer of ours, who drank tea and read the Bible regularly three times a week, after living on Heaviside, Harrison, and myself for a fortnight, refused us a cupful of sugar, and wrapped up his refusal in a thumping lie; and yet the major is respected and the privates called rascals.'[206]

The officer accused of this parsimony has to be either Robert Howard or Matthew Ryan since they were the only field officers (of brevet rank) present with the battalion at the time. Years later, Howard identified himself as the parsimonious officer but also denied the accusation. Furthermore, Macready was a young man of strong feelings which boiled unchecked in the heat of the moment. Also, while caustically critical of his fellow officers, he viewed the misdeeds of the men with tolerant amusement.

This tolerance was extended to men of other units. 'We had very strict orders against plundering of any description, and all marauders taken by the provosts marshal were to be immediately executed. Two of our men had been taken, but the Duke released them, as his note expressed, "in consequence of the excellent behaviour of our corps." – However, neither compliments nor commands can fill empty stomachs, and as our commissariat only served out three rations in twenty days, our men were obliged to forage or starve. I had myself mounted Ryan's horse, and was reconnoitring the district of Caulaincourt, when I heard a confused noise of pigs squeaking and men swearing, behind a hedge very near me. I rode up and discovered four soldiers of the 33rd cutting the throats of an old sow and her litter, "Hallo!" said I, "what are you gentlemen about? Don't you know that if the provost sees you, you'll swing for this?" "Yes, sir," answered the spokesman, "we do, but then, there's no rations – and, perhaps, your honour would like a pig." "Why, as the pigs are killed, I have no objection; but I assure you, my good fellows, this is a very serious business, and I wish I could have prevented it. I'll thank you for that pig to the left. Good morning." I galloped off with my prize, and the ramrod was through him immediately.'[207]

On 30 June Bailey took over command, having recovered from the severe contusion he received at Waterloo. Andrews and Pratt rejoined on the same day. Still incapacitated by their wounds were Hamilton, Vigoureux, Rumley and Lockwood, while Finucane, Machell and O'Halloran were all on detached duties.

The battalion spent two days at Annay from where they could see Montmartre and hear the Prussian guns. On 2 July news arrived that the main French force had capitulated, a day before the planned allied assault on Paris. As the French forces prepared to withdraw beyond the Loire, the allies advanced. On 5 July the 30th marched to Bau Bigny and the next day they occupied La Chapelle in the suburbs of Paris. A day later they marched to the Bois de Boulogne, where they bivouacked with the rest of the British troops. Elkington congratulated himself on obtaining a good quarter near the regiment, which meant the sick were within reach of their officers, and the accommodation was sufficient to house both himself and his friend, Bailey. Meanwhile, the men made themselves huts, to the detriment of the trees.

Macready's account of the entry into Paris is typically irreverent: 'Our division marched through the suburbs of La Chapelle, where crowds of Parisians came out to see us. As our Grenadiers were in front, they all agreed that England had picked her finest men to beat them. They laughed at our ragged colours, and called our riflemen, whose clothes were discoloured, *des ramoneurs de cheminee*. Nothing is too high or too low for the laughter of a Frenchman.'[208]

This may have been the occasion when the regiment was decked with laurel leaves. There exists a memorandum, enclosed in a piece of flannel, written by Howard. 'A part of laurel worn in Major Howard's cap on entering Paris immediately after the battle of Waterloo.' Macready, however, wrote that 'on the 22nd July, the anniversary of the battle of Salamanca, our whole army paraded on the road to Neuilly, in contiguous columns, every soldier with a leaf of laurel in his cap. The Sovereigns of Russia, Austria and Prussia, surrounded by a staff of some hundred officers, galloped down the line, and we afterwards broke into open column at half distance, and marched past them, the Duke at our head; our road was under the new triumphal arch, down the Elysian Fields, through the Place Louis XV, and home by the Porte St Denis. The leaves of laurel were sadly distressing to the poor Frenchmen, it was certainly insulting; but it is pleasant to remember the day on which an English army marched through Paris proudly bearing this badge of victory.'[209]

It is possible that laurel leaves were worn on more than one occasion. The Salamanca commemoration was certainly an important event, which Elkington also recorded. 'The whole army, under the command of the Duke of Wellington, passed in review before the Emperors of Austria and Russia and the King of Prussia, they were formed up in close columns of companies, having their front rank on the road, and reached from the Place Louis XV to the Bridge of Neuilly. The Head Quarters rode down the line, then the Army marched past in the Place Louis XV in quick time and occupied from eleven o'clock till three p.m., the rear was brought up by six pieces of twenty-four pounders, escorted by the Black Brunswick Hussars.'[210] In Elkington's opinion, these displays of military strength explained the passive response of the Parisians.

The huts in the Bois de Boulogne were soon replaced by tents, forty-seven for the battalion, which meant fifteen men to a bell-tent, although officers were less crowded, as Macready records. The encampment attracted sightseers. 'Heaviside, Harrison and myself had our tent in a fine grove of old trees beneath which we built huts and enclosed the whole with a staked hedge. Numbers daily stopped to admire our little establishment, and among the rest Lady Castlereagh. The comfort of the interior was not, however, strictly correspondent with the elegance of the outside appearance. We had not an article of furniture, but an old camp stool; the ground was our bedstead, a bundle of straw our mattress, and Harrison's blanket, for I had none, our covering. I always turned in completely dressed, and was generally awoke near daybreak by the arrival of my comrade from the gambling-house; his unvarying account of his losses, and his determined resolutions in favour of reformation, kept me awake until he dropped his head on the pannier, which served us for a pillow, and murdered my sleep by his melodious snoring. At this time the morning dew began to pinch my finger ends, and I employed myself in fretfully lamenting the unfortunate infatuation of my friend, and the accommodating harmony of his nose till breakfast time.'[211]

The march to commemorate Salamanca was not the only occasion when the allied rulers were entertained by British troops. 'In consequence of the increase in our numbers, we began to entertain the Sovereigns with field days. We generally manoeuvred on the plain of St Denis, and represented different occurrences in the Peninsular War. Sometimes on our arrival at the ground it would begin to rain, and we were faced about, and ordered to parade on the next fine day. As our camp was some miles from the plain, and as an army of our numbers took some time to get into position, we were generally out ten to twelve hours; during half this time we were standing in lines or columns, and for the rest half stifled with dust or bespattered with mud, and heartily cursing the deliverers of Europe. I have positively marched past in such a cloud of dust, that I have neither seen Duke, King, nor Emperor. How they stood it I cannot conceive. When the Duke did not require us, Sir T. Bradford and Sir P. Belsen [in command of the third division, and fifth brigade respectively] had us out and when their fantastic tricks were finished, old Hamilton [who had rejoined in August] paraded us to caricature light infantry movements.'[212]

By the end of September the pleasures of a summer encampment were over. 'During our stay in the Bois de Boulogne,' Elkington noted, 'the most exact discipline was observed. At length the weather became extremely bad, heavy rains with fogs, quite equal to those that occur in London, and we were almost washed out of our bivouacs. Until the heavy rain we felt no annoyance in our station but the distance the fatigue parties had to go for water.'[213] The change in the weather led to fevers and dysentery, although, owing to the use of anti-fever remedies, brandy and tobacco, the officers were unaffected. Nevertheless, there were only two natural deaths for each month the battalion spent in the Bois de Boulogne.

The officers could spend their leisure time pleasantly in Paris. Macready later recorded that Elkington was one of his companions on these excursions, so it is no wonder that their journals describe similar diversions. The surgeon visited all the sights, including the theatres and the gaming houses. The latter, he noted, ruined many English officers.

Macready's account is more detailed. Having described the Palais Royale as 'a high temple of vice and obscenity,' he proceeded to outline a typical visit. 'When we left camp for a day of pleasure we generally drove to the floating baths near the Tuilleries called les Bains de Vigier – had a tepid wash, swallowed a cup of chocolate, and moved to the Café de France where a gorge upon oysters and a pint of [illeg.] recruited us for Maury's heaven – we generally left this about five for Gunion's or Berry's – dine on a vol au vent diluted with a bottle of La Fitte – called at 144 Palais Royal to throw down a few five franc pieces – if successful Maury had the profit and if not we usually adjoined to the Hotel d'Angleterre where champagne was to be had on tick – got glorious, went to bed, forgot the Cardinal's niece [a reference to an infamous brothel] in the arms of the fille de chamber – were called up at four o'clock – galloped back to camp – were on parade at six and then quietly vegetated for some weeks on ration beef and sutler's brandy. All my pay and money I drew from home for a bit was swallowed in this vortex – I was only seventeen – and when I couldn't raise another sou I began to make virtue of necessity and rail at dissipation like a good young man.'[214]

A letter to his father, written in July, confirms that he was already outrunning the tipstaff. 'Croasdaile [the regimental agent] must have made a mistake about the £70, I think if you were to write to him for a copy of my account, you would easily see it . . . I am sorry that you think I would draw far more than I know he has to credit me with, as the bill's being sent back would effectively do any young man's business in the army; and Mr C. is the least obliging of agents in that particular.' Mr Croasdaile obviously took care not to let young officers fall deeply into debt by borrowing against the value of their commission. Nevertheless, it is safe to assume that Macready was not the only one to encounter financial difficulties as he was seduced by the pleasures of Paris.

Meanwhile, as the inspection return for October 1815 makes clear, the men also succumbed to temptation. Between July and October there were three cases of theft, and two of being absent without leave, as well as the usual cases of drunkenness, using disrespectful language and unsoldierlike conduct, yet these totalled only eleven regimental courts martial, against thirty-one in the period between 16 April and the battle of Waterloo, which is the highest number in the battalion's history. Furthermore, in the later period, two of the eleven were found not guilty, one was pardoned, and six had their original sentence reduced.

The normal business of military life continued for the army of occupation. On 29 October the inspection referred to above took place. The report was wholly complimentary to the battalion, although the inspecting officer, Colonel Belsen, commented that the colours 'which have been carried for twelve years, are so bad that they are not capable of receiving the badges and names of the actions in which the regiment has been engaged and as a substitute Lieut.-Colonel Hamilton has annexed silk streamers on which such names, etc, are placed.' These were the colours the battalion had received upon its formation, and carried into action ever since in the Peninsula and Flanders.

At the end of October the British forces moved into cantonments. The battalion marched to Clichy 'where the Prussians had been, so we had not much beyond the bare walls, my landlord stated his house had been quite stripped in 1814, on the first advance of the Allied Armies, he had scarcely re-furnished before our return after Waterloo took place; every particle of iron and lead was removed from this really fine house. Clichy is on the North of Paris not far from the Seine. *November 1st* We marched to Clamart, South of Paris. *November 3rd* We marched to Vauve, one league nearer Paris. *November 11th* We again moved to Mont Rouge, about one mile from the Barrier d'Enfer on the Orleans road. This town had suffered severely, having been occupied by the Prussians even since the capitulation of Paris.'[215]

Because there was no need for such a large army of occupation in a country which had accepted defeat or rather, with French pragmatism, had consigned that defeat to the vacuum of history, some of the British battalions were pulled back into Belgium while others, second battalions like the 30th, were directed to England where they could resume their proper function of recruiting for their senior battalions. Having been thanked by Colonel Belsen for their good conduct, the 30th left Mont Rouge on 4 December. 'The natives, who never attended our reviews, came in crowds to rejoice at our departure. We smiled a farewell at them, and the quick step of "Bon voyage Messieurs les Anglais," and that known to them as "ça ira," but called by us the "Downfall of Paris," soon hurried us from their gaze. We marched through St Denis, and after a long, wet, and dreary day's journey, arrived late at a miserable village, which furnished, however, tolerable poultry. Five more marches, with execrable weather, through wretched villages, brought us to Beauvais. The men and officers of our regiment fared particularly ill; as we moved with the 12th, whose colonel was senior to ours – he always occupied the best places, and his men were, of course, about him. We were consequently sent off the road to country houses in the neighbourhood, and besides going three or four miles to our billet at night, we had to go the same distance to head quarters the next morning before daylight.'[216]

During this march to the coast the 30th were brigaded with three other battalions under the command of Colonel Stirke of the 12th. They reached Calais on 24 December. 'On Christmas Day we marched our three hundred gallant bloods on board miserable smacks, of from sixty to a hundred tons burthen. The government had contracted with a house at Dover for the transport of the troops at a very cheap rate, and consequently lost two-thirds of the cavalry horses for want of accommodation. Our men were so crowded on and below deck, that there was barely room, if there had been hands, to work the vessels properly. The master of the one I went in assured me, that if we encountered such a breeze as the 12th Regiment had weathered a few days before, we should founder, and added that he would give a hundred pounds to be off his agreement.'[217]

It is probably no wonder that the officers chose to dine, and drink deeply, on shore. Pratt became most outrageously drunk and was soon taking issue with his fellow officers. Macready backed him up, both in talk and in drink, until they had insulted every officer in the party. As a result, Pratt and Macready found themselves abandoned by everyone except 'Johnny Roe'[218] whom even insults could not separate from his bottle. Having no-one at hand to quarrel with, the two young men went into the town to look for further trouble. Supporting themselves against a large door, they tried to batter it open. As a result, they were taken up by the National Guard, after a brawl which left Pratt with a wound to his temple. They were fortunate to escape without charge. If the provost marshal had come upon them, they could have been cashiered.

Drunkenness might have been the ideal state for the voyage that followed. Elkington succinctly described how a violent gale blew up, causing all but one of the ships in the fleet to run for Ramsgate. The onset of nightfall, the wild weather and the lack of water in the harbour made entry perilous but their pilot risked it, bringing them to safety after twelve hours at sea. Elkington lost a horse on the passage, but was relieved to have survived.

In Macready's more histrionic account, the voyage started mildly enough, with a fair breeze and a choppy sea, but in mid-Channel conditions freshened into a gale. 'Smack went our mainbrace, and roll came the seas over our weather quarter. In a few minutes we were in imminent danger; but, providentially, the wind lulled, and we repaired our rigging. We tried in vain to make Dover, and towards night changed our course and stood up for Ramsgate. When we reached its offing, the gale was stiff, and momentarily increasing, so that, though the high water flag was not hoisted, the masters of our vessels, trusting to their trifling draught of water, dashed for the harbour. The first vessel came crash aground between the two piers, the next ran her bowsprit into the stern rigging and swung broadside onto the sea – all followed, and all got foul of each other. The piers were covered with crowds of all sorts of people, running here and there with lights, and appearing by their gesticulations (for the roaring of the elements drowned their voices) to recommend us to take to our boats. We were twelve crank ships locked together, with our gangways, bowsprits, and timbers crashing with every heave of the water; the spanker booms were lashing right and left with each kick of the vessels, and the uproar of the wind, rain, waves, speaking-trumpets, ropes and sails creaking, and crews shouting was indescribable ... At length part of us were landed in boats, and the remainder ascended the piers by rope ladders thrown down. Two men fell and were crushed to pieces between the vessels.'[219]

Regimental records state that Thomas Roycroft, a labourer from Golston, Norfolk, was drowned during the landing at Ramsgate. Another man, Daniel Foley, a labourer from County Kerry, died in Dover at the beginning of February; he may be the second casualty, who eventually died of his injuries. There were two desertions in Calais but since these men rejoined on 29 December it is probable that they had celebrated their last night in France too freely.

The battalion was ordered to march to Margate, which they reached at midnight. The following day they returned to Ramsgate, to collect their arms and kit, and to witness the aftermath of their perilous crossing, ruined vessels and the drowned horses of the Inniskilling Dragoons piled in heaps on the quay. They then marched to Sandwich, and the following day on to Dover where they were quartered in the castle. By this time Macready was thoroughly disgruntled. 'I can't say the *amor patriae* was very strong within me for these three days. We were barbarously treated at Ramsgate, overcharged by the inn-keeper at Margate, misled by our guide, and wrongly directed by a ploughman on our road to Sandwich; drenched to the skin every day, and looked crossly on by every one but the waiters at the inns whose grins and grimaces were so much out of our pockets. As to the peasantry, the ones from Kent – if I ever come across them in the execution of my duty [illeg.] shall fly about their ears – a civil word could not be extracted from them.'[220]

This ungenerous reception may have surprised Macready but others would have recognised the attitude. The 30th were heroes of Waterloo and at a distance they could be applauded as such. At closer quarters they were merely an expensive and unruly inconvenience.

On 29 December the battalion was inspected by Major General Sir George Cook. Two days later they embarked for Cork, having been joined by the depot of seven drummers and 116 rank and file. A draft of thirty-eight men and eight officers was detached to sail for India, considerably less than the first battalion required but it was felt unreasonable to send out men who had just returned from France, while many at the depot had been invalided home after Waterloo. The draft contained ten Waterloo veterans, those most fully recovered from their wounds, but the majority had not seen active service. Since more men were needed, the prison ships anchored off the Isle of Wight were raided for deserters who were guilty of no other offence, and fifty were drafted into the 30th. As deserters, their likely punishment was foreign service for life but these men and boys were told that if they satisfied their commanding officer for seven years they could then return to England in the normal way.

Meanwhile, the second battalion had already sailed for Ireland. Thus, this 'English' battalion spent only a year of its fourteen-year existence on English soil.

Chapter 17
Ireland Again

The crossing from Spithead to Cork was another of those sea voyages which was long remembered by those who experienced it. Conveyed in the transport *Alexander*, the battalion suffered an uncomfortable experience, as Elkington recorded in his journal. '*December 31st* We embarked for Cork. *January 1st 1816* West wind, could not sail. *January 2nd* The wind coming fair at 2 p.m., left the Pier and sailed, we had baffling winds, only off Portland on the 6th, when a gale from the West came on and we put back through the Needles to Spithead. Here we remained for three weeks, it blowing from the West hard. *January 22nd* Weighed anchor but wind backing brought up again. *January 23rd* Sailed with an Easterly wind. *January 27th* The wind North, came to anchor in St Mary's Sound, Scilly Isles. I went on shore and called on the Governor, a brother of our Col. Vigoureaux [sic]. *January 28th* Sailed, wind South-East. During the night it came to blow a tremendous gale, nearly South, the weather was very thick when we made land, that the mate declared to be Ballycotton Island, the wind was right off shore and we with difficulty stood close hauled, about 8 p.m., picked up a pilot having first seen a ship run into Cork harbour. We anchored at Monkstown about 3 p.m., 29th, just before dark. This same evening two Transports with troops were wrecked in Tramore Bay and many lives lost, some hundreds of the 82nd and 59th Regiments. *January 30th* Attempted to land, but it blew up hard and such a swell that the boats were nearly swamped, and the men were ordered on board again, that in a part so landlocked as Monkstown was almost unprecedented. *February 1st* The wind having moderated we landed and marched at Cork. I went by water with Major Howard, who was commanding.'[221]

Macready, meanwhile, had taken advantage of the enforced stay at Spithead to spend time ashore, a privilege enjoyed by the officers but not the men. He stayed at the George Inn and drank fervently to the Queen's birthday. Unfortunately, he also fell in with a party of naval officers, spent all his money, risked his commission, and suffered a severe headache. He also missed the boat when the transport sailed. He was not alone, however. James Gregg found himself in the same situation, probably for a similar reason since Macready admits that he and Gregg had sown a few of their wild oats together in Paris.

Macready was able to cash a ten pound bill on the agent, and the two of them then travelled to Bath where Macready's brother, William, was performing. From there they went to Bristol and took the packet, *The County of Cork*, on 7 February. Having remembered that the regimental returns were dispatched on the twelfth day of each month, Macready calculated that they would have three days for the crossing and another day to make their peace with Howard. Unlike the rest of the battalion, the two subalterns enjoyed a fast sail, 254 miles in twenty-five hours. After spending a night in Cork, they caught up with the rest of the battalion at Buttevant, in barracks on a bleak moor.

It is not surprising that those who experienced the crossing in the *Alexander* needed to celebrate their safe delivery from the gale which claimed so many lives from the 59th and 82nd. There is no record of how the men marked their return to dry land, but the officers of the headquarters wing certainly observed the occasion with some deep drinking. While the left wing marched to Mallow, they 'had supper at the Inn at Cork, most of the party took too much whiskey punch. I slept in a double-bedded room with the Major [Howard], who when called the following morning could not recollect anything about the route. *February 3rd* Head Quarters marched off with one Officer only, about ten we were on the alert and in Post Chaises, started off after the Regiment, and overtook them before they reached Mallow.'[222] It would be interesting to know the identity of the one sober officer. Howard's lapse (which seems to have been uncharacteristic) may explain why when Macready arrived 'Major Howard came forward in his kindest manner and received me with a cordiality and a total silence as to my faux pas which gave me more pain and did me more good than all the terrors of big looks or even arrest. His conduct entitled him to my grateful recollection particularly as he was one of the party with whom I quarrelled so recently at Calais.'[223]

From Mallow the battalion marched on to Limerick, by way of Buttevant, Charlesville, Bruff and Kilmallock. Such a march should have been safe enough but dangers of a not strictly military kind could be lurking for the unwary. At Charlesville Lieutenant Freear, who seems to have been susceptible to female wiles proposed to a Miss Lowe after meeting her at a ball. Fortunately, he was able to extricate himself from this rash engagement.

Elkington was not impressed by the New Town Perry Barracks in Limerick. His main objection seems to have been the mess room, which was so small that nearly half the battalion officers were obliged to dine in the reception room. This may seem a trivial complaint but in a corps where relations between officers of all ranks seem to have been particularly cordial it would have been regarded as a serious inconvenience.

Nor did Macready find the city a particularly congenial place. Although the society of Limerick was genteel, they did not welcome the new officers with much enthusiasm. Limerick was full of officers, so that those of the 30th found themselves vying with the 93rd Highlanders, the Cavan Militia, two troops of the 4th Dragoons, and a detachment of Artillery for the citizens' attention. It was at this point that Macready began to formalise his journal, to counteract the boredom of garrison life. 'The diary of a single day will serve with a very trifling variety for a detail of many months employment. To rise at 8 – parade at half past 9 – read, write or shoot snipe till one – play backgammon, dress and lounge till half past five – brush up again for dinner and sit down at six – rise from table at 8 – read or write till half past ten and then to bed was my usual routine. Our mornings were occasionally diversified by a drill and our evenings by a drink.' It was necessary for the officers to dress fashionably and expensively, since this was expected of them. 'I insinuated myself into habilements which hardly allowed me to move and put running quite out of the question. I dared not stoop even to conquer.' Unfortunately, the young ladies were not interested in subalterns when 'a brace of epaulettes' was on offer.[224]

Special occasions enlivened the tedium of garrison duty in an Irish provincial town, however. St Patrick's Day was celebrated with great enthusiasm, not surprisingly considering the Irish presence in the battalion. Macready and his fellow light company subaltern, John Rumley, who had only just recovered from wounds received at Waterloo, were returning from the mess when the 'Light Bobs seized us and carried us back to their barracks, swearing we must see how happy they were. These days are the Saturnalia of our poor fellows, so we could not refuse them. They brought us to our room on their shoulders, preceded by a blind fiddler, torturing his catgut into "St Patrick's Day in the Morning".'[225]

The Waterloo medals which had been awarded to all combatants were presented to the battalion on 2 May, 1816. The event was reported in the *Limerick Evening Post* a week later. 'Thursday last, the 2nd Battn 30th Regt, quartered in this garrison, who bore a distinguished part at Waterloo, received the medal which is conferred by the Prince Regent upon every officer, non-commissioned officer, and soldier of the British army present on that memorable day. The medal is silver, very neatly finished, has "George Prince Regent" on the right side, on the reverse "an Eagle", in the centre the words "Wellington Waterloo, June 18, 1815;" on the rim, the name of the individual whom the medal is presented to is engraved.' Not only is the description of the actual medal somewhat inaccurate but the reporter does not seem to have been aware of subsequent events.

The occasion was marked by a speech to the battalion by Hamilton which, presumably, was similar to the words contained in the regimental orders. 'Lieutenant Colonel Hamilton feels the most sincere satisfaction in communicating to the Battalion the very high honour conferred on them by the Prince Regent, in having ordered them a Medal, for their steady conduct in action with the Enemy in the Netherlands, and with heart felt pleasure congratulates them on this Noble Reward for their gallantry.

'The Commanding Officer trusts, they will be *inviolably* and *most sacredly guarded* and preserved. He cannot but for a moment doubt but they will ever operate on the minds of the Men, as a guard against committing an act, that would in any way *disgrace the badge of distinction* now granted to them; but, that it will stimulate them, steadfastly, and shew by their good conduct how greatly they appreciate this inestimable mark of Royal favour.'

After this, the day turned sour when fighting broke out between the cock-a-hoop Waterloo veterans and the men of the 16th Regiment, who had recently replaced the Cavan Militia in the garrison and who had spent the last ten years either in the West Indies and Surinam, or on home service. 'The 16th had seen no service, our men had passed through a great deal; they were irritable, we were insulting. Our fellows showed their medals, their opponents knocked them down, so that confusion worse confounded disturbed the purlieus of Garryowen, till [Major General] Barry, by decisive measures, in which he plainly showed himself our partisan, put a stop to these irregularities. Though at the moment we were gratified by his partiality, yet I never heard anyone speak on the subject after we left Limerick who did not censure him, and applaud the independent conduct of Colonel Tolley, of the 16th.'[226]

General Barry, whom Macready described as fat, red-faced, vulgar and good-natured, had already proved himself a friend to the battalion, giving it a glowing inspection report in which he commented on the men's soldierlike appearance and competent manoeuvring. He noted their exceptionally clean barracks, remarking that such cleanliness had never been surpassed. He commented on the infrequency of courts martial and asked Hamilton, his officers and the men to accept his best thanks. He may have been influenced in his partiality for the 30th by the many excellent dinners he had enjoyed in their company. Even before the presentation of the Waterloo medals, this partiality had already provoked the hostility of the 16th. However, it won for the 30th a compliment from the Commander of the Forces, Sir George Hewitt, who noted Barry's report on the rarity of courts martial and commented approvingly on the good behaviour of the battalion.

The principal celebration in 1816, however, was the first anniversary of Waterloo. Invitations were sent out by an organising committee consisting of Major Howard, Paymaster Wray, Lieutenants Andrews, Elliot, Neville and Pratt, and Surgeon Elkington. Two days before the main celebration the battalion were already in full fling, as Macready reported. 'On the 16 June the day of the action at Quatre Bras, our good men got drunk – so did the sergeants – so did the officers – so did the garrison staff – the Commandants of Corps and our worthy General, and all at the expense of the officers of the 30th Regiment.' The next day the NCOs gave a ball at O'Brien's Tavern at which there was, reportedly, a little drinking and a great deal of fornication. On the actual anniversary, the festivities began when the soldiers assembled 'at an early hour, neatly dressed with white trousers, uncovered caps, and side arms, bearing numerous chairs, lavishly and really tastily ornamented with flowers, ribands, and laurels, and declared their intention of carrying their officers round the town. Entreaties were of no avail, resistance had a worse effect; accordingly, the band drew up, the men of our respective companies, after fixing a leaf of laurel in our caps, hoisted us up, and away we went to the quick steps of "Waterloo", "The Downfall of Paris", "Garryowen", and the "White Cockade". Thousands of people joined our fellows, and every five minutes greeted us with thunderous cheers. The Irish have a vivacity not unlike that of the French. Women would dash from their houses, and try to push through the crowds to shake hands with us, or give us an audible "Arrah, God bless your good-looking face, honey! I'm sure ye're a brave one." We halted opposite General Barry's door, he came out, bowed to us all, and, giving a hip, hip, set three such cheers agoing as I never heard before or since.'[227]

By early afternoon tables had been set out in the barrack yard, in the form of a hollow square. The whole battalion sat down to an excellent dinner of rounds of beef, legs of mutton, and bacon-hams, with an abundance of good beer. They were joined by a hundred friends from other corps, and there was also a cold collation for the ladies of Limerick. Buckets of whisky punch were emptied as toast after loyal toast was proposed by Sergeant Major James Woods as president, so it is no surprise to read Macready's opinion that within two hours the majority were happily drunk. The *Limerick Evening Post* described the scene more poetically: 'In the course of a short time, many of these brave fellows before whom the conqueror of Europe fell, surrendered, in their turn, to the rosy God, and at every table songs of war and love, anecdotes of the past and enjoyments of the present, given when the heart is soft, added to the interest and novelty of the scene. The square being thrown open to the Public, a number of carriages and a vast concourse of our fellow-citizens moved round the several tables; the order observed and the unexceptionable good conduct of the men, were highly gratifying.'

The reporter from the *Evening Post* then gave his account of the evening celebration. 'These scenes, though beyond any description we could give, were secondary in style and magnificence to the grand Ball and Supper given at the Assembly-Rooms by the Officers. The preparations had, for some days, excited such a curiosity and interest as to render it difficult, even with cards, to gain admission. At 11 o'clock the Rooms were opened, and presented a combination of rural enchantment, military trophies, and courtly splendour beyond any thing we have seen. The Hall and Stair-Case were covered with arbours of laurel and other shrubs; in the various compartments were fixed 1,500 variegated lamps, which were so placed as to astonish and delight. On entering the ball room, a number of transparencies, painted by Mr Gubbins, gave an elegant appearance to the room; among these we particularly noticed, a full length of the duke of Wellington decorated with his numerous orders; in the background the bastion of *St Vicente*, with the French flag flying on the battlements. A full length of the Prince Regent, in a Field Marshal's uniform, and a highly finished portrait of our venerable King, with the Crown, Sceptre, etc. Over the door was a large sphinx, *couchant*, resting on a pedestal with the word *Egypt*. Various smaller transparencies were placed round the room, presenting, in variegated letters, the names of the different other scenes of British Valour, in which the 30th were particularly distinguished: such as *Salamanca*, *Badajos*, *Madrid*, *Villa Neave* [sic], *Fuentes d'Honor*, *Quatre Bras*, *Waterloo* etc ... A number of bronze figures, holding lights, mirrors, with wreathes of laurel and a profusion of natural and artificial flowers had a major influence on a first view. The floor was chalked in the best style – dancing Nymphs, piping Satyrs, with innumerable Figures, were in humble readiness to receive the animated guests that, shortly after, screened them from general observation. Cards of invitation, as we stated in our last, were sent to and accepted of by nearly 300 of our Fashionables, and a more brilliant assemblage of beauty and elegance we have not witnessed. At twelve, General Barry and Mrs Hamilton (the Colonel's Lady) opened the ball. The dancers were relieved from pressure by standards intersected with silken lines, the card room was ruralised by a variety of rare exotics – here, and in the refectory, the company occasionally enjoyed a delightful promenade. Col. Hamilton, from his many wounds, was unable to join in the merry dancing.

'At 2 o'clock the Supper-Rooms were thrown open, to which the company ascended by a shrubbery of evergreens. The brilliancy and taste with which the rooms were lighted, and the arrangements and splendour of the tables so eclipse description, that we can only say, that every thing, which could bewitch the fancy, or satisfy the taste, was here placed in rival excellence. Grapes, Melons, Ices, and Confectionary, of every kind, and in every shape, interspersed with all the delicacies of the season, with the richest viands and the most delicious wines. The entire under the arrangements of Mr Talbot.' At this point the reporter became carried away by military metaphor. 'An engagement even more gratifying to our heroes and heroines than even the victory of Waterloo, now menaced the entire line – the right, left, and centre soon gave way – and in the order of attack, pillars and pyramids were levelled, legs and arms were scattered on the field; in short, every thing surrendered at discretion, and the entire Corps were either killed, wounded or missing. During the engagement some of the arch cupids hovered in the air, and no sooner was the battle ended than "the vivid flash from beauty's eye" irresistibly cheered and wounded the victors. Two rounds of grape were discharged to the Ladies of Limerick "and the heroes of Waterloo".

'After supper the dancing recommenced, and the party did not separate until a late hour next morning, delighted, not only with the excellence and variety of the entertainment, but with the minute attention and finished elegance of the Corps who entertained them.'

There was a price to pay, however. Excused from duty during the extended celebrations, the battalion was required to parade 500 men for duty on 19 June, but only twelve were sufficiently sober. As a result, a punishment march of twelve miles was ordered to sober up the rest. Nor did such jollification come cheap. Macready estimated that the total cost was a thousand pounds and wondered how a corps with few men of property could have squandered so much money. Questions were asked, 'but it was now too late – all we could do was to economise and forswear unrestricted committees for the future. Nothing is more dangerous for an unmarried Corps than to possess a few dashing fellows within it – they mislead young fellows of high spirits and thoughtless good nature by the specious argument of the credit of the Regt – the honor of the old and bold.'[228]

In September the battalion left Limerick for Tralee where the barracks were better and there were entertainments throughout the winter: balls and suppers in the mess room, public balls every fortnight, private family parties, a visiting company of actors, and regular shooting parties. Detachments were stationed at various posts along the coast, from Kenmare to Skibbereen, their principal business being to curb the activities of the gangs of smugglers which infested the coast. Once again, the battalion, like many others, was fulfilling the punitive tasks which kept the army occupied when there were no wars to be fought. These duties could prove both uncomfortable and hazardous, however. Lieutenant Pratt contracted a serious illness, from which he made only a slow recovery, as a result of being posted for some days without proper shelter or rations.

Macready was touring the Lakes of Killarney with Captain Heaviside and Lieutenants Warren and Moneypenny when he was summoned to sit the court martial of Private John Riley who was accused of having deserted from the regiment while on the march near Madrid, on or about 17 August, 1812. He then compounded the offence by making claims for arrears of pay and allowances to which he declared himself entitled as a prisoner of war. He had insisted upon receiving these payments before he would let himself be transferred to the first battalion.

The prosecution quickly established that Riley had been confined as a prisoner on 16 August 1812 for absenting himself from the regiment and had then disappeared from the march while under guard. Upon his return, in 1816, he was recognised by Sergeant Donnellan as a deserter. No date was given for this, but several witnesses testified that at the muster on 24 October (1816) they heard the prisoner make claims for back pay, showing Colonel Hamilton some papers which he said supported his claims. Hamilton refused to accept them. He would let Riley go to India without the charge of desertion being followed up, but only if he would acknowledge in writing that he had no valid claims. Riley refused.

At this stage it must have seemed a routine case with a predictable verdict, but the court had yet to hear Riley's defence, which is recorded in the court papers in reported form.

'On the march from Madrid in the month of August 1812 about the 16th or the 17th he was Prisoner in the Rear Guard of his regiment, and obtained leave to fall out, and private Cox of the Rear Guard was ordered to remain in charge of him, shortly after from a violent flux he had he was unable to proceed, and sat down by the side of the road, he frequently endeavoured all in his power to overtake his Regiment which he could not effect from the weak state he was in, at last the man in charge of him, (after asking him if he was able to proceed, to overtake the Regiment which he said he was not) left him saying he could not stop any longer, although he did all in his power to persuade him [Cox] to stop with him [Riley], telling him it would be better for them both – just before Cox left him and while this latter conversation passed Private Charles Connell of the 30 Regiment and another man passed he thinks Private Shearman also of the 30 Regiment – but towards evening [he] was obliged to sit down, unable to proceed further, when three men on horseback, dressed like the Spanish Brigands, and who afterwards proved to be Spaniards, came up to him and asked him if he was English, to which he replied he was, they then asked if he was going to join the Army. He said he was, at which they laughed, and one of them then placed him on a horse behind another man at which he rejoiced at first, thinking they were going to take him to his Regiment, but they then turned back, and shortly quitted the High Road and continued travelling till about 12 o'clock at night selecting unfrequented places to rest at till at length they reached Saragossa, when they gave him up to the French who put him in prison in the Castle, he got over the wall there, in order to effect his escape, but hurt himself so much that he could not, and was taken, and again put in prison and next day was taken to a French General Hospital where he remained some months very ill – a long while insensible.'

He was eventually marched to Montpelier, where he was held in prison for about six weeks before being sent on to Lyons, where he was held for nineteen months. His next place of detention was Selines, for a further ten months. Here he suffered further sickness and was put into the city hospital for about ten months, before being sent back to prison. He then heard news of the peace [which followed Napoleon's first abdication]. He was now a free man but the travel pass given to him by the commandant of the prison sent him to Hanover rather than England. From Hanover, which he reached six months later, he travelled on a German pass to Kitzbuttel, near Cuxhaven. He located the English Consul, who sent him to the Packet Agent, and the following morning he sailed to Harwich, landing in England about 1 May. Officials at Harwich then directed him to Colchester, where he was attached to the 69th Regiment. He now knew that the depot of the 2/30th was on the Isle of Wight. Before making his way there, he visited the regimental agent who 'at his request advanced him £2.0.0. in money on account; the next day on showing him his Pass etc and also the Papers [which he produced to the Court] – being printed forms to be filled up for – remuneration for clothing and also others for arrears of Pay etc as prisoner of war – which are the papers he showed his Commanding Officer. He denies most positively having deserted from his Regiment, his absence from it having been altogether unavoidable, as he has endeavoured to prove.

'With regard to the 2nd charge, he hopes that it will not be considered by the Court either unjust, or unsoldierlike his claiming for himself the same allowances, other Prisoners of War have received, when he knows and declares he never was a deserter – that if he had been one, he would certainly not have been so anxious to join his Regiment as he ever has been – for he thinks it must be clear, he might have easily avoided joining his Regiment if he had any fear on that head; on the contrary he was not even marched a prisoner from the Isle of Wight, and had charge given him at Cork by the Sergeant Major of that Depot, of the Route of the men he marched with from there, which Route he handed over to the Adjutant of the 30 Regiment, who said he was sorry to inform him, he was obliged to confine him.'

The crucial witness was Private Cox and Riley actually sought the court's permission to establish his whereabouts. He probably knew what Sergeant Watkins, the clerk to the battalion, now told the court, that Cox had been struck off dead. He also asked for the route from Cork to Tralee to be produced, since it supported some small part of his story. Other than that, he could only put his trust in the good judgement of the court.

Riley had transformed a clear-cut case into something as obscure as Irish mist. The court's deliberations lasted several days before the members decided there was insufficient evidence to convict Riley on the charge of desertion, which meant that he could not be found guilty of making false claims. Major General Gordon, the local commander-in-chief, was less convinced when the papers and sentence were passed to him for confirmation. He instructed the court to examine carefully Riley's claimed route from Spain to Germany. They did so and still found him not guilty, although whether out of bemusement or conviction is not clear. Either way, Riley got his money.

At the beginning of 1817 there were further reductions of the army. An order was received that one subaltern per company in the 2/30th was to be transferred to the half-pay list. Seven were put on English half-pay and two on Irish. More specifically, in March the Colonel of the regiment, General Manners, was informed that the complete disbandment of the battalion only awaited the return of some regiments from France. The date for its disappearance was 24 April, although the officers put on half-pay were to be paid in full until 24 June. Henceforth, the officer establishment of the regiment would be that of a single-battalion corps, with the addition of a recruiting company.

Had the two battalions managed to sustain seniority, this reorganisation would have been simple to effect. All the officers of the second battalion would have gone on half-pay, except for one or two required to bring the first battalion up to strength. Over the years, however, the complication of first battalion officers serving with the second, and vice versa, had become increasingly confused. In December 1816, the last month to be unaffected by the reorganisation, forty-one of the regiment's ninety-one officers were serving with the wrong battalion. The officers of the second battalion who were serving with that battalion were easily removed. It took months, though, to notify the officers in India of their altered circumstances and effect the changes, so that even in January 1819 the first battalion was still describing some officers as on attachment from the defunct second battalion, although some of these were still waiting to learn if all the first battalion officers who had been in Ireland intended to come to India or to opt for half-pay.

Even among the seven field officers serving with the two battalions there was some necessary adjustment. Of the two lieutenant colonels in India, Vaumorel and Maxwell, the latter belonged to the second battalion and officially went on half-pay in June 1817. Of the four majors, only Bircham, the junior, was in India. Bailey, the senior major, was returned as absent without leave and seems to have been looking for an exchange, as well as a divorce from his wife. In December he exchanged with Major Dalrymple of the 80th Foot. For Dalrymple the timing was fortuitous. Had the exchange taken place earlier in the year he would have been junior to Hawker and Bircham, both of whom had been placed on half-pay by the end of the year. Bircham's case is particularly interesting. This promoted sergeant (Toulon 1793) had risen steadily through the ranks; as a son of the regiment, who enlisted as a ten-year-old boy, he seems to have enjoyed particular favour. According to his own half-pay statement, completed some years later, he did not actually go on to half-pay until June 1820, while in the Presidency (Madras) for his health. Three years later he joined the Royal Veteran battalion, still with the rank of major, and then, in 1827, he transferred to the Ceylon Rifles, where he finished his career as lieutenant colonel, a rare distinction for a man who had risen from the ranks.

Major Vigoureux, second in seniority, and officially attached to the first battalion since 1815, eventually joined the regiment in India in 1819. A year later, upon Vaumorel's death, he was promoted to lieutenant colonel, junior to Hamilton.

Of the twenty-two captains, nine were attached to the wrong battalion but their reorganisation was comparatively straightforward. Only William Stewart of the first battalion chose to leave the regiment, retiring rather than going on half-pay. His departure and the extra captain allowed to a recruiting company (a duty performed by Robert Howard) meant that the two second battalion captains in India, Skirrow and Cramer, were able to remain with the regiment. The remaining second battalion captains, whether in Ireland or India, went on half-pay, with the exception of Richard Heaviside, who transferred into the 57th Regiment.

The greatest confusion existed among the lieutenants. There were forty-six serving with the two battalions in 1816 and twenty-four were with the wrong battalion. As subalterns, they (and the ensigns) were the first to be removed from the regiment but there seems to have been considerable bartering between those who were nominated for and those who actually wished to go on half-pay. Both James Poyntz and Macready were able to exchange back into the regiment. Four first battalion lieutenants opted for half-pay: Barlow, Perry and Penefather were already in Europe on private affairs; Andrew Baillie, although serving in Ireland, had marital and business interests in Antwerp. Hamilton was reluctant to lose Baillie, and tried to persuade him to stay but Baillie cited the intense pain he suffered from wounds received at Badajoz as his reason for going on half-pay. George Teulon, with the first battalion, also went on half-pay but not before he had purchased a captaincy. His later half-pay statement implies no reluctance to leave the regiment but it may be significant that in 1820 he exchanged into the 35th Foot.

Fortunately, the situation among the sixteen ensigns was relatively straightforward. Only two from the first battalion, Gregg and Deane, were on attachment with the second battalion and they joined the regiment in India after disbandment. Ledge, of the second battalion, was with the first in India. He had been a quartermaster sergeant with the senior battalion and was subsequently appointed quartermaster. When Kingsley arrived in India in 1815, Ledge became a supernumerary and was given an ensigncy, which he retained after the reduction of the regiment.

There were no problems with the staff officers, since they were all attached to their respective battalions. As a result of disbandment the paymaster, Wray, the quartermaster, Wilkinson, Surgeon Elkington, and the two assistant surgeons, Huggins and Palmer, went on half-pay. The case of Andrews, the adjutant, was more complicated. As adjutant to the second battalion he was junior to Stephenson, in India, but as lieutenant he properly belonged to the first battalion and he eventually served in India. Wray also rejoined the regiment when Jones, paymaster with the battalion, was invalided home in 1818.

Meanwhile, the men of the second battalion received the unsentimental treatment meted out to old soldiers which was typical of the period. There were small pensions for those entitled to them. Half the younger men were transferred into the first battalion. The others were discharged as 'unfit for the active military service of the line'. Some undoubtedly were unfit for active service, particularly men who had been invalided back from India but had failed to satisfy the Invaliding Board of their incapacity. They now found themselves cast off without reward, as did others who were merely surplus to requirements.

In February 1818 a detachment of nine officers and 203 other ranks sailed from Sheerness for India. In June a sergeant and twenty men joined them. Apart from the men at the depot and recruiting, this was all that remained of the second battalion as it passed into history, if not into oblivion. As Macready wrote: 'This brave corps ... will be remembered as long as the names of Fuentes d'Onoro, Badajoz, Salamanca, Muriel, Quatre Bras and Waterloo are emblazoned in the highest pages of British achievement.'[229]

Chapter 18

Meanwhile, in India . . .

The first battalion, it will be remembered, left Ireland in 1805 to join Lord Cathcart's abortive expedition to North Germany. In February 1806 the five companies which had completed the voyage to Germany and the four companies driven back by storms into east coast havens were reunited at Margate. They then marched to Portsmouth, arriving in the middle of April to learn that their new destination was India. East India Company ships were waiting for them, as was a strong draft from the second battalion which brought them up to strength. On 6 May the first battalion embarked at Portsmouth Hard for a posting which would last twenty-three years.

India might not quite rival the West Indies as the graveyard of British regiments but it still decimated the forces sent there and ruined the health of many who survived the posting. Most of the men and many of the officers never returned to Europe, while those who did often came home broken in health. The casualty returns attest to a continuous loss of NCOs and men, and discharge papers tell a melancholy tale of hepatitis and liver disorders. Even by the time the battalion reached the Cape of Good Hope there had already been several deaths, including one of the assistant surgeons, Ben Maxwell, and 163 men were lost in the first nine months in India.

The intended destination was Madras but the battalion was diverted further east as part of a naval expedition against some Dutch-held East Indies ports. French control of the Netherlands meant these had become convenient bases from which French pirates preyed on British shipping. Sir Edward Pellew, however, achieved a significant victory over the Dutch fleet at Batavia Roads and decided to delay his attack on the ports. As a result, the 30th continued their interrupted voyage to Madras, where they landed in January 1807.

What followed were years of inactivity, punctuated by sporadic moments of active service. Not surprisingly, there seems to have been a sense of lassitude and tedium, as Macready recorded in his journal after his arrival in 1819. 'The men of the 1st battalion appeared well drilled and set up, but were terribly emaciated and had a very dissipated (or what the French would call demoralized) appearance. They were considered superior in conduct to the other regiments on the Madras establishment, but being accustomed to the strict discipline and orderly behaviour of our troops at home, and totally unacquainted with the licence which custom has made the right of the English soldier in India, I must confess I was sadly prejudiced against them on our first acquaintance – much, however, of this wore off on finding that the deterioration of the soldier did not proceed so much from any inner depravity in himself, as from the silent but too certain working of a system which has originated in thoughtless and senseless indulgence, and been perpetuated by that servile spirit of imitation, and that paralyzing inertness which are almost general among our Anglo-Indians. I was still less inclined to think unkindly of the poor fellows when I had seen other regiments of His Majesty's service in India.

'Notwithstanding this I do still maintain that a battalion may be kept in as good order here as at home, if its commandant and his officers land with an immoveable determination to persevere in a strict observance of their duties, and to avoid as they would the pestilence, that relaxed system (so accommodating to the idle officer but so ruinous to the thoughtless soldier) which they will find pursued in every regiment ... The officer who has not been in India (for all who have been there must know it too well) when I mention that drunkenness, off duty, so far from being a crime is generally adduced as a palliation of almost every offence, and if bad conduct is conceived to be venial in the habitual drunkard, it becomes still less reprehensible in him who can boast of years of unblemished servitude. Disrespect appeared frequent, and though the officers were more free in their speech and indulgent in their practice towards the men than we had been in Europe, we looked in vain for that readiness to serve, and evident attachment to their leaders, which is the brightest trait in the character of the true soldier.'[230]

Macready's comments are borne out by the far greater number of courts martial recorded by the first battalion, and may also explain why Thomas Walker Chambers, a talented officer but a stickler for proper conduct from both officers and men, had such an unhappy time with the first battalion.

To return to the early years in India, in May 1807 Pellew resurrected his plan for an attack on the Dutch ports. He sought reinforcements from the 30th, initially a sergeant and fourteen men to act as marines. A month later another fifty-five men under Lieutenant C.S. Watson joined the expedition. At the end of August there was a successful action against the remnants of the Dutch fleet which Pellew had defeated at Batavia Roads. This resulted in the capture of a corvette, an armed brig, and a merchantman. The next month a further fifty men joined as marines, commanded by (former quartermaster) Ensign Poyntz, while in October the headquarters wing, under Lieutenant Colonel Lockhart, embarked at Madras before the fleet sailed for Malacca under the command of Vice-Admiral Troutbridge.

The Dutch ships *Revolutie*, *Pluto*, *Kortenaar*, and *Ruttkoff* were discovered at Grezzie and Captain Sir Charles Burdett of the 30th, accompanied by a naval officer, was sent to the Dutch naval commander under a flag of truce to negotiate their surrender. Ignoring the flag, the commander imprisoned the two officers and then fired red-hot shot at the British ships, although without doing any damage. The Governor of Souraybava, however, decided to surrender the ships, and the matériel, which had been the purpose of the expedition. As Pellew wrote to the Admiralty, the ships had been scuttled, so they were burnt, but Grezzie was ransacked of its stores and ammunition. Pellew also commended the 'zeal and perseverance' of the officers and men involved in the expedition.

The headquarters wing now returned to Madras, although sixty-three men, under the command of Lieutenant Watson and Ensign Washington Carden continued to serve as marines.

Meanwhile, another naval expedition was making use of seven officers, six sergeants, three drummers and 200 rank and file of the 30th. Rear Admiral Drury's objective was the Portuguese enclave of Macao. With the French in Portugal, there was an urgent need to gain control of Portuguese Macao. Major Wright of the 30th was required to persuade the Portuguese that their capitulation was politically necessary, even though no animosity existed between Britain and Portugal, who enjoyed the longest-standing alliance in Europe. Wright, however, never reached Macao, dying in Penang on 16 August, but the rest of the detachment from the 30th, commanded by Captain Beaumont, was present when Macao passed peacefully into British hands.

Back in India there was some brief excitement early in 1809 when the Rajahs of Travancore and Cochin rebelled against the East India Company. The 30th were kept at Fort St George, Madras, to defend the Presidency until reinforcements from the north and from Ceylon eased the situation. The battalion was then sent south to Nagapatam where it formed the field force of Colonel Wilkinson, former lieutenant colonel in the regiment who had reapplied to join when he could not obtain an active service posting. By April, though, the threat was over and the battalion was garrisoned at Trichinopoly.

Although the men of the 30th were regular soldiers enlisted in the service of the king, they still found themselves involved in the affairs of 'John Company'. The East India Company had its own forces, officered by Europeans, but regular forces were always called upon when additional troops were required. The greatest source of concern was the Mahratta Confederacy, where prince manoeuvred against prince or leagued against the Company. As the 30th discovered in 1809, regular forces were then drawn into Indian affairs.

Later in 1809, however, it was the European officers in the Company's service who provoked a crisis. The Governor of Madras, Sir Thomas Barlow, provoked them to mutiny, a dangerous situation because the officers had the support of their sepoy soldiers. The Company immediately required its British officers in Madras to sign a declaration of obedience. Colonel Wilkinson, still in command, made the same demand at Trichinopoly, where half the officers refused to sign. They were ordered by Wilkinson not to communicate with their sepoys. Again they refused, and were placed in the custody of 200 men of the 30th, armed with loaded muskets and fixed bayonets which they were to use should the prisoners attempt to escape or should their sepoys try to rescue them. The officers were then sent to Nagapatam and on to Madras to be disciplined for their disobedience but by this time Barlow's behaviour was so notorious that the Governor General decided upon leniency. Indeed, it was Wilkinson who was castigated for the rigour of his actions, even though Trichinopoly alone was spared outright mutiny.

Officers of the regular army were often sent on detachment to Company units or to support Company residents in the various allied states. During the period of the mutiny, Major Christopher Maxwell was sent to the 6th Native Cavalry, with Lieutenants Cane and Lewin in support, and Captain Bircham went to the 16th Native Infantry, accompanied by Lieutenant Napper.

There was a brief disturbance involving the native ruler of Travancore in 1810. Captain Murray, with a force of seven officers and 343 men, was sent to deal with it but returned within a month. Nevertheless, such intervention was typical of how the Company relied on regular forces. Upon Murray's return, the battalion sank into the monotonous routine of Indian military life. Any disruption tended to be caused by the battalion's own internal tensions. Quarrels between officers, duels, and the inevitable courts martial, punctuated regimental life. Macready himself got into a quarrel with his friend, Neville, and found himself fighting a duel, even though he regarded the practice as ridiculous. The cause might be trivial, in Macready's case impatience with Neville's boasting, but the consequences could be serious. Four officers, the principals and their seconds, were court martialled for a duel and were lucky not to be cashiered. One of them, Captain French, was foolish enough to repeat the misdemeanour, with the result that he lost his commission in 1814.

An event which revealed a disturbing underside to the regiment was the court martial of Lieutenant Nicholson. Problems began when a small detachment under Captain Jackson was sent to Vellore in 1808. Something about Jackson's conduct offended his second-in-command, Chambers. Words were exchanged, which led to a duel, Chambers's court martial, and his suspension from rank and pay for three months, a mild sentence which suggests that the court had some sympathy for him. Chambers subsequently signed a resignation from the regiment, possibly already intending to join the second battalion in Spain. His friend, Nicholson, who was also involved, was not so accommodating. He refused to sign a resignation without first receiving a promised recommendation. He was also heard to say that blood would be spilt, which led to a charge that he had urged Chambers to fight another duel. The resultant court martial revealed deep animosity in the battalion.

Despite every attempt by Lieutenant Colonel Vaumorel to have Nicholson found guilty, the court condemned him only on the minor charge of saying that blood would be spilt. At this point Colonel Wilkinson intervened. He refused to endorse the sentence and required the court to reconsider its decision, presumably because Nicholson's conduct offended his concept of loyalty. The court reconsidered but still reached the same decision and sentenced Nicholson to a reprimand, which was delivered by letter.

Command of the battalion during these early years in India passed through a sequence of officers who had long-standing connections with the 30th. Colonel Wilkinson was promoted to major general in October 1810, thus severing a direct association of thirty-seven years. He was succeeded by Lieutenant Colonel Lockhart, who had been with the regiment since 1784. In 1812 he was given command of the Malabar and Canara districts and temporary command passed to Lieutenant Colonel Vaumorel, who had already been with the regiment for nineteen years, and remained until his death while on sick leave in 1820.

Despite the dominance of the East India Company and the presence of so many regular units, India was essentially an unstable place and a disputed succession in the tributary state of Karnal caused another flutter of excitement. The battalion was withdrawn from Cannanore towards Madras, and attached to a force assembling at Gooty, three hundred miles north of Cannanore. By September, however, the situation had been resolved and after a six-week halt at Vellore the battalion marched to Madras.

This non-event, contemporaneous with the Waterloo campaign, emphasises the different experiences of the two battalions and may explain why the remnants of the second battalion, when they finally reached India, were granted a less than fulsome welcome.

From 1815 until 1818, when Hamilton and his second battalion detachment reached Fort St George, the first battalion saw no further action, even though several regular units were engaged in the Pindari War of 1817. Since they were subsequently involved in the mopping-up operation, however, some explanation of this war will provide a context for later events at Asseerghur.

With the decline of the Moghuls power passed to the princes of the Mahratta Confederacy, although their first attempt to challenge the East India Company ended in defeat in 1803. Nevertheless, the situation in central India remained volatile. By 1817 the nominal head of the Confederacy was Peshwa Baji Rao but the main destabilising force was Daulat Rao Scindia. One weapon which all the Mahratta powers were prepared to use, against the British or against each other, was the Pindaris. A commentator wrote of them: 'Every horseman who is discharged from the service of a regular government, or who wants employment and subsistence joins one of the *darras* (principal divisions) of the Pindaris; so that no vagabond who has a horse and sword at his command can be at a loss for employment. Thus the Pindaris are continually receiving an accession of associates from the most desperate and profligate of mankind. Every villain who escapes from his creditors, who is expelled from the community for some flagrant crime, who has been discarded from employment, or who is disgusted with an honest and peaceable life, flies to Hindostan, and enrols himself among the Pindaris.'[231]

This military tribe of bandits, embracing all races and religions, operated as a secret state within a state, as many as 30,000 strong. Their objective was plunder; they would descend without warning, torturing, pillaging, wounding and killing their victims. Lightly armed horsemen, they resembled a plague of locusts, disappearing as quickly as they arrived, carrying off everything that was portable. They were undoubtedly a useful weapon in the internecine strife of the Mahratta princes, and in their quarrels with the Company.

By 1817, however, their outrages had extended into the Presidency of Madras. The Governor General, the Marquis of Hastings, organised a military campaign which not only extirpated most of the Pindaris but also dealt a serious blow to the power of those Mahratta princes who foolishly seized the moment to oppose the British. Only Appa Sahib of Nagpur and a Pindari leader, Chitu, remained as a threat, eventually bringing the 30th to Asseerghur in 1819.

Hamilton reached Fort St George in June 1818. Macready, who was with the detachment, sensed that its mainly junior but battle-experienced officers were resented by the officer establishment in Madras. 'Our men were safely landed and we marched into Fort St George preceded by the two bands of the 1st and 2nd Battalions, which relieved each other alternately. Many of the officers of the Regiment came to see us, and remarked that they had never seen such a detachment land in India. We had two hundred as fine fellows as ever stepped, and nine officers, of whom seven had seen good service. Next day we were told off to companies, and all our men put to drill. This was not a measure calculated to produce much cordiality between the men of the two

Battalions, as a soldier who had seen such days as 6th April 1812, 22nd July and 25th October of the same year, and the 16th and 18th June, 1815, could hardly be supposed very deficient in the knowledge of his duty, nor could he feel particularly gratified to see men who had never heard an angry shot or seen an enemy, lolling and enjoying themselves in their cots, while he was called on to exhibit himself three hours a day for many weeks as a young and ignorant recruit. However, our lads knew the men had nothing to do with this . . . Of the officers we met many were gentlemanly men. A few were old soldiers, great talkers and hard drinkers, and some were strange fellows who required to be well known in order to properly appreciate. None of them, however, eyed our medals with very great complacency, or appeared cordially to forgive us for having gained them . . . Our old friends who had known us "in happier days and on a happier shore" were very glad to see us, and we were entertained very hospitably.'[232]

It is difficult to guess what Vaumorel's motives were for subjecting experienced soldiers to the regime of raw recruits, unless it was to acclimatise them to the rigours of India. A less charitable interpretation of his actions might question his attitude to these newcomers, and his relationship with Hamilton.

Meanwhile, Appa Sahib, the deposed Rajah of Nagpore, was conducting irregular warfare in the hills to the north of Jalna and Ellichpore, where a force under General Doveton was based. Appa Sahib had been a prisoner of the British but escaped in May 1818. In October he joined the Pindari leader, Chitu, and together they fled towards Asseerghur, which was a possession of the Mahratta prince, Scindia, and was held by his Killador, Jeswant Rao Lar, in his master's name. Scindia had submitted to the British, so Asseerghur should have been in friendly hands. Nevertheless, Appa Sahib was offered refuge, although Chitu chose to flee elsewhere.

By this time the left wing of the 30th, under the command of Major Dalrymple, was on the march to join Doveton's force despite suffering seriously from dysentery. Macready recorded that he was reduced to the condition of a walking skeleton. Eventually they reached the ancient fortress of Asseerghur, situated at the western end of the Satpora hills. The upper fort, a thousand yards by six hundred, was perched on a hill 'scarped and precipitous, accessible only at two places, which were strongly fortified. The fort contained an abundant supply of water. It was, in spite of its natural strength, easily approached under cover by numerous ravines. In one of these, terminating in the upper fort, is the northern avenue where the hill is highest; and to bar access at that point an outer rampart, consisting of four casements with embrasures, 18 feet in height and thickness, and 190 feet in length, crossed from one part of the interior wall to another . . . The principal approach to the fort was on the south-west side . . . the entrance was through five gateways by a steep flight of stone steps. Here a third line of works, called the lower fort, embraced an inferior branch of the hill immediately above the town. The wall was about 30 feet in height, with towers, and at the northern and southern extremities it ascended to connect with the upper works. The town had a partial wall on the southern side where there was a gate; but elsewhere it was open, and surrounded in every direction by ravines and deep hollows.'[233]

Doveton, in command of the attacking force, was described by Macready as 'an old officer of great character. He had been tried for his behaviour, during the most unsoldierlike proceeding of the officers of the Madras army in 1809 [when Colonel Wilkinson intervened in Trichinopoly], which common sense must designate as mutiny, but which must have some palliating circumstances in it, unknown to the multitude, as those concerned in it have been since especially favoured . . . He was acquitted, and distinguished himself last year in

The Siege of Asseerghur, 1819

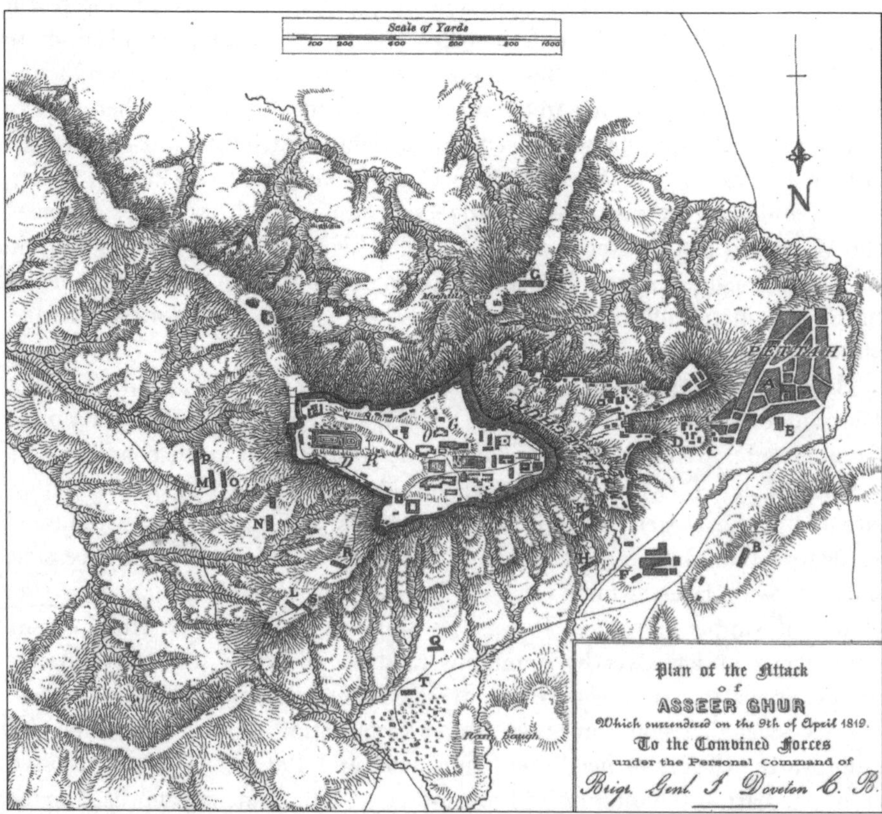

Nagpoor. He is very able in procuring information, he lives retired, sees little society, and seldom moves without a posse of staff and horsemen.'[234]

Doveton's force began its advance towards Asseerghur on 3 February 1819. Four days later news arrived that Appa Sahib had narrowly escaped capture by riding his horse down a precipitous slope before taking the road to Asseerghur. At daybreak the next day the British force, part Regulars, part European Company, part Native Company battalions, marched for Kandeish. On 10 February they reached the territory of Scindia, a wild country of jungle heath and ravines. By 3 March they were within reach of Asseerghur. Doveton immediately engaged in negotiation with the Killador, to the frustration of his troops, even though most of them were inclined to regard the fortress as impregnable.

During the second week in March, the Madras European Regiment and some Native Infantry brought up the Nagpoor artillery train, while the 67th, with another artillery train from Saugor, was daily expected. This probably explains the patently unprofitable negotiations.

With everything in place for an attack on the lower fort, the assault troops, including the flank companies of the 30th, assembled at midnight on 17 March. Lieutenant Colonel Fraser of the Royals was in command, while Major Dalrymple commanded the reserve, which included the remaining companies of the 30th. The aim was to break the walls of the lower fort. At the same time a diversionary force would attack from the north.

At 1.00 a.m. the assault force moved out of camp, rushed the town, and overwhelmed the defenders. They then sheltered in the streets, which ran parallel with the lower fort. They proceeded, wrote Macready, 'over the wilderness, taking advantage of the hollow ways and ridges – one of which was so steep as to require our scaling ladders – established ourselves under a rock at the end of a ravine or nullah bed, near seven hundred yards from the Pettah, at about four in the morning . . . Torches were repeatedly seen moving in different quarters of the fortress, and, just before we ascended a height towards the end of our march, some particularly large ones were exhibited, and we received the word of command from the head of the column: "Halt – prime and load." At these moments the whole host of memory flash as it were before us, there is a strange hollow sensation between the chest and the throat; it is not a feeling of apprehension, but really a sort of shudder of the flesh, at the resolutions of the nobler mind, and I can recollect myself laughing in pride of heart as I considered myself rising superior to my nature.

'The spot where we halted was destined for the reserve as soon as we should quit it. Above us a little stream divided and prattled down each side of a vast mass of rock behind which we lay, and by its plashing from break to break in the stone, drowned the occasional murmurs of impatience which were growled by the cold and anxious soldiery. As we sat and dozed, wishing for morning, and muttering curses against the chill dew, which was cruelly penetrating, two shots roused us, and Doveton, who had accompanied us hitherto, after a pause of a few seconds, stood up and gave the word, "Fix bayonets! Now then, upon 'em my lads!"

'We dashed up each hollow of the nullah, and as we advanced in double quick time, formed regularly, the Royals leading, and our company next. An irregular fire of wall pieces commenced as we left our halting place, but without any effect. We soon reached the gate, burst it open and rushed into the Pettah, with three cheers. As we pushed thro' the gateway, the clashing of our bayonets made the fellows in the rear think we were hard at work, and they shouted loudly, "Stick it into 'em, my boys; don't give an inch [for] your souls!" We were soon clear in, formed, and cleared the streets before any effectual resistance could be offered. One or two fellows were bayoneted in the main street, and towards the end of it nearest the fort some Arabs brandished their swords and shields, and drew the head of the column on some exposed ground, by which Major Mc'leod and Bland were wounded, with about a dozen men, and three killed; but the Arabs were driven into the gateway with some loss.

'We now got the men under cover of the houses and banks, as the fire became heavy, particularly to the left of the Pettah, where we occupied a flat hill, from which we returned the tiraillade. They threw rockets, and occasionally discharged their overgrown ordnance, which we called the gram-kettles, but we had few casualties, and those chiefly from the matchlock fire, which was directed at every one who passed the streets which ran up to the fort. I was much pleased with one of our fellows, named McGrath. He received a shot in the right shoulder and fell. We raised him up, and I remarked to one of his comrades, "He'd better be sent off, for if the wound is not dangerous, he can't use his musket," when the brave soldier faintly replied, "No, no, your honor, let me stay, I always fire left-handed." This work – sniping – continued all day, and towards evening an howitzer battery opened from our rear, but did not seem to answer. It was tedious and tiresome.'[235]

At this point, Macready, who was still suffering from dysentery, collapsed, and was thought to be dying. The 30th, however, had been left to hold the town with the Royals, so he had to stay put.

The next day the garrison of the lower fort counter-attacked, but was repulsed. The following day the same thing happened at sunset with the same result. The defenders then abandoned the lower fort, but at 7.00 a.m. on 21 March a magazine exploded, killing thirty-four sepoys and their officer, and wounding another sixty-six. This brought the defenders back into the fort and they 'began firing their guns and manning the works, clashing their shields and yelling like devils; but a few hints mildly delivered as salvoes soon convinced them of the incorrectness of their conjecture.'[236]

The arrival of the heavy gun battery from Saugor changed the situation. Once a breach had been achieved the defenders abandoned the lower fort – just as well in Macready's opinion, because the breach would have proved impracticable. The battery was now moved into the lower fort in order to batter the upper fort. On 5 April, the north-eastern tower collapsed with all its guns, which prepared the way for a breaching battery. Two days later this battery fired at the retaining wall, which collapsed. There now followed a fierce argument as to who should have the honour of heading the storming party, the grenadiers of the 67th or the light company of the 30th. Before it could be resolved, however, Jeswant Rao Lar entered into negotiations, surrendering the fort on 9 April. He and his forces departed with their possessions but the fort remained in British hands after a discovered document proved that Scindia himself had ordered his deputy not to give up the place when summoned.

In Macready's opinion, the Killador made a poor resistance: 'Instead of plying us with his jinjauls and wall-pieces (excellent weapons of which he had abundance), he contended himself with throwing rockets, which seldom strike within an hundred yards of their mark, and occasionally discharging his gram-kettles, to the infinite terror of his own artillerymen.'[237] The respective losses, however, suggest that the assailants definitely received the worst of it. They had 323 killed and wounded, while the defenders suffered forty-three killed and ninety-five wounded. The 30th had nine men wounded, a sergeant and eight rank and file, none of them seriously.

The two renegades who had brought the British to Asseerghur suffered varying fates. Appa Sahib, who was rumoured to have fled early in the proceedings disguised as a fakir, finally found refuge in the Punjab. Chitu, hiding in the jungle after he failed to get into the fort, was said to have been killed by a tiger which devoured all but his head. The remnants of the Pindaris continued their marauding in a desultory fashion for some years, particularly in Hyderabad, but they had lost their power to terrorise. Significantly, this area, the Rajputana States, remained loyal during the Mutiny.

The 30th had arrived late on the scene, but they received commendations for the part they played. Doveton, in his report to the Commander-in-Chief in Madras, Lieutenant General Sir Thomas Hislop, wrote: 'The conduct of the detachment of H.M. Royal Scots, under the command of Captain Wetherall, and of H.M. 30th, under the command of Major Dalrymple, during the siege of Asseerghur, has been most exemplary, as to reflect the most distinguished credit on their several commanding officers, as well as the whole of the officers and men composing those detachments.' Doveton subsequently referred to the left wing of the 30th as 'this exemplary detachment'.

The East India Company attempted to have Asseerghur added to the actions, fought between 1803 and 1826, for which the general service medal was awarded in 1848. Their request was turned down by the government of the day, however, on the grounds that the application had been made too late.

The remainder of the regiment's Indian period can be dealt with in a few words. Their social life, which lies beyond the scope of this work, provides the only interest for the remaining nine years.

Vaumorel's death in 1820 left Hamilton in command of the regiment and this had an interesting effect on its discipline. There had always been a marked difference between the number of regimental courts martial listed in the inspection returns for each battalion. This was partly due to the junior battalion seeing so much active service, although the frequency did not rise in Ireland. Under Hamilton's command in India, the rate decreased markedly and subsequent inspection reports congratulated him and his officers on their efforts to reduce the number of offenders.

From 1820 to 1826 the 30th were at Secunderabad, where nothing of any moment occurred, so that the casualty figures for this period can be ascribed only to the hardship of service in India. A monument erected upon their departure from Secunderabad commemorates the 708 men, women and children (including seventeen officers) who died during those years. These grim figures take no note of officers sent home for the recovery of health or men invalided home, who died on the voyage or soon after.

From Secunderabad the regiment returned to Madras and then in August 1827 they moved to Trichinopoly. By this time Hamilton was no longer in command, having been promoted to commander of Fort St George (Madras) in May 1827. Like Lockhart and Vaumorel before him, however, his health had been ruined by India and he finally sailed home in December 1827 on two years' sick leave, his first period of extended leave since 1811–1812.

The regiment soon followed him, embarking for England on 14 February 1829. They left behind five sergeants and seventeen other ranks, time-expired men who opted to receive their pensions in India. These were men who had Indian wives, whom they were unable to bring back to Europe. Men in the same situation who were not time-expired transferred into other regiments which were still serving in India.

The 30th reached England in June 1829, disembarking at Gravesend. A month later they were on the Isle of Wight, where they were reunited with Hamilton as their commander. It was a short-lived reunion, however, since Hamilton went on leave in August, preparatory to retirement. As the one officer who was with the regiment throughout the period covered by this study (1793–1827) it is fitting to end with Bannatyne's words on a man whose career was inexorably associated with the 30th. 'No man had ever exercised a stronger influence in a regiment. He commanded the second battalion, except for a few months, from the time it left Cadiz in October, 1810, till it was absorbed by the first in 1818, and he commanded the regiment in India, from October 1819, till he went sick in September, 1827. He was as kind-hearted and generous as he was brave, and under him the regiment knew that it was efficient and capable of great things, but during the last year in Madras the climate and age had begun to tell and he was no longer the same man. He died at Woolwich on June 4th, 1838, aged 63.'[238]

For both Hamilton and the regiment the glory days of the Revolutionary and Napoleonic wars were long over. But as Macready so pertinently remarked, the memory of those days and those deeds would survive for as long as stirring heroism aroused the interest and admiration of succeeding generations.

Notes

Chapter 1

1. Quoted in Neil Bannatyne, *History of the Thirtieth Regiment* (Littlebury Bros. 1923) p. 18.
2. Quoted in *Red Roses over the Veldt* (Carnegie Publishing 2000) p. 213.
3. James Aytoun, *Redcoats in the Caribbean* (Blackburn Recreation Services Dept. 1984) p. 7.
4. Aytoun, p. 41.
5. Alex M. Delavoye, *Life of Thomas Graham, Lord Lynedoch* (Richardson & Co. 1880) pp. 57–58.
6. Delavoye, pp. 71–72.
7. Aytoun, pp. 34–35.
8. From a handwritten account at Fulwood Barracks, Preston.
9. One of them, Sergeant Major Samuel Bircham, was subsequently commissioned into the regiment, serving until 1817 and rising to the rank of major. He was a child of the regiment, having been born in Gibraltar in 1770, the son of a corporal, and enlisting as a twelve-year-old drummer in 1782. It is not clear why the other sergeant, who has never been identified, did not receive a similar reward. He may have been illiterate, a Catholic, or too old for a commission. He was, however, promised an enhanced pension when he finally retired.
10. Aytoun, pp. 42–43.
11. From a handwritten account held at Fulwood Barracks, Preston.
12. Quoted by Bannatyne, p. 189. In addition, Bannatyne cites the later comment, written by General Hislop (deputy-adjutant general at Toulon) to Vaumorel when they were both in India: 'On that occasion you and the brave soldiers with you who nobly did your duty fell into the hands of the enemy while the officer who was intrusted with the command of the post abandoned it early in the contest and soon after quitted the service.'

Chapter 2

13. This tower, of course, gave its name in a corrupted form to the Martello towers which were soon to line the south-eastern seaboard of England.
14. *Historical Records of the XXX Regiment* (William Clowes & Son, Ltd. 1887) p. 57.
15. Thomas Walsh, *Journal of the Late Campaign in Egypt* (London 1803) p. 45.
16. Mackenzie Macbride (editor), *With Napoleon at Waterloo; the unpublished diary of Sergeant Daniel Nicol* (G. Bell & Sons, Ltd. 1911) p. 21.
17. Walsh, p. 52.
18. Nicol, pp. 43–44.
19. Walsh, pp. 113–114. This is one of the first references to opthalmia, a disease of the eyes which, being highly contagious, was to plague the British army for many years to come.
20. Nicol, p. 61.
21. *Historical Records of the XXX Regiment* p. 78.
22. Walsh, pp. 214–216.

23. Nicol, p. 63.
24. Quoted in Walsh, Appendix pp. 117–118.
25. Quoted in Bannatyne, *History of the Thirtieth Regiment* p. 221.
26. Walsh, pp. 252–253.

Chapter 3

27. Bannatyne, *History of the Thirtieth Regiment* p. 228.
28. Bannatyne, p. 227.
29. Sir Henry McAnally, *The Irish Militia 1793–1816* (Dublin and London 1949) p. 191, note 65.
30. This list was appended to the appropriate pay list/muster roll, the only time wives are mentioned by name in the contemporary records of the regiment.
31. *A Military History of Ireland* (Cambridge University Press 1996) p. 358.
32. These details come from WO 119.
33. *Historical Records of the XXX Regiment* p. 84.

Chapter 4

34. The Journal of Lieutenant William Stewart, Thirtieth Regiment.
35. Walsh, *Journal of the Late Campaign in Egypt* pp. 4–9.
36. Delavoye, *Life of Thomas Graham, Lord Lynedoch* p. 338.
37. Delavoye, p. 418.
38. Sir William Maynard Gomm, *A Staff Officer in the Peninsula* (Napoleonic Archive) p. 11.
39. Andrew Leith Hay, *A Narrative of the Peninsular War* (London 1834, second edition) Vol. I, p. 265.
40. Leith Hay, Vol. I, p. 266.
41. Stewart's journal.
42. Stewart's journal.
43. Stewart's journal.
44. Stewart's journal.

Chapter 5

45. The Journal of Lieutenant William Stewart.
46. Stewart's Journal.
47. Stewart's Journal.
48. Gomm, *A Staff Officer in the Peninsula* (Napoleonic Archive) p. 12.
49. Stewart's Journal.
50. Stewart's Journal.
51. Stewart's Journal.
52. *The Royal Military Chronicle* Vol. III, pp. 256–257.
53. William Tomkinson, *Diary of a Cavalry Officer* (London 1894) pp. 102–103.
54. *The Royal Military Chronicle* Vol. III, p. 10.
55. *The Royal Military Chronicle* Vol. III, p. 14.
56. *The Royal Military Chronicle* Vol. III, p. 124.
57. *The Royal Military Chronicle* Vol. III, pp. 241–243.

Chapter 6

58. *The Royal Military Chronicle* Vol. III, pp. 419–420.
59. *The Royal Military Chronicle* Vol. III, p. 422.
60. *The Royal Military Chronicle* Vol. III, p. 422.
61. *The Royal Military Chronicle* Vol. IV, pp. 42–43.

62. James Hale, *The Journal of James Hale, late Sergeant in the Ninth Regiment* (republished by the IX Regiment 1998) pp. 76–77.
63. See Sir J.T. Jones, *Journal of Sieges in Spain* (Ken Trotman Ltd. 1998) Vol. I, pp. 11–12.
64. Jones Vol. I, pp. 149–150.
65. *Dispatches of the Duke of Wellington* Vol. IX, p. 36.
66. Jones Vol. I, p. ix.

Chapter 7

67. Leith Hay, *A Narrative of the Peninsular War* Vol. I, p. 291.
68. Jones, *Journal of the Sieges in Spain* Vol. I, p. 218.
69. Leith Hay, Vol. I, pp. 294–297.
70. Captain McCarthy, *Recollections of the Storming of the Castle of Badajos* (London 1836) pp. 97–99.
71. Lamare, *An Account of the Second Defence of the Fortress of Badajoz by the French in 1812* (London 1824) pp. 32–34.
72. Jones, Vol. I, p. 385.
73. W.F.P. Napier, *History of the War in the Peninsula and in the South of France* (London 1840, reprinted Constable 1993) Vol. IV, p. 431.
74. Sergeant John Douglas, *Tale of the Peninsula and Waterloo 1808–1815* (Leo Cooper 1997) pp. 38–39.
75. *Dispatches* Vol. IX, pp. 40–41.
76. The following verses appeared in a London magazine:

On the Death of Colonel Gray at Badajos April 1812

At Badajos the dreadful fight
Raged fiercely, and the darksome night
Lit by the meteor shell.
By the bayonet's gleam, and the cannon's flash,
As onward o'er the breach they dash,
The Briton fell.

On that fell breach lay Britain's pride,
The scarlet yet was deeper died
In British blood.
And Gallia's brave in deadly strife
Mingled their purple stream of life
In one dark flood.

But 'mongst the many brave who fell
Was one who loved his country well;
For her he died.
And 'midst the groans of wounded dying,
That round him there were lying,
He death defied.

Brave Gray! The first in glory's van,
Cried, as amidst the fire he ran,
"On, brave 30th, on!"
On, on they went, the Frenchmen fly,
He fell – but still his dying cry
Was – "On, my 30th, on!"

The battle's o'er; the sword is sheathed,
And he, who late in manhood breathed,
Now low does lie.
His comrades bare him to his grave,
The 30th his last volley gave,
With many a sigh.

Farewell, brave Gray, a last farewell!
Thy comrades all that loved thee well
Bid thee farewell!
Each drops a tear – a soldier's tear,
In one whom all had held most dear,
Farewell! Farewell!

[Ap Thomas].

77. Napier, Vol. IV, pp. 432–433.

Chapter 8

78. Leith Hay, *A Narrative of the Peninsular War* Vol. II, p. 6.
79. Leith Hay, Vol. II, p. 10.
80. Leith Hay, Vol. II, p. 16.
81. *The Journal of James Hale* p. 86.
82. Douglas, *Tale of the Peninsula and Waterloo* pp. 41–42.
83. Hale, pp. 86–87.
84. Douglas, p. 42.
85. Hale, pp. 87–88.
86. Leith Hay, Vol. II, pp. 38–39.
87. Leith Hay, Vol. II, pp. 45–46.
88. Douglas, p. 42.
89. Leith Hay, Vol. II, p. 47.
90. Leith Hay, Vol. II, p. 49.
91. Leith Hay, Vol. II, pp. 50–51.

Chapter 9

92. Leith Hay, *A Narrative of the Peninsular War* Vol. II, p. 52.
93. Douglas, *Tale of The Peninsula and Waterloo* p. 45.
94. Leith Hay, Vol. II, pp. 52–58.
95. Douglas, pp. 45–46.
96. Douglas, pp. 46–47.
97. Hale, *The Journal of James Hale* pp. 91–92.
98. Douglas, p. 47.
99. see Rory Muir, *Salamanca 1812* (Yale University Press 2001) p. 135.
100. Douglas, p. 47.
101. see Adrian Lewis, "The Eagle of the 22nd" (*The Lancashire Lad* May 1995).
102. Leith Hay, Vol. II, pp. 59–60.

Chapter 10

103. Leith Hay, *A Narrative of the Peninsular War* Vol. II, pp. 70–71.
104. Napier, *History of the Peninsular War* Vol. V, pp. 256–257.
105. Hale, *The Journal of James Hale* p. 96.

106. Douglas, *Tale of the Peninsula and Waterloo* pp. 52–53.
107. Jones, *Journal of the Sieges in Spain* Vol. I, pp. 305–307.
108. Bannatyne, *History of the Thirtieth Regiment* pp. 283–284.
109. Napier, Vol. V, pp. 298–299.
110. Hale, p. 97.
111. Douglas, p. 58.
112. Douglas, p. 57.
113. see Napier, Vol. V, pp. 300–302.
114. Hale, pp. 97–98.
115. Hale, p. 98.
116. Napier, Vol. V, p. 301.
117. Hale, p. 98.
118. Napier, Vol. V, pp. 301–302.
119. Douglas, p. 59.
120. Hale, pp. 98–99.

Chapter 11

121. The normal arrangement in a three-battalion brigade was for the senior unit to take position on the right, the second in seniority on the left, and the junior in the centre. The officer casualties for the second brigade at Villamuriel reflect this sequence.
122. Hale, *The Journal of James Hale* p. 100.
123. Douglas, *Tale of the Peninsula and Waterloo* p. 62.
124. Napier estimates losses of nine thousand, which includes the siege of Burgos and about four hundred men in Hill's army (see Napier, Vol. V, p. 336).
125. William Grattan, *Adventures of the Connaught Rangers* (Henry Colburn 1847) Vol. II, pp. 134–135.
126. Grattan, Vol. II, p. 152.
127. Hale, pp. 101–102.
128. Hale, p. 103.
129. Richard Cannon, *Historical Records of the 13th Light Dragoons* (London 1837) p. 37 footnote.
130. Another casualty of the summer campaign, although not fatal, was William Stewart, brigade major with the second division, who was seriously wounded during the siege of Pamplona. He received a temporary pension of £100 a year.

Chapter 12

131. *The Royal Cornwall Gazette* 29 January 1814.
132. *The West Briton* 21 February 1814.
133. The Journal of Edward Neville Macready, chapter 2.
134. Macready's Journal, chapter 3.
135. Macready's Journal, chapter 4.
136. J.W. Fortescue, *A History of the British Army* (Naval and Military Press 2004) Vol. X, pp. 50–51. A recent account of the failed assault has been written by Andrew Bamford, "Wellington's Infamous Army" (*Military Illustrated* Vol. 238).
137. Macready's Journal, chapter 6.
138. Macready's Journal, chapter 6.
139. Macready's journal, chapter 7.
140. Bannatyne, *History of the Thirtieth Regiment* p. 308.
141. Macready's Journal, chapter 7.

Chapter 13

142. The Journal of Edward Neville Macready, chapter 8.
143. Macready's Journal, chapter 9.
144. Macready's Journal, chapter 10.
145. Macready's Journal, chapter 10.
146. Macready's Journal, chapter 10.
147. Macready's Journal, chapter 10.
148. The Journal of Surgeon J.G. Elkington.
149. Macready's Journal, chapter 10.
150. Major General H.T. Siborne (editor), *Waterloo Letters* (Greenhill Books 1993) p. 320.
151. Siborne, pp. 337–338.
152. John Selby (editor), *The Recollections of Sergeant Morris* (The Windrush Press 1998) p. 68.
153. A.T.L. Mullen (editor), *The Military General Service Roll 1793–1814* (The London Stamp Exchange Ltd. 1990) p. 255.
154. Siborne, p. 320.
155. Bannatyne, *History of the Thirtieth Regiment* p. 316 (unfortunately, Bannatyne does not give his source).
156. Elkington's Journal.
157. Macready's Journal, chapter 10.
158. Macready's Journal, chapter 10.
159. Elkington's Journal.
160. W.B. Craan (translated with explanatory notes by Captain Arthur Gore, *An Historical Account of the Battle of Waterloo* (London 1817) p. 33.

Chapter 14

161. General Sir James Shaw Kennedy, *Notes on the Battle of Waterloo* (John Murray 1865) pp. 17–18.
162. Macready's Journal, chapter 11.
163. Elkington's Journal.
164. Macready's Journal, chapter 11.
165. Macready's Journal, chapter 11.
166. Elkington's Journal.
167. Macready's Journal, chapter 11–12.
168. David Howarth, *Waterloo, A Near Run Thing* (Collins 1968) p. vii.
169. Shaw Kennedy, pp. 99–102.
170. Siborne, *Waterloo Letters* p. 233.
171. Elkington's Journal.
172. Siborne, p. 327.
173. Shaw Kennedy, p. 106.
174. Macready's Journal, chapter 12.
175. Macready's Journal, chapter 12.
176. Macready's Journal, chapter 12.

Chapter 15

177. Captain J. Kincaid, *Adventures in the Rifle Brigade* (Leo Cooper 1997) p. 165.
178. James Shaw Kennedy, *Notes on the Battle of Waterloo* pp. 114–115.
179. Shaw Kennedy, pp. 115–116.
180. Macready's Journal, chapter 12.
181. BL Add.Ms 34706 ff. 445–450.

182. Macready's Journal, chapter 12.
183. Alten's dispatch, quoted in Bannatyne, *History of the Thirtieth Regiment* p. 331.
184. Craan, trans Gore, *An Historical Account of the Battle of Waterloo* pp. 90–92.
185. Lieutenant G.W. Picton, *The Battle of Waterloo* (London 1816) p. 231.
186. Macready's Journal, chapter 12.
187. Bannatyne pp. 331–332.
188. Siborne, *Waterloo Letters* p. 329.
189. Craan/Gore, pp. 90–92.
190. Shaw Kennedy, pp. 126–127.
191. Macready's Journal, chapter 12.
192. Shaw Kennedy, pp. 128–129.
193. Macready's Journal, chapter 12.
194. Shaw Kennedy, pp. 142–143.
195. Macready's Journal, chapter 12.
196. Siborne, pp. 330–331.
197. Macready's Journal, chapter 12.
198. Macready's Journal, chapter 12.
199. Craan/Gore, pp. 92–93.
200. Macready's Journal, chapter 12 (Picton combines Gore and Macready's accounts without naming the officers, Picton p. 209).
201. Macready's Journal, chapter 12.
202. Macready's Journal, chapter 12.
203. Macready's Journal, chapter 12.

Chapter 16

204. The Journal of Edward Neville Macready, chapter 13.
205. The Journal of Surgeon Elkington.
206. Macready, chapter 13.
207. Macready, chapter 13.
208. Macready, chapter 13.
209. Macready, chapter 13.
210. Elkington's Journal.
211. Macready, chapter 16.
212. Macready, chapter 15.
213. Elkington's Journal.
214. Macready, chapter 15.
215. Elkington's Journal.
216. Macready, chapter 16.
217. Macready, chapter 17.
218. There were two John Roes in the battalion, one of whom figures in Macready's journal as a deep drinker, while the other is presented as unpleasantly sanctimonious – only Macready's impression, of course.
219. Macready, chapter 17.
220. Macready, chapter 17.

Chapter 17

221. Elkington's Journal.
222. Elkington's Journal.
223. Macready's Journal, chapter 19.

224. Macready's Journal, chapter 19.
225. Macready's Journal, chapter 19.
226. Macready's Journal, chapter 19.
227. Macready's Journal, chapter 19.
228. Macready's Journal, chapter 20.
229. Macready's Journal, chapter 22.

Chapter 18

230. Macready's Journal, chapter 40.
231. Captain Sydenham, quoted in *The Mahratta and Pindari War* (Simla 1910) p. 4.
232. Macready's Journal, chapter 33.
233. Lt-Col R.G. Burton, *The Mahratta and Pindari War* pp. 107–108.
234. Macready's Journal, chapter 38.
235. Macready's Journal, chapter 40.
236. Macready's Journal, chapter 41.
237. Macready's Journal, chapter 41.
238. Bannatyne, p. 378.

Select Bibliography

National Army Museum Sources

NAM 6112 – 33 Journal of Captain William Stewart 1810–1811
NAM 6807 – 209 Journal of Edward Neville Macready

The National Archives

WO4 – Correspondence relating to officers' compassionate fund 1803–1860
WO12 – Pay lists and muster rolls
WO17 – Monthly Returns
WO23 – Register of half-pay officers
WO23 – Register of officer pensions for wounds
WO25 – Casualty Returns
WO27 – Inspection returns 1750–1857
WO71 – Courts martial proceedings
WO97 – Men discharged and awarded Chelsea pensions
WO119 – Men discharged and awarded Kilmainham pensions

Primary Sources

Dispatches of the Duke of Wellington
General Orders, Spain and Portugal, Volumes II–V (London 1811–1814)
Faulkner's Journal, Dublin
The Battle of Waterloo by a Near Observer (London 1815)
The Leinster Journal
The Limerick Evening Post
The Royal Cornwall Gazette
The Royal Military Calendar 1820
The Royal Military Chronicle, Volumes I–VI
The West Briton
Britain Triumphant on the Plains of Waterloo (Burslem 1817)
Aytoun, James, *Redcoats in the Caribbean* (Blackburn Recreation Services Dept. 1984)
Batty, Captain, *An Historical Sketch of the Campaign of 1815* (London 1820)
Boutflower, Charles, *The Journal of an Army Surgeon during the Peninsular War* (Spellmount 1997)
Burroughs, George Frederick, *A Narrative of the Retreat of the British Army from Burgos* (Bristol 1814)
Craan, W.B., (translated with explanatory comments by Captain Arthur Gore), *An Historical Account of the Battle of Waterloo* (London 1817)
Douglas, John, (Stanley Monick ed.), *Douglas's Tale of the Peninsula and Waterloo* (Leo Cooper 1997)

Gomm, Sir William Maynard, *A Staff Officer in the Peninsula* (Napoleonic Archive)
Grattan, William, *Adventures of the Connaught Rangers* (London 1847)
Hale, James (Peter Catley ed.), *The Journal of James Hale* (republished by IX Regiment 1998)
Hope Pattison, Frederick (Stanley Monick ed.), *Horror Recollected in Tranquility* (The Naval and Military Press Ltd. 2001)
Jones, Sir John, *Journals of Sieges in Spain* (Ken Trotman Ltd. 1998)
Jones, John T., *Account of the War in Spain and Portugal and the South of France* (London 1821)
Kelly, Christopher, *A Full and Circumstantial Account of the Memorable Battle of Waterloo* (London 1817)
Leith Hay, Andrew, *A Narrative of the Peninsular War* (London 1834 second edition)
Mackenzie Macbride (editor), *With Napoleon at Waterloo* (G. Bell & Sons 1911)
McCarthy, Captain, *Recollections of the Storming of the Castle of Badajos* (London 1836)
Picton, Lieutenant G.W., *The Battle of Waterloo or, A General History of Events* (London 1816)
Shaw Kennedy, Sir James, *Notes on the Battle of Waterloo* (London 1865)
Tomkinson, William, *The Diary of a Cavalry Officer* (London 1894)
Walsh, Thomas, *Journal of the Late Campaign in Egypt* (London 1803)

Secondary Sources

Adkin, Mark, *The Waterloo Companion* (Aurum 2001)
Arcq, Alain, *Les Quatre-Bras 16 Juin 1815* (Historic'one 2005)
Bannatyne, Lt Col Neil, *History of the Thirtieth Regiment* (Littlebury Bros 1923)
Butler, Captain Lewis, *Wellington's Operations in the Peninsula* (T. Fisher Unwin 1904)
Buttery, David, *Wellington against Massena* (Pen & Sword 2007)
Cannon, Richard, *Historical Records of the 13th Light Dragoons* (London 1837)
Carter, Thomas, *Historical Records of the Forty-Fourth, or the East Essex Regiment* (1887; Naval and Military reprint)
Chandler, David, *Waterloo, The Hundred Days* (Osprey 1980)
Chartrand, René, *Fuentes de Oñoro* (Osprey 2002)
Chesney, Col Charles, *Waterloo Lectures* (Greenhill Books 1997)
Dalton, Charles, *The Waterloo Roll Call* (London 1904)
Delavoye, Alex M., *The Life of Thomas Graham, Lord Lynedoch* (Richardson & Co. 1880)
Downham, John, *Red Roses over the Veldt* (Carnegie Publishing 2000)
Esdaile, Charles, *The Peninsular War* (Allen Lane 2001)
Fletcher, Ian, *In Hell Before Daylight* (The Baton Press 1984)
Fletcher, Ian, *Badajoz 1812* (Osprey 1999)
Fletcher, Ian, *Salamanca 1812* (Osprey 1998)
Fletcher, Ian, *The Lines of Torres Vedras 1809–1811* (Osprey 2003)
Forczyk, Robert, *Toulon 1793* (Osprey 2005)
Fortescue, The Hon. J.W., *A History of the British Army* (Naval & Military Press 2004)
Fortescue, The Hon. J.W., *The County Lieutenancies and the Army 1803–1814* (The Naval & Military Press Ltd. reprint)
Hunter, Archie, *Wellington's Scapegoat* (Pen & Sword 2003)
Glover, Gareth (editor), *Letters from the Battle of Waterloo* (Greenhill Books 2004)
Glover, Michael, *Wellington's Peninsular Victories* (The Windrush Press 1996)
Glover, Richard, *Peninsular Preparation – the Reform of the British Army 1795–1809* (Cambridge University Press 1970)
Grehan, John, *The Lines of Torres Vedras* (Spellmount 2000)
Grocott, Terence, *Shipwrecks of the Revolutionary and Napoleonic Eras* (Chatham Publishing 1997)

Houssaye, Henry, *Napoleon and the Campaign of 1815 Waterloo* (The Naval and Military Press Ltd. 2004)
Howarth, David, *Waterloo, A Near Run Thing* (The Windrush Press 1997)
Ireland, Bernard, *The Fall of Toulon* (Cassell 2006)
Lawford J.P. and Young, Peter, *Wellington's Masterpiece* (George Allen & Unwin 1972)
McAnally, Sir Henry, *The Irish Militia 1793–1816, A Social and Military History* (Dublin and London 1949)
Muir, Rory, *Salamanca 1812* (Yale University Press 2001)
Mullen, A.L.T. (editor), *The General Miltitary Service Roll 1793–1814* (The London Stamp Exchange Ltd. 2000)
Myatt, Frederick, *British Sieges of the Peninsular War* (Spellmount 1987)
Napier, W.F.P., *History of the War in the Peninsula and in the South of France* (Constable 1993)
Nofi, A. Albert, *The Waterloo campaign June 1815* (Combined Publishing 1993)
Oman, Sir Charles, *A History of the Peninsular War* (Greenhill Books 1996)
Oman, Sir Charles, *Wellington's Army 1809–1814* (Greenhill Books 1986)
Siborne, Maj Gen H.T. (editor), *Waterloo Letters* (Greenhill Books 1993)
Siborne, Captain W., *History of the Waterloo Campaign* (Greenhill Books 1990)
Uffindell, Andrew and Corum, Michael, *On the Fields of Glory* (Greenhill Books 1996)
Weller, Jac, *Wellington in the Peninsula* (Greenhill Books 1992)
Weller, Jac, *Wellington at Waterloo* (Greenhill Books 1992)

Index

BRITISH ARMY

EAST INDIA COMPANY ARMY

FRENCH ARMY

PORTUGUESE ARMY